THE SCIENCE OF
GETTING
RICH *for*
WOMEN

SARA CONNELL

YOUR
SECRET
PATH TO
MILLIONS

THE SCIENCE OF
GETTING
RICH *for*
WOMEN

The Science of Getting Rich – for Women is not a passive experience. I want to ensure not only do you have access to every strategy, idea, practice and tool in this book, but that you are able to easily implement what you learn here and use it swiftly to create more wealth, riches, abundance, joy and success in your life.

You can access our interactive SCIENCE OF GETTING RICH – FOR WOMEN PORTAL to:

- Download a workbook to make it easy for you to do the exercises
- Watch the video sequences and follow the guided exercises for the key strategies and tools;
- Access resources that add to the stories and strategies in the book
- Watch interviews with the amazing women who started from nothing and became millionaires

Access everything from The Science of Getting Rich – for Women HERE:

You can also join our community for our next Science of Getting Rich – for Women Abundance Accelerator

Or talk to one of our Success Coaches to help you implement what you are learning.

You are going to break through that next glass ceiling …

… We've got you!

Request a session here

CONTENTS

Introduction

The day I signed up with my first business coach, she sent me a copy of *The Science of Getting Rich* by Wallace Wattles. The second business coach I worked with two years later (also a woman) recommended the same book.

Wallace wrote the book in 1910, and in the personal growth space it is considered a seminal text to improve one's money mindset and create wealth. At that time, my money mindset had me stuck at earning $20,000/year as a writer and coach so all recommendations were welcome.

The premise of Wattles' *The Science of Getting Rich* is that, regardless of geography, background, education, talent, intellect or physical strength, every individual is capable of creating great financial abundance, wealth, prosperity and more—and that it is, in fact, each person's responsibility to do so.

Money Mindset:

Your attitudes, thoughts, ideas and beliefs about money (that dictate how much and with what ease money will come into, or not, your life).

What a wonderful premise! I agree completely. Yet for its thrilling claim, Wallace was a white man writing in the early 20th century and the tone of the book reflects its time.

Rhonda Byrne, the founder of film and book *The Secret*, credits Wallace's book as the change agent for her meteoric rise from struggling filmmaker to being named Time 'Magazine's "100 most influential people of the year."

Rhonda tells people to whom she recommends the book, "Remember the book was written 100 years ago . . . some of the language is dated."

While I agree with Wattles' metaphysical teachings, the book's tone is rigid and straight up masculine. Over and again, the reader is told "you must." Readers wade through a sea of "he" pronouns. "A man must ..." "A man knows ..." "A man's highest happiness is ...". While the book is useful and worth reading for any student of metaphysics and using the mind to create wealth, I longed for the women leaders in my life to refer to another type of book. A book on creating abundance and wealth that was both powerful *and* feminine, a book that spoke directly to the female experience of abundance creation.

Toni Morrison says if you don't see the book you wish to read in the bookstore, you must write it yourself. I needed less imperious "you musts" and more intuitive soulful "ways of showing," with specific strategies that would support me in unburdening the generations of oppression, suppression and squelching of female power. *The Science of Getting Rich – for Women*, is the book I wished my coaches had recommended.

There is already a superb abundance of books written by women, for women. I've loved and learned much from Jen Sincero's *You are a Badass at Making Money*, Rachel Rodgers' *We Should All Be Millionaires* and Amanda Frances' *Rich AF* just in the last year. So why should I write another book on women and financial prosperity?

After decades of unconscious replaying of patterns of lack, unworthiness, underearning, undervaluing myself, moving from struggling to make $20,000 a year as a writer and coach to making $1,000,000 in a year as a writer and coach did not happen in a day, or by reading one book. It took a full life-makeover approach. It took a bombardment of money-positive and women-positive and worth-positive messages. I'm still a newbie as a CEO of a seven-figure-a-year company. Some of the women whose stories you will read in these pages have created multiple millions of dollars, despite personal and cultural adversity.

The goal is not for this book to be any kind of absolute authority. (However, the clients and friends with whom I have shared what is in this book *have* created collectively millions of dollars using these exact steps.) And I fully believe if you take action on The Science of Getting Rich for Women equation—the roadmap—I share here, you *will* create more abundance and continue doing so for the rest of your life. The intention is to add another voice to the symphony, a note to the rising, resounding chorus of the amazing women's wealth, prosperity and empowerment movement that's taking place on this planet.

For years, I avoided doing the work to transform my life from one of financial lack to one of richness and abundance, because I did not want money to be the focus of my purpose-driven work, my life or my art. But that "excuse" stemmed from a lack-based money mindset. I approached life as if I couldn't do both: purposeful work that was of immense service to others *and* wildly financially lucrative.

The truth was, I was living out old family messages and cultural programming that said pursuing money or having abundance was bad, that it was unspiritual to care about material things, that caring about money meant I was greedy or a "bad" person, superficial, wrong. The truth was, I was broke and disempowered with money, because I'd guzzled cultural, religious, familial, ancestral societal and gender "Kool-Aid" from my earliest cell development that said I was not allowed, that I shouldn't, that I wasn't worthy, wasn't capable, didn't deserve and wasn't good enough to have it.

I played these limiting ideas and patterns out for decades until I had the opportunity to speak at a conference with author Marianne Williamson and began to read her work. On the subject of women and wealth, Marianne does not sugarcoat her message; "Your being broke does not serve anyone."

In her book *A Return to Love,* she also famously said,

> There is nothing enlightened about shrinking so that other people won't feel insecure around you. We are all meant to shine, as children do. We were born to make manifest the glory of God that is within us. It's not just in some of us; it's in everyone. And as we let our own light shine, we unconsciously give other people permission to do the same. As we are liberated from our own fear, our presence automatically liberates others.

These words are exciting! When I see them, I feel them ring through my body ... maybe you do too. Our hearts recognize the truth. I could see, once I looked closely, that my repeating the messages and patterns I'd taken on about myself—as a woman, a writer, an abuse survivor and coach—and turning them into financial lack was not serving anyone!

It was not serving me to be unable to contribute to my household in any significant way, leaving my partner with that whole responsibility.

It was not serving my professional community to be unable to attend conferences, invest in editors, to let people hear about my writing, once it was written.

It did not serve my community to be unable to help a friend in need or contribute to a cause I care about deeply.

It did not serve the world to live my life in a little box, because I had no resources to travel and learn from others and contribute to life outside the box I'd built for my life.

And, most of all, it did not serve my clients, my child, my niece, my fellow artists, coaches and friends, to perpetuate the long worn-out stereotype of the struggling artist. Or by me being yet another woman on this planet who earns far less than the men in her life, which cuts her off from access to the greater power that economic abundance provides.

I repeat: Living in financial lack doesn't serve anyone!

Not for me and not for you. *That* is why you're reading this book.

And the timing could not be more important for us to make a global shift! With a pandemic that has economically cost women and women of color $800 billion dollars in lost income, according to a 2021 Oxfam International study, we can no longer afford to do anything but make this issue a top priority.

You're here and I'm here doing this work because it's time, and women at large need your participation—and because you deserve to finally access, or exponentially increase, the riches and abundance of life.

Depending on your starting point, you may have some deep mindset work to do, or you may just need a few little tweaks to create the abundance of fireworks that come when you reach that next level (whatever that is for you) with ease and joy. Wherever you are, it is my hope that this book will help shorten the path, amplify your success and create a fast track to the vision of abundance and prosperity and financial security you deserve.

You *get* to have financial abundance. You *get* to use this book to increase your current and long-term financial prosperity. You will hear the stories of the women who started without seed money, without financial support, without investors, without startup capital and, in some cases, without anyone believing in them and are now millionaires and multi-millionaires. You will learn exactly what they did and will be able to follow in their footsteps.

My deep desire is for this book to be a love letter and a lighthouse for any woman who has been told or believed she can't, she shouldn't, she's not allowed, she's not good enough, she's not worthy, not deserving; that women can't make as much as men, that women earn less than men and they'll never "catch up."

There is an abundance of research that shows that women who have a mentor who believe in a bigger vision for their mentees increase confidence and success exponentially. *11 Ways Mentors can Help you Succeed* (The Glass Hammer) and *3 Reasons Mentoring Helps the Mentor, Not Just The Mentee* (Forbes) are just two of a plethora of articles expounding upon this. If you don't have a friend, family member, mentor, coach, community, colleague to tell you the truth, I am now that mentor for you. This book is that voice and a clear, specific path forward to break you out of any glass ceiling, box, room or confine you are in.

In Part I, I will share my specific Science of Getting Rich for Women *Equation* that I developed to go from struggling to make $20,000 a year as a writer and coach to bringing in over $1M in a single year as a writer and coach. These are the exact strategies and practices I created for our clients in our Thought Leader Academy, where I have the gift of helping hundreds of mission-driven women create abundance, *while* they change lives and our planet by becoming best-selling authors and in demand speakers.

The science in this book and what I teach in Thought Leader Academy is a science of the *mind*. Like the original *Science of Getting Rich*, the scientific practices in *Science of Getting Rich – for Women* are metaphysical and reside in the realm of quantum and neuroscience. I'll share the exact neuroscientific practices that have allowed those seven figures to come in faster than any business strategy alone would have. You'll learn how to reprogram your brain for wealth from badass female neuroscientists and neurotherapists.

In Part II of the book, you'll hear from 25 women millionaires and multimillionaires. You'll learn how they overcame their own limiting beliefs and external challenges. You'll have access to their secret tips, and their mindsets, so you can add another tool or tools in your toolbox from each woman.

I specifically sought out women who were self-made. I say "started with nothing" because most of us did not begin with investors or seed money or a trust fund or capital or things we hear so much about in a male-dominated entrepreneurship world. Many of us didn't have families or patterns or society or culture or religion or teachers who believed in us. For many of us, from our beginnings, creating multi-million-dollar businesses doing what we love and what brings good to others seemed next to impossible.

But I must state the obvious here: None of us actually started with nothing. I didn't have seed money or a trust fund. But I am white, grew up middle class, had food every day, a home, two parents, good public education, and four years of college. Like most women, I also had challenges: a learning disability, was sexually abused at six, raped at eight and other traumas. Although not many people feel comfortable talking about their painful past experiences, trauma always and dramatically impacts adult earning and financial health.

The women in this book come from a variety of backgrounds, ethnicities, sexual orientations, identities and experiences. Most of us started with some level of privilege. But even if we didn't—even if you didn't—the thrilling truth is that you have everything inside that you need to break the cycles and patterns that were unfairly put on you, and you *can* create a rich life!

Here is what you need to know as we prepare to embark:

You are Worthy.

You are Capable.

You are Supported.

You get to have financial and all levels of richness, abundance and wealth.

You deserve it.

The shift is already happening, just from reading this book.

My goal is for this book to be an antidote to the challenges and obstacles, both conscious and unconscious, that women and other marginalized groups may contend with as they release the conditioning of our society and experience, break limiting family patterns and agreements, release patriarchy from their money and truly *rise*. Rachel Rodgers says, "Women's wealth is a protest." This book is my picket sign. It is a movement into greater empower-ment, abundance, health, success and *joy* for all!

Another important note. This book is not designed to be something you read and pop on your virtual or actual bookshelf. A number of years ago, Participant Films set a bold intention that their documentaries not just inform or entertain, but that their films would move people to new actions and create social change. *The Science of Getting Rich – for Women* shares this intention. My greatest desire is that you create financial breakthroughs and big abundance using this book. To accomplish this, you must practice the techniques in the Science of Getting Rich for Women Equation, and take the action steps your awesome mind will present to you, once you learn them. The action will produce your new results! And I want to make this easy for you to do! In Thought Leader Academy, I facilitate these directly, and I want you to have as close to that experience as possible. Some of the strategies I rec-ommend are interactive: visualizations, affirmations and other sequences that have created rapid and lasting shifts for our clients. I've compiled the inter-active exercises into a portal—your Science of Getting Rich toolkit. You can access these tools throughout the book when you see the link, or go straight to the *Science of Getting Rich – for Women* Book Portal now:

The Universe *wants* you to fulfill your heart's desires—including financial abundance—and will support you every minute of your quest.

Now is your time.

It's your turn.

And if you feel any sense of trepidation (I get it—I felt squeamish, ner-vous, fearful and judgmental too), think about the legacy you want to leave for the young women in your life. Each woman who liberates herself from lack lifts all of us. Money is energy, flow, a form of power, a symbol of success. Money is not the most important force. But it is important. Once we learn how to attract, share and create it limitlessly, it returns to its true place, simply as energy. Your vision of abundance is not, and never needs to be, the same as any other women, man or organization.

What I want to ensure is that you know how to create your money ideal. If you love to live simply in a cabin with a zero-carbon footprint, I want you to create it with total security, with all your needs met and with a huge celebration of your badassness. If you want to create a business with thirty team members and lead a global transformation movement, making tens of millions each year so you can roam the planet, give to causes you care about, empower others and fulfill your destiny, I am going to cheer and help facilitate every step of the way.

The Science of Getting Rich – for Women practices are not those of comparison and competition. You having more creates more for others. We're not going for "more" just for some American, capitalistic endeavor. *The Science of Getting Rich – for Women* is about authenticity, you living as big and powerfully as you desire to live. It's about *you* being all you came here to be, owning your absolute worth and power—whatever that means to you. If you don't want more, then own it! But if you have visions that require abundance—people you will hire, an audience or community to promote your mission, travel, a more self-loving home or vehicle, the creation and distribution of a book, a business, more time to play, a not-for-profit, artistic creation that the world has never seen—getting that into the hearts and hands of people who need it often requires investments. It requires money. And every woman whose story you will read in this book is waiting breathlessly for you to create it.

You are an essential part of this evolution of our species.

Thank you for joining this wave. Congratulations on breaking the cycle of lack and limitation for your family, community and world. This gets to be fun! And we get to do this together.

So, let's not waste a single moment.

Let's be the rising tide that raises all ships!

Let's do this!

ORIGINS

There is a saying that goes something like: If you want to understand your current finances, look to your upbringing.

As a child, I was told:

- You aren't good with money.
- You have a learning disability that makes you bad at math and numbers.
- You'd better make sure you meet someone with money, you like nice things.
- You're ugly and bad (and therefore unworthy of anything good).
- Women can't make as much money as men.
- Writers are broke.
- You can't have Abundance.

You might have heard messages like these. Or maybe yours were different. You may have heard limiting ideas about yourself, your worth, your gender, your race, your physical and mental or creative attributes or abilities—from family, siblings, parents, caregivers, teachers, authority figures, religion, society and culture.

It may feel painful to reflect on the messages we received as a child. Very few of us, particularly any of us that did not grow up as the previous standard of power (white, male, affluent) were given 100 percent positive messages about ourselves, our options and lives.

However, it is precisely in excavating these messages that we will begin the process of liberation and financial success. I was told these limiting things (and many more) by a variety of people and sources, and I believed them. Not only did I believe them, I spent the first few decades of my life proving those messages right.

What are your negative early or significant memories about money?

Second grade: my Great Aunt Mary with her clear-frame glasses and floral shirt dress presses a $100 bill into my hands in my bedroom at Thanksgiving. I've never seen a $100 bill. Benjamin Franklin's face grins at me. What Abundance! Like something out of a fairy tale! I run to show my dad.

"What? Oh no! She's old. You can't take advantage of her."

Ben is now in my dad's pocket. My hands tingle empty. I watch my dad wait until Aunt Mary's purse sits by the door, then he slips Ben into her wallet and walks her to the old Pontiac for the drive back to Philadelphia.

Takeaway: If you are given Abundance it will be taken from you. A man will take it from you. You don't deserve Abundance.

Third grade: I sleepover at a friend's house and her father rapes me in his bedroom. He says that if I tell anyone I'll be taken away from my family— he'll make sure of it. I don't tell.

Takeaway: I've done something very bad and it must have been my fault because he picked me. I'm not a good girl or a good person and I don't deserve anything good ever again, certainly not prosperity or success.

Fifth grade: Sun dancing on the kneelers during Stations of the Cross. Slight gag when the incense reaches our pew. Jesus swims above me in the stained glass. We hear stories of St. Francis, the pampered, rich, spoiled cloth merchant's son who was bad in Assizi before he heard god's voice telling him to give all his money away and become good.

Mother Teresa, Padre Pio, Saint Augustine, Isioadore Bakanja, Saint Catherine, and Saint Bernadette, who grew so poor in following God's will, she had to move her entire family into a single room in an old jail that had been deemed unfit for criminals to live in.

Takeaway: Poverty is the way to God and to be good.

Sixth grade: New public school. I'm given a test with a psychologist to determine if I will be placed in the TAG—Talented & Gifted Program. During the test the doctor stops taking notes. "I've never seen this before. When did you find out you have a learning disability?"

I begin to sweat through my clothes. I don't understand what he means. I wonder if I will be taken to a different school, or a shorter bus, leave all my friends. The doctor tells my parents that while I made it into the talented and gifted program because my score was high, the abnormal way I do numbers and spatial relations is defined as "disabled." I am put in talented and gifted for all subjects except math where I sit in the back row and don't raise my hand anymore.

Takeaway: I am abnormal. I have a disability, which puts me behind others. In any area where numbers are concerned, I will struggle.

Junior High: I love anything to do with theater. I get leads and supporting parts in plays, I don't care, as long as I'm in that rehearsal room with these amazing people, drunk on Shakespeare and courtroom dramas and The Twelve Dancing Princesses. I fill fifty journals, writing and writing, staying up late in my room, my blue Bic pens going fast against the hum of the air conditioner. "I'm going to England to study drama. I'm going to write books. I'm going to be on TV." Adults comment: "That one's not very practical. Not great with money. Hope she finds someone well off."

Takeaway: an artist's life equals poverty. If any money is to be in my life it will come through someone else, through a marriage. There is not a scenario in which I will be a successful artist, one that actually makes money.

News stories: Women make .75 cents to every dollar a man makes. Women freelancers make 25 percent less than equally qualified male peers. Until 1974, women were not allowed to get a credit card without a man's signature.

I could go on. I bet you could too. What came up as you read my list of money and worth messages? You may have read this list and thought, *Good God Sara, I didn't have food to eat, my parents died or abandoned me, I had real money issues.* Or maybe you read this list and some of your own memories are rising up in your mind. Whatever you experienced and have believed about yourself and money it is welcome here. Your origin experiences are important in creating wealth from now on.

Making a list of our memories and programming around money is not an exercise in how bad it was or to blame anyone for any struggles we've had with money. No one intended to imprint negative beliefs on us. My father, who marched for women's rights, didn't want me to think I was unworthy of money or that women don't deserve abundance. Yet without any context or ability to see from other perspectives, I interpreted these things the way I interpreted them. We make meaning out of every experience. The point of this exercise then is not blame or guilt, it is *awareness* about our origins with money and worth because awareness is the first step in change.

If I knew as a child and young woman what I know now, I could've seen all those limiting messages for the falsehoods they were. I could've even laughed at them all and gone right ahead and been awesome with money, created wealth and had a hugely prosperous life by twenty-five. But I didn't. I believed those thoughts and then felt terrible and incapable and unworthy and ashamed which led to me proving every one of them right—for two decades!

I took underpaying jobs, I didn't charge what I was worth, I shied away from doing positive business building and wealth generating actions that would have created more abundance. I avoided looking at my bank balance. I overdrew my checking account. I lived the bad-with-money, starving artist, vague, unpractical, powerless, limited financial life that I'd been told and I believed I would live.

The key to your liberation is in identifying these ideas and programs, seeing them as false. Then releasing and transforming them so you can have new, real, founded on truth-thoughts-emotions-actions and *life*.

I'll walk you through exactly how to release and transform these limiting ideas in this book. (If you want to start immediately, go to the portal and I'll walk you through the Money Positive/Money Negative tool to begin your transformation now.)

The great news is that every belief you've developed is *revisable*. You're reading this right now because you are ready to shift into a Money Positive mindset and life. You're ready to break these lies and mixed messages and *Abundance Blockers* off your life, your gender, your community and your ancestral line.

So, yes. I was told:

- You aren't good with money.

  And yet, I now run a seven figure a year business with excellent records, clear financial reports, all cash (no debt) and paid my entire team and myself on time, every month, including throughout the entire pandemic.

- Your brain is a-typical and you have a learning disability that makes you bad at math and numbers.

  And yet, (see above) + I have a Master's Degree and several professional licenses and certifications in mental health and holistic healing that required me to take science-based board exams. I scored in the top 5 percent on these exams and maintained a 4.0 throughout my master's program at a top 20 university in the US.

- You'd better get together with someone with money, you like nice things. (Implicit: You would not be able to make your own money.)

  And yet, I now make equal and soon to be more than my partner and am able to buy a new house for and support our family even when his work slowed due to the pandemic.

- You are unlovable, unworthy and ugly.

  This one does not deserve a comment. Today, I do my best to accept, support and be kind to myself. To like the way I am made, inside and out. To tell myself, I am a kind, generous and beautiful human and show up as one.

- Women can't make as much money as men.

  And yet, see above with me becoming a high contributing earner in my household.

- You don't deserve Abundance

  Again, here I am. I spent years struggling to make $20K as a writer and coach but when I began to do the process and strategies you will learn in this book, my entire life transformed and I broke through six, multi-six, half million and now into the million+ a year income bracket.

- If you become a writer, you will be poor

  And yet, again, see above with the million dollars + a year as a writer and coach.

Whatever limiting belief you were told or made up internally gets to *go* … now! Like a bad spell in a fairy story, you will clear these false, limiting ideas one by one, or in big groups like rocks falling off the side of a mountain after a dynamite blast, until you have your "and yet" list, after everyone one of those lies and your life is a living example of the truth of your unlimitedness, innate ability and power!

Your Turn

Use the workbook, via the portal below, or take a piece of blank paper or doc on your computer, and free-write on your early programming about money, and your worth and abilities to have it.

If you uncover any money negative beliefs know that even writing them down will begin to dissolve their power and that you've taken a courageous and important step into your new *rich life*.

THE
SITUATION

I doubt we need any convincing that women, globally, are not equal in economic power to men, and that things would be better if women were more financially empowered.

Women as a whole have never experienced economic equality around the globe or in the United States. We've heard for decades about the pay gap. In 2020, the Ellevest team pulled together some whopping stats in their *60+ Stats About Women and Money* article. Stats such as a woman's average pay to a man's dollar is: 86 cents for Asian women, 82 cents for women overall, 75 cents for white women, 61 cents for Black women, 58 cents for Native women, and 52 cents for Latinx women. One in four women has a disability; on average, people with disabilities are paid 37 percent less than non-disabled people. (We don't have reliable stats yet about non-binary people's pay gaps.)

Due to these pay gaps, women on average lose some $900,000 over a 40-year career, according to a recent estimate.

In recent years, 37 percent of the CEOs on the Fortune 500 list were women, which is a record from previous years. There are zero Black or Latinx women on the list, and zero non-binary people.

Women retire with two-thirds the assets that men do. Black women run an 80 percent chance of being impoverished in retirement.

In an online business article, *The Atlantic* revealed startling statistics that women's earning has been impeded by what's called "The Confidence Gap," a phenomenon where women through cultural and individual conditioning underestimate their worth, skills and performance by about 25 percent (men overestimate by about the same amount leaving a 50 percent gap between the two groups). Studies show confidence directly leads to income and career success. Intuitively, this makes sense; the more confidence we have, the more likely we are to charge what we're worth, pitch the bigger opportunities, ask for and receive a promotion. Over time, confidence could affect a woman's income by hundreds of thousands—even millions of dollars.

Last year, while reading and article from *FreshBooks*, I discovered that women freelancers make 28 percent less than equally talented and qualified male counterparts. I was so upset, I went on a media tour to share tips on how to "smash this new glass ceiling," and teamed up with a colleague to create free trainings for freelancers that we published in Forbes.

This book takes the work we started for women freelancers and provides the entire road map. It's imperative each of us find the solutions, strategies and practices that will help us each breakthrough the limits and achieve our full financial potential and abundance. And we can't have accessed this a moment too soon.

If the confidence and pay gaps were boiling in 2019, the 2020-21-22 pandemic brought the blaze sweeping down the hilltops like a brush fire. The most recent statistic as of the writing of this book is that the pandemic has cost women globally $800 billion in lost income. That's Billion.

A few more stats: According to the *U.S Department of Labor Blog:* "In June 2021, there were 7.2 percent fewer adult Black women, 5.9 percent fewer adult Hispanic women and 4.8 percent fewer adult white women employed compared with February 2020. Among mothers with children under the age of 13, 1.2 million fewer mothers were working, representing a loss of about 7 percent of employed mothers ages 25-54."

From a March 2021, Gallup Report: "The gap in labor force changes amounts to roughly 493,000 more women than men being absent from the labor force since the pandemic began. This is the difference between the roughly 2.3 million women missing from the U.S. workforce as of February 2021, compared with about 1.8 million men."

From the National Bureau of Economic Research, April 2020:

In "The Impact of COVID-19 on Gender Equality" we learn:

- The pandemic has battered industry sectors in which women's employment is more concentrated—restaurants and other retail establishments, hospitality, and health care.
- Working women are also at a greater disadvantage compared with working men in the current crisis because fewer women have jobs that allow them to telecommute: 22 percent of female workers compared with 28 percent of male workers.

The U.S Bureau of Labor Statistics quoted the American Time Use Survey in their *Monthly Labor Review*:

- Single parents face the greatest challenge. Only 20 percent of single parents reported being able to telecommute compared with 40 percent of married people with children. In two-parent households where only one parent works in the labor market, the stay-at-home parent, usually the mother, is likely to assume primary childcare duties during coronavirus-related school closures. However, in 44 percent of married couples with children, both spouses work full-time. Among these couples, mothers provide about 60 percent of childcare. Men perform 7.2 hours of childcare per week versus 10.3 hours for women.

Here are some real-life examples for women who were lucky enough to have good jobs pre-pandemic:

- After her daycare was canceled every other day for three weeks, Andrea in Hyde Park, Illinois quit her job as editor of a magazine and stayed home to care for her three-year-old daughter, cutting the family earnings down to one salary.
- After home school proved ineffective and unmanageable, Rachel in Atlanta Georgia gave up her freelance clients to take over full time zoom link hunting, re-learning pre-algebra, troubleshooting to the school, teaching essay writing and ensuring her children did not spend all day playing Minecraft.
- Erin in New York City was furloughed in her job as a physical therapist because her medical practice lost patients and couldn't pay full salaries.

- Tara's yoga studio where she made 100 percent of her income shut down. She offered virtual classes but also as a single mother was in charge of her teenage son's virtual schooling and her clients were overwhelmed as well. Her income dropped to 25 percent of what she'd been earning.

Takeaway: In terms of work and earning, women got f-ed hardest by the pandemic. But the great thing about a *setback is* that it's also a *set up*. Like an archer pulling back an arrow and by doing so infusing it with massive energy, so we have an enormous opportunity to clear out the limiting patterns internally and externally and truly fly further than we've ever gone on the other side.

But as you'll continue to hear from me and the women in this book, you don't have to be a statistic of disempowerment. In fact, you found *The Science of Getting Rich – for Women* because you are *destined* to become abundant, rich and wealthy in all areas of your life and empower other women to do the same.

• • •

At the beginning of 2022, my husband lost his biggest client. Four years ago, this would have been a crisis for our family was now a moment of shared courage and support. I was able to say, "I've got you. I've got us." We don't have to wake up at 4:00 in the morning wondering if we can stay in our home, keep our son in his school or buy groceries.

One of my greatest joys in the past year was seeing not one, not two, but *many* women in Thought Leader Academy and my coaching practice have this type of experience. To become the primary earners in their households—*during* the pandemic.

Whatever the world conjures up—pandemics, sexism, pay gaps or anything we might see in the future—the opportunity to reclaim our power and create a new reality of women's wealth and richness exists *now*.

We don't have to wait on the world or systems or anyone else to change and change ourselves. Tony Robbins says, "Our decisions determine our destiny." So we get to *decide* to chart a new future—for yourself, as well as every human on this planet. This is the alchemy-the metaphysical *science* of getting rich!

Without spending another second on how it's been, or what's happened or what led to us being in a disadvantaged place, let's release the arrow and hit that bullseye.

THE
SOLUTION

BE

In January of the first year our company reached 1 million mark. I had one virtual assistant working with me and I'd made a hiring error. She was an acquaintance who had terrific passion and I thought a well-matched skill set for the position, but for personal reasons, she shut down and essentially stopped working, without telling me. She was spinning two dozen plates in the air, and they all came crashing down. The silver lining was I'd met a new virtual assistant through the experience, and I could feel she and I were a real match. The first assistant and I parted ways with love, and the new team member and I were left deep down in a pile of administrative and systems rubble without lamps on our hardhats. I understood that serving our current clients without lapse, while building new systems and developing new team members, was going to take time and a lot of our energy. This was not a situation where one could count on revenue growth or expansion; best case scenario, we'd be able to maintain the business we had.

But I'd set a goal—felt it burning in my heart—to double the business, to help at least twice as many women change the world by writing and publishing best-selling books, speaking on new stages, speaking at TEDx and expanding their income that year. I had a vision of making seven figures and my heart wouldn't compromise.

My coach said, "You can do it as long as you can see it. As long as you can put the numbers into a spreadsheet and clearly see how you will get to the million."

I could not see it.

There was no spreadsheet scenario, based on our two-person team and my bandwidth, whereby we could reach that number. I stood at the "choice" point: I could revise my goal, commit to helping half as many people that year at half the income, or I could go against reason and logic and go for the goal anyway.

We went for the 7 figures. Every day when I set my feet on the floor next to my bed, I said, "I am sooo grateful I am now a 7-figure business owner of a world class company where my clients get phenomenal results." At every choice point, instead of doing what my overwhelmed, shaking with fear, imposter syndrome feeling, self-doubting self would have me do—cut back the goal, get back into a comfort zone, dive into bed and watch Netflix for five hours—I asked, "What would the 7-figure CEO do here?"

When I told my business best friend about my new habit, she started asking me the same questions whenever doubt seeped in, "What would the 7-figure CEO do here?" I'd answer her by identifying the calm, decisive action someone who already ran their 7-figure business would do. Then I would do it. Clearly, I engaged with both the being the doing part of the equation to get to $1M/ year but in this chapter, I will teach you the foundation being steps that made this jump possible.

That year was highly uncomfortable.

The step I took to calm my brain that January, when I had no rational plan, was the first part of the Science of Getting Rich equation. The first step in the equation is *BE*.

Most of the time we jump to *doing* when we set a new goal. But, as you'll see in the coming pages, doing first can be perilous. *The Science of Getting Rich – for Women* asks us to do things backwards from what our ego or rational mind prefers. I mean, wouldn't it be fantastic if we could have the goal achieved (or at least a money, time, confidence-back guarantee)? Then we'd feel comfortable doing the actions that would get us there and, *voila*, we'd *be* the kind of person who lives this wonderful new life.

The *Science of Getting Rich – for Women* asks us to invert the process. We begin with *being* the version of ourselves who've already achieved that goal, which is living our rich, abundant, fulfilled and impactful life. Then we *do* the things that kind of person/version of ourselves would do, and then we *have* the result we desire.

The Science of Getting Rich – for Women way of doing things is not comfortable. You will likely want to swear, give me the middle finger, throw the book across the room. *Being* the 7-figure business owner before the money was in the bank, before we'd met the awesome clients we'd support, meant *doing* things before I was ready, tripling our team (and paying them all), investing in better systems and tech so our processes would work in an excellent way and not doing everything in the business myself (where I had the illusion of control and overhead was super low). I'm a financially low-risk person. My skin itched and my back ached with this insane task of *being* something I had no proof would come to pass. I wanted comfort, I wanted assurance, but in the *Science of Getting Rich – for Women* equation, we are asked to summon courage from the deepest part of ourselves. Somewhere in a micro section of my gut I believed this could be the way, and I walked with faith through the fire of fear.

Be comes first because change happens fastest at the level of identity. Starting with *be* opens a magic portal. Like some kind of awesome time travel machine, *being* the vision taps you into the version of yourself who has already accomplished the goal. You are no longer asking *if* you are worthy, capable, deserving, willing, disciplined, smart, old, young, talented, *good* enough to achieve it. *Be* says you've already done all that. You tried and you triumphed. It's as if you're asking your brain and life to simply "remind" you of how you did it, what that next step was. The amazing thing is that, when you do this, the answers will come. Always!

Even if you don't believe this in the least, acting as if you can be this person will produce the same effect.

One of my clients had tried to improve her health, drop some extra weight and become active for almost fifteen years. She'd made vision boards, signed up for Weight Watchers, joined gyms, kept a food and exercise journal, worked with a therapist, made vows, done hypnosis—she had tried everything! When she met with me to work on her writing, she said she'd accepted that she was never going to change her health behaviors and was resigned to the eating whole bags of salty snacks, losing the weight, then putting it back on plus ten pounds, the same roller coaster she'd lived on for years. I teach an Epic Year Workshop every January, which coincided with the start of her coaching.

"Just for kicks," she told me in our next session, "I put a woman riding a bike on her vision board alongside the words: active, fit and healthy."

We proceeded with the writing coaching, and she went on eating her super-sized bag of chips every evening. Then something odd happened. We'd talked about *Be, Do, Have* in terms of writing and thought leadership. "What would the best-selling author do next?" our clients ask themselves if they start to feel fear. One afternoon, instead of ripping open the Lays, my client said, "What would the fit, active, healthy woman do right now?"

The answer was instant.

"Well, she wouldn't eat these chips," my client said and was astounded to see herself pushing the bag, unopened, into the cabinet. "She'd probably go for a bike ride," came next. But my client didn't own a bike. She settled for a walk.

On our next call, she was exuberant. "It's as if I've been possessed—in the best possible way!" That week, she'd walked every day. First around the block. Then for fifteen minutes, and the day before our session she'd walked two miles. By December that year, she'd bought a bike and was riding three times a week, walking every morning, had lost the weight she'd always hoped to lose. "But the best part," she told me, "is that I'm not trying to do anything. I just ask with each choice, 'What would a fit, healthy, active woman do next?' and I do that. I have so much energy. I feel confident I can do things now. I know I will finish my book!"

Being the vision before it happens jumps us right to our new identity. Like the Hindu god Ganesha, who cuts through obstacles with his sword, *Being* the vision shows us exactly what choice to make at each fork in the road and removes inner resistance. We tap into the genius and power of the entire universe.

Of course, *Be* is only the first part of the Science of Getting Rich equation. If I had just asked my magic question and then sat back without taking action, I would not have broken the 7-figure mark. And my client would not have enjoyed her fit, active, healthy body if she had simply envisioned someone riding a bike or taking a three-mile walk. But starting with *Be* will fast track your progress and exponentially increase your results.

How to BE Your Vision

As uncomfortable as *The Science of Getting Rich – for Women* equation may make us, *Being* the vision can be one of the most exhilarating parts of the process. The *Being* practices fire the imagination, stimulate creativity and expand your mind.

I could fill an entire book with *Being* strategies, but to ensure you most expediently get to your rich life, I will share the five that have brought me and our clients the most immediate and substantial results.

1. VISION

We cannot *Be* something until we are clear on the vision, the goal, the "what we really, really, want." Take a moment and ask yourself, "What is the goal that you want most with your body, heart and soul? Since this is *The Science of Getting Rich – for Women*, I encourage you to set a financial goal. Know, however, that you can use the exact process I'm sharing here to achieve any goal, in any area of life. Write your vision in a journal, or, if you'd like me to walk you through the vision process in real time, go here to access the video version

Prompts to identify your Abundance Vision:

- What is the income/amount of money that would fill me with joy and change my life this year?

- What I really, really want in terms of financial abundance now is _____?

- If I could make/receive the amount of money that would match my inner potential, it would be _____?

- What other goals will reflect my awesome, *rich* life? (This could be launching a business, certain # of clients, retreats, courses or classes you will take, books you will write, a conference or stage on which you want to appear, a trip you will take, a house you will buy or rent. Paint a gorgeous, radiant, five-sensory picture of your *rich* life.)

Then write your vision in one or a few sentences. Write these in the present tense (remember you already *are* this vision). Once you have your vision written down crystal clear, say out loud: "Yes! I am ... I get to live this abundant new life."

Post the vision somewhere visible (your bathroom mirror, refrigerator door, as the screen saver on your phone). Every time you see it, keep saying *yes*!

2. I AM

Each morning—or anytime you have a few minutes—sit quietly and focus on your breathing. See if you can slow your breathing and bring it deep into your stomach. Next, think of the quality or specific part of your vision you most want to manifest *now*. Set a timer on your phone for 1-5 minutes (you can start with one and work up to 5.) With each inhalation say, "I am one with (insert your goal/quality that aligns with your goals). To amplify the effects, spread your arms open and lift your chin and chest as you breathe and affirm.

- Example: When I first committed myself to creating financial abundance (after that awful meeting with my accountant), I couldn't envision a big, juicy amount of money. The best I could do was say I wanted Abundance. So that's where I started. Every morning, before anyone else in my household was up, I sat on the floor, spread my arms open and said: "I am one with all the Abundance of the Universe." I did this for 3-5 minutes a day. For a few days nothing happened, then, about a week later, a client called "out of nowhere." She said, "I attended a workshop you taught two years ago, but I wasn't ready to write my book yet. Do you have space for me?"

I continued the practice and similar events took place. Within a month, I'd received over $2,000 of unexpected income.

You can breathe in a specific amount of money "*I am*" as you inhale, and perhaps, "$100,000" as you exhale. You can breathe "I am a multi-seven figure CEO" or "Confidence" or "best-selling author" or "$10,000 a week."

In the face of high resistance or self-doubt, author and teacher Esther Hicks recommends, "going general versus specific." When I coach a client who has never experienced financial abundance and finds it hard to imagine her situation ever changing, I suggest this general Abundance *Be* practice. 1 minute, 5 minutes. *I am one with all the abundance in the Universe.*

Yes, you are.

3. WHAT WOULD?

I've already shared the power in asking the question, "What would the me that's already achieved my goal do next?" Or if that question feels too big of a jump, try "What would the person who has achieved this goal and lives this rich life do next?"

Once you begin asking this question, you'll receive all kinds of guidance; you'll attract the person who will show you your next step, and it will begin to appear as if you're a magnet for success.

You can amplify this practice in fun ways. Ask, "What would the million-dollar-a-year you wear? What would she do for exercise or movement? What restaurants does she frequent? With whom does she hang out for fun? Get to know this *rich, abundant* you.

- Practice: Free write in your journal for three pages without editing or analyzing what you write. Explore the prompts above and these:

  - What would the *rich* you who has achieved your vision wear, eat, connect, express? Where does she live, travel? Is she presenting in the media, building schools around the world, publishing white papers, leading a retreat in Bali? Does she only work three days a week while her team runs many aspects of her business? Does she go away for two weeks to write in a cabin in the woods? Has she hired assistants so she can pick up her kids every day from school and never works weekends while still making $300,000 a year? $3 million? $35 million? What else is different and better in her life now that she's unleashed the abundance of the universe?

• • •

To do this process with me in real time, click the portal and I'll walk you through the powerful guided visualization I do with our Thought Leader Academy clients.

4. IMMERSION

Coming from a money negative upbringing, creating a financially abundant life was akin to learning a new language. The *Being* stage of the equation of *The Science of Getting Rich – for Women* is about being different, thinking differently, speaking differently, feeling differently. Different here is good; if you keep thinking, feeling, and acting the way you have, you'll get the exact results you've already created. You're reading this book because you want and deserve more!

When people set out to learn a new language, they may take a class, get a workbook, listen to language videos or make flashcards. However, most people agree that the most effective and expedient way to learn a new language is through immersion.

Live in a country or with people who speak that language or take a job in a company that uses your new language as their primary mode of business communication. Immersion makes sense, as opposed to doing regular life 98 percent of the time and then practicing the new language one hour a week at the language lab. Instead, you're shopping for groceries, buying a bus ticket, ordering at a restaurant, talking to the dentist, and watching TV in the new language. Your brain is inundated with the language, and you don't have the option to default to your comfort zone. Eventually, you start to even think and dream in French or Swahili or Czech.

Abundance is a language and a way of life. Money is energy, and to accelerate change we want to immerse ourselves in audio, visual, written communication, activities and interactions, all in our new language of abundance. Because of generous leaders, authors and experts, this is now easy to do. Go to YouTube and type in Abundance and you'll see hundreds of audios and videos, interviews and other recordings there for you to access completely free. A quick internet search will connect you to podcasts, paperbacks, audio books, conference recordings, live streams, panels, meditations, hypnosis, visualizations and affirmations about abundance. You can listen or read almost all of these for free and by checking out materials from the library.

I think of this process as steeping, like a teabag. Imagine steeping yourself every day in a sea of abundance. What we take in, we become. Listen while you fold laundry, walk the dog, wait in the pick-up line, take your parent to the doctor. Listen when you wake up in the morning, while you're washing your face, and with headphones while you fall asleep at night. At one point, I recognized that I felt anxious about money when I showered in the morning. So I stuck some ear buds under a shower cap and listened to abundance audios while the water washed away my fear. Read, watch and participate in some abundance content at least once a day, and you'll feel the resistance dissolve like rock in the ocean. Listen, read, take in … *become*.

For a list of my favorite abundance resources, go here:

In addition to abundance immersion, you may also consider the complementary action of abstaining from lack thinking. Here's what I mean.

When someone enters a 12-step program to stop using drugs, smoking, overeating, drinking, having sex with strangers or working 24-7, they immerse themselves in recovery. They read recovery books, attend meetings, spend time with other sober people and do daily practices to connect to their spirit and wellbeing. They're also sometimes encouraged to avoid (at least at the beginning of their sobriety), bars and parties where people are drinking, tailgating at sports events, reunions, holiday booze fests, sometimes even friends of partners, who are still engaging in addictive drinking.

As you are learning the new language of abundance and developing a new abundant lifestyle, you may want to abstain from conversations, habits and certain relationships that revolve around a belief in lack or unworthiness. Remember the scene from the film *Mean Girls*? Regina George (the queen of the school) invites the clique to her house. The girls take turns looking in the mirror and naming their physical flaws. Friendships often, without meaning to, develop a negative locus. They could easily have transformed the energy of their group and their school community by focusing on their positive attributes, unique abilities and empowering values, but the agreement was to objectify each other and criticize.

If you have friends who consistently complain about rich people, the economy, money struggles and resentments, consider saying "Hey, would you play a game with me? Just for this week, let's share something great that happened today or something positive we heard in the news." If your friends/colleagues/family tell you to f-off and want to continue complaining and focusing on lack, you can send them love while changing the subject or spending a little less time with them while you're moving your life over to Abundance Land. You can respect their right to choose lack and go right back to immersing yourself with content and people who "speak abundance."

Samantha

My client Samantha had a money-negative upbringing. Her father abandoned the family and her mother stuffed dollar bills in boxes under the bed and in the back of her sock drawer, because she feared if she couldn't touch the money, it would be taken from her. Samantha grew up feeling there would never be enough. She was afraid to spend on herself, always finding the cheapest car or hotel room or clothing item. But she had a dream to help people with her health coaching work. She had an intuitive ability to sense where they were blocked and help them reverse even chronic conditions and chronic pain that doctors said they'd just have to live with. She began writing articles and taking the business actions I'll teach you in the CHAPTER on "Doing." But every time she'd make money, she'd get a home repair bill or a client would ghost her. Her head would drop into her hand. "See?" she'd say. "I get money and then it's gone; I'm right back to struggling."

I understood her frustration. She was doing the "right things" for her business. But she was playing out the old script and her father's fear. I encouraged her to focus on the *Being* work you're doing in this chapter. I asked if she was willing to speak, and eventually think, in a new language. I offered her the immersion approach.

For the first month, not much changed. Then she had three clients renew with her before they'd finished the first three-month program. Two others referred family members. "I love the new clients," she said. "But I'm still not making much profit. I'm scared if I raise my rates, no one will work with me." I understood. I'd felt exactly the same way when I asked my first client to go from investing $50 for one session at a time to $1,500 for a 3-month program.

I taught her the releasing work I'll teach you in the next chapter. She started listening to 30 minutes of money-positive content each day and saying, "The Universe is my Source." every time she thought about money. She posted money-positive sticky notes around her home and on her computer. She set her phone to send her abundance messages such as "Money comes to me easily" or "I receive and abundance of money effortlessly" and "I am worthy of abundance" every day at 12:00 and 3:00. When a new client inquired about working with her about a month later, she found herself quoting a new rate—double what she'd been charging. She messaged me: "I blew it. I quoted a really interested potential client my doubled my rate, and she didn't even respond."

We did some deep breathing. "She may just be busy," I said. "Keep doing the abundance immersion."

Samantha called, jubilant, the next day. "Guess What?!" Samantha showed me the text from her new client:

"Sounds good. How do I pay?"

Samantha increased her income by over 200 percent. Today, her clients pay her five figures for a single day of private coaching. She no longer questions her access to abundance; she has now *become* abundance.

Olives

In my journey to become fluent in abundance, one of the prosperity teachers I studied was a five-foot-tall woman with fiery, strawberry-red hair named Edwene Gaines. She told mesmerizing stories about her climb from a single mom on welfare to her world travels and many-acre estate, where she held abundance retreats for women.

My favorite story was about her best friend who, when they met, was as down and out financially as my teacher. This was years ago, so I may not have every detail exactly as Edwene described it here (pardon if I miss anything, Edwene!); this is how I remember it.

As they sat holding food stamps for the grocery store, Edwene asked her friend to imagine what her life would be like if she were rich. 'Her friend described an ice-cream-white luxury convertible, trips to countries far outside North America, a great school for her child, who was floundering in his pub-lic school. Family vacations in the summer, a home where she never worried about paying the electric bill. A pantry stocked with a fancy brand of olives she'd seen in a magazine. Then her friend stopped. "What's the point of this? I can't have any of this. Imagining it makes me feel worse."

"You can have the olives," Edwene said and counted out some of her own food stamps. "Get the olives and put them on your kitchen counter. Every time you see them, say, 'This is my life now. I have an abundant life.'"

The teacher and her friend bought the olives. They had to eat cheap pea-nut butter and beans to make up for the olives but kept them on the counter while the water was turned off and the stack of bills piled next to the tele-phone. They immersed themselves in Abundance books they checked out of the library. They each found a job. The water was turned back on. On week-ends they test drove convertibles. They kept driving their crappy cars but pre-tended the cars had the automatic locks, wide leather seats and shiny rims that made the vehicle feel like a boat sailing through water. They lay at the public pool and pretended they were at the Hotel Beverly Hills. They said Abun-dance mantras one hundred times a day. They over delivered at work. They donated 10 percent of any money they made as a gift back to the Universe.

They got better jobs. Edwene wrote a book. She devoted her life to healing the abundance consciousness on planet earth. Suddenly, people from all over the world wanted her to come and speak at their churches, their community centers, their schools. Her friend saved enough to get her son into a private school. They both moved into a neighborhood with rolling hills and vast green yards stuffed with flower bushes. They stocked the fancy olives jars deep in their pantries. When guests came over, they ate the olives with champagne.

Action: Choose a tangible item to represent your *rich* life and buy it for yourself. If the item is beyond your current means, find a smaller or "look alike" version, or even post a picture of that item in your living space or office. When I was doing my abundance transformation, I decided to pay cash for everything and to live debt free. If that resonates with you, buy your rich items when you have the cash to do it, use a picture until then. Seeing it every day is the key. You're *Being* your rich-life self by having that item. Start wherever you are and bring that *rich* life into your reality now, and you'll have the real thing lightning-fast.

To help bring all the *Being* techniques together, I'll introduce my favorite technique: The Future Pull.

5. FUTURE PULL

A future pull takes place when you create a conversation or experience of having the thing/goal/dream/desire/abundance *now*, before it's in your physical reality.

Here are examples of future pulls I've done for myself and with clients:

- When I pitch an article to a magazine, I send myself an acceptance email the same day. I put the magazine and editor name in the subject line. The email reads the way I would be *thrilled* for the real response to read. "Dear Sara, we loved your piece and will publish it in our next issue. Congratulations! Forbes Editors" (I've published every article, short story, poem and book I've future-pulled. When I keep getting rejections, I ask if I've been sending the future pulls and usually I haven't. I start the practice up and the piece gets published.)
- My client Erin was divorced with three teenagers and working a job she hated at a financial firm. "I want to work at a company I respect, but I have to make over six figures, plus benefits and flex time, so I can be with my girls if they need me. I want to switch to a not-for-profit company with a great mission, but those companies don't pay my level of salary. And I want an iPhone."

I raised an eyebrow.

"All my companies have been PC based," she said. "I like Mac's."

We future pulled during the next two sessions. For several months she found jobs she liked that paid less than she could live on, or financial jobs that she felt would suck her soul dry. Then one afternoon, her name lit up on my phone.

"Guess where I'm calling from?" she said. "My NEW company. With the whole salary, PPO benefits, flex time. And check out the number."

I pulled up "recent calls" on my screen. The call came from her new suped up Apple iPhone.

- My client Joelle wanted to get married. She kept meeting unavailable men. She drove down to Oak Street and tried on wedding dresses and took photographs of the one she would buy if she was getting married that day. She borrowed my engagement ring and wore it for the duration of every session we held in my office. I went to her wedding a year later.

- A good friend wanted to change careers from being an actor to being a doctor. This required two years of undergrad classes in math and science (she'd majored in drama the first time around), then MCATs and being accepted at age 40 to med school.

  "They'll never take me. I'm too old. They won't think I'm serious when they see I've been an actor."

  Plenty of people would've told her she was crazy, but our friends rallied around her with zeal. When she began applying to medical school, we each took one school and created an acceptance letter for her. We used the school letterhead, looked up the name of the dean of admissions and mailed her the "Congratulations, you've been accepted" letters. She strung them up over her desk, and that's what she saw every day as she wrote essays and filled out financial aid forms. She has now graduated, completed her residency and is working full time as a doctor.

Future Pulling for Abundance

I'd been future-pulling for a few years and had seen astounding results for my clients and in my writing career. Then I met Catherine and Geri in a mastermind for women entrepreneurs.

The three of us loved our work and our families and had seen growth in our income but wanted to make a big leap. We agreed to future pull every day for three months as an experiment. We each declared a specific financial goal that seemed like an unattainable fantasy. Catherine wanted to make $200K in passive income through the e-course she'd created. I wanted to bring in $100K and write all six figures in a check that I'd share with my husband as a demonstration that he no longer had to bear the burden of being our sole financial provider. Geri wanted to pay off $150K in debt and surprise her husband with a gold membership to the club he'd given up when she took on debt to start her business.

We created a message group and each day left a message celebrating these three goals. We talked about the Italian restaurant with the framed paintings of birds on the walls Geri would take her husband to when she shared the news that their debt was gone and handed him his golf club card. We gushed over the trip to Italy Catherine booked after she hit the $250K mark through her automated funnel, without doing a single sales call. We "awwwwed" at that moment when my husband Bill's mouth hung open at the sight of that check he didn't know was coming. We didn't ever say we hope, we wish, I want. We never "broke character" from the future selves who'd already done these things. We simply gushed over the airwaves every day about how awesome it was that these financial miracles had come to pass, how grateful we were, how fantastic it felt to be empowered.

On day 85, Catherine hit the $200K mark. On day 88, I wrote out that check to my joint family account with Bill. And on day 90, Geri took her husband to the Italian restaurant we'd visualized almost one hundred times, and he cried as she handed him the gold membership card and showed him the positive balance in their bank account, debt gone.

•   •   •

You can future pull yourself through texts, voice messages, vision boards, and emails. If you want to amplify your results, then future pull in conversations with a buddy or small group like Catherine, Geri and I did. To join me for a live demo of a group future pull go here:

Here's exactly how to do it:

1. Invite each person to share her abundance or other goal in one sentence. Specific clear goals work fastest, i.e., "$25K this week" vs "more abundance."

2. Count to three and inhale/exhale deeply a few times.

3. When you open your eyes, transport yourself to a place where you have achieved your goals.

4. Without using "I hope, I wish, I would like, someday…," but speaking entirely in the present, talk about how awesome life is now that this goal is actualized, and abundance is your new reality.

5. The key is *feeling* the emotions, sensations and thoughts that arise when you're already living this life—where it's already done.

6. Speaking and feeling in the present moves you past any resistance, doubt and fear, and into the place where we began this chapter, where your goal is your new life. You did it. It worked out. It's as good or better than you imagined.

7. Notice any changes in your posture as you step into your new reality.

8. Continue the conversation for a few minutes, then go about your day. See if you can adopt the posture you felt during the future pull while doing your daily tasks. This will act as a magnet for change and empowerment. Watch for the miracles to begin!

Future Pull Party

If you want to supersize the future pull power, try this: At our Thought Leader Academy retreats, we host a party where everyone comes dressed as their future self. Women bring props like photos from recent trips to awesome places, cars they've purchased, their dream house and their best-selling book covers. The group energy is electric. Gather a group of friends wacky and open enough to play with you and spend an entire night in a future pull, dressing, eating, thinking, speaking, smelling (maybe your future self wears amazing perfume or essential oils) your new rich life. The group is greater than the sum of the parts. Have a blast in your new energy and let the manifestations roll in! I know multiple people who manifested houses, trips, relationships and millions of dollars out of a future pull party- try it!

RELEASE

On April 15th, 1912, two lookouts on board the Titanic stood high above the glassy, black Atlantic water. You know the story. The night was moonless. Neither lookout had binoculars. They didn't see a thing until right before the iceberg tore a hole in the side of the ship.

It's nearly impossible to think of the Titanic and not hear Celine Dion play in your head (and see Leonardo and Kate leaning out over the bow, pretending to fly), but stick with me because there's an important detail about icebergs and *The Science of Getting Rich – for Women.*

Scientists have determined that only 1/10th of an iceberg is visible above the water—a phenomenon that has to do with ice having lower density than seawater. Because of this, icebergs have been ubiquitously used as a metaphor for the conscious and subconscious mind. The idea is that our conscious mind is the 10 percent of the iceberg we can see above the surface and the subconscious mind and the subconscious is the 90 percent that resides, invisible, below the water. According to and *Inc.com* article, research from one Harvard professor showed that 95 percent of our purchasing decisions are made by the subconscious mind. I believe at least 80 percent of all decisions are determined by this mysterious part of our brain.

The Titanic effect is what happened with all my initial attempts to make six figures in a year—I hit an iceberg every time.

New Year's Day: my friend Joanna invited five friends to her photography studio to set our goals together and make vision boards. Her studio was a vast loft space in the West Loop of Chicago. We meditated, lit candles, journaled our goals, then blasted music, drank herbal tea and spent the rest of the day pasting images of our visions fulfilled onto foam core board. I taught them how to future pull. Our visions expanded. It was an awesome day, epically inspiring. We felt unstoppable.

We'd made a good start. We'd embodied the first step in the equation: *Be.* The problem was that we then went right into *Do,* and I quickly got stuck. If I'd been asked on a polygraph if I wanted to make $100,000 that year, I'd have responded with an ecstatic yes! and passed. My conscious mind absolutely wanted to make $100,000 as a writer and coach that year. I visualized myself with the money. I read abundance books with zeal, but hanging out beneath the surface, a good bit of the 90 percent of me under the "water" was saying, "No, no, no! You're not worthy. You're not capable. You're not allowed. You don't deserve it."

Jumping from *Be* to *Do* comes at a high price. Reaching our goals, financial or otherwise, becomes like swimming upstream. We are like Sisyphus pushing his eternal boulder up the mountain. I set the goal to hit six figures at least five times. That year in Joanna's studio, I didn't even come close.

However, when I employed the strategies I will teach you in this chapter, I smashed through the 6-figure goal and have doubled my revenue every year since.

In his many books on the subject of wealth creation and attraction, Joe Vitale calls this "The Missing Secret" (to manifesting wealth). Amusingly, he was also featured in the movie "The Secret," which focuses primarily on Part 1 of my Science of Getting Rich for Women equation. Like me, Joe discovered that, if you leave out what I will teach you in this chapter, only a very few people will achieve their money goals.

You already made a start on this step in the first CHAPTER of this book, when you looked at your first memories and impressions of money. Our early conditioning from family, religion, culture, peers and even our ancestry can point us toward potential blocks to wealth and abundance. The fascinating thing is that these blocks can show up as subconscious resistance or as outer obstacles.

Laurece West, founder of easilycreative.com, is a true polymath: formerly a nurse, medical researcher, massage/energy therapist, now she's a singer/songwriter/performer/recording artist, voice coach, and business consultant. She explains:

> From before we were born to age 7 particularly, our brains function largely in a theta state (the brainwave associated with hypnosis and imagination). Our minds are designed to quickly assimilate hundreds of things our parents and society teach us and play, like baby animals. Unfortunately, in this state, we also integrate family limiting beliefs and negative self-belief from our own challenges. These programs run subconsciously behind the scenes and determine our reality.

As it had in mine, the phenomenon of subconscious blocks manifested in my friend Alex's life.

I met Alex in a prosperity class in Chicago. She was a make-up artist working at a department store and wanted to work with high-end clients on TV shows. She started *Being* her vision and took more action than most of us in the class. She had coffee with people who could possibly refer her new clients, networked with colleagues who'd broken into TV make-up and offered her services pro-bono to a TV station in Chicago to build her resume. She was *being* a total badass. But the class didn't give us the *Release* step of the equation. It was do, do, do. And Alex had success. She manifested three new high-end clients, one a TV personality in Chicago, and increased her income by several thousand dollars in a month. She was feeling thrilled until someone hit her car in a parking lot and didn't leave a note. Her insurance went up, and her mother called to ask for a loan. The total in unanticipated expenses was more than her increased income. She left the class in disgust.

I believe if Alex had the *Release* step of the Science of Getting Rich equation, those unexpected expenses would have stopped, or she would've made the money back quickly and kept going without experiencing many setbacks. Alex consciously wanted abundance and fulfillment, but she discovered later that, subconsciously, she believed she was too old, not worthy of success and guilty for having more money than her mother. I'm happy to report she *did* find a way to release the inner blocks and is now living in LA working on several TV shows.

• • •

How do we find out if we have limiting beliefs or inner blocks to abundance? Again, you made a start in the first CHAPTER when you explored and excavated your early memories and programming around money and wealth and your worth. You can do this exercise again:

Or you can use one of my favorite techniques to reveal limiting beliefs called "2 Columns."

2 Columns

Find a blank piece of paper or start a new doc on your computer or tablet. Draw a vertical line down the center of the page. On the left side of the page, write your desired financial goal. Hold that number in your mind and check how likely you feel you'll achieve that goal in the next month, six months, year?

On the right side of the page, list every reason you don't believe or fear you can't make or have that amount of money in the timeframe you desire. Don't try to be spiritual or wise here. You want to let your fear thoughts, your ego, the parts of you that worry have a voice. If you're not getting anything in column 2, consider taking a bold action toward your big financial goal. This could be pitching a new client, raising your rates, hiring someone to work with you or turning away work you don't enjoy. Take the action. If any fear, judgment, worry, procrastination or resistance arises, write down the message that goes with the resistance.

Example: I know it would be helpful for me to reach out to three potential clients this week. I find myself organizing my dishes and giving my dog a haircut instead.

So, I do 2 columns:

"Sign three new clients."	"I might get rejected."
	"I might find out no one wants to pay for what I offer."
	I will feel ashamed if they say no."
	"I'll have to give up this business idea."
	"The economy is bad."
	"People won't be willing to pay what I charge."
	"People aren't investing in high-ticket services right now."
	"I don't know how to find ideal clients."
	"Other people do what I do, only better."
	"Other people are more well-known."
	"I don't have enough experience for people to pay me."
	"Other people have big advertising budgets."

The ideas do not have to be rational; they may or may not be. The goal is to let the scared, small, conditioned, judgmental, critical, fear-based voice out. One of my mentors Fabienne Frederickson told me that, "Success is simple. Roust out every limiting idea and belief you have against your goal. Then take them to a mindset expert to clear them out." Every time I've done the release step, I have been set free. However, you don't have to wait to find an expert to release your beliefs. Once your limiting beliefs (fears) are on the page, you can change them using the strategies I will teach you in this chapter.

Sometimes my clients tell me they don't think they have any limiting beliefs, and I share what another mentor told me: "If you were totally aligned with your goal (no subconscious blocks) you'd already have achieved it." The idea is that, if we are going for something more, bigger, new, different than what we've had in the past, we likely will encounter limiting beliefs because we are asking our being to change or up-level our identity. Change of any kind can feel threatening to the brain. If you sense you have limiting beliefs about abundance, then take comfort in the fact that every belief can be revised. None of them are ultimately true. They are illusions, distortions, tricks of the mind. They are a false spell under which you've been operating. This is the point in the story when the spell is lifted and all the life, good, love, abundance and *joy* flow back into the land.

How do we release these limiting ideas? There are many, many ways to clear subconscious and conscious money blocks, and I am going to share my four favorites with you.

But first a very quick story.

A few years ago, I had the opportunity to speak with Marianne Williamson, author of the best seller *Return to Love* and eventual presidential candidate, at a women's conference. I had just turned thirty and was one of the "opening acts" for Marianne, who gave the keynote.

Although I can't find this written in her work online, what I remember most is her mentioning a phenomenon in nature whereby anywhere a poisonous plant grew, the antidote to the poison could be found growing within twelve feet. Marianne must have talked about many things, but I kept replaying the twelve-feet phenomenon over and over in my mind, for weeks. The idea felt awesome to me. Essentially, whatever wound, deficit or problem we encountered, the solution (the antidote) was also present. The concept excited me, gave me ballast. I took from this that whatever we need is truly at hand.

I share this story because I want you to know that your antidote to any internal or external resistance to richness, wealth, abundance, joy, purpose and success is also here- now. I am going to share my top four favorite strategies to clear and align all levels of your being to richness and success, but know there are infinite ways to do this work. The four found in this CHAPTER have proven the most potent, the most efficient and the most enjoyable for me and my clients, and I encourage you—whether you've sampled these before, or this work is completely new and feels ludicrous—to try them all.

I'll walk you through all four strategies (and one bonus strategy) step-by-step. I've invited several women neuroscientists and mindset experts who specialize in wealth work for women to provide additional explanations of the way these strategies work. To ensure you get the maximum benefits from the *Release* step of the equation, I've also created a fully guided experience for each strategy, which I'll coach you through in real time. If you prefer to jump right to the guided strategies go:

1. Emotional Freedom Technique (aka Tapping/EFT)

I met Nancy Linnerooth, my EFT/tapping guide, through a community of women entrepreneurs. I'd watched a few tapping videos on YouTube and was intrigued by the therapy's track record of helping heal PTSD, which I'd been diagnosed with twice. Nancy helped women with all kinds of issues, but she specialized in using tapping to help women overcome money and success blocks.

After one session, I knew I'd stumbled into something special. I was halfway through the year in which I'd declared $1M in sales, yet the first four months of the year had been abysmal. Every day I heard my inter-nalized childhood messages: "You don't deserve it. You're not good with money. You don't know what you're doing. You'll never make a million in sales. It's bad to want money, to focus on wealth. You can't build a team. You're a weak leader." I did my best to push past the critical thoughts, but I felt as though I was swimming with weights strapped to my legs. After two sessions with Nancy, I felt a physical, palpable release. Within eight weeks, my company had our first-ever consecutive $100K months in sales. As the false beliefs loosened, I felt more empowered. All sorts of other neat things emerged too: confidence, self-love, and more joy in each action I took. I felt more present. I felt expanded. All from tapping my fingers on a few spots around my body.

Here is Nancy's explanation of EFT in her own words:

"My journey has been interesting. After college, I earned a degree from Harvard Law School and practiced law for nine years in Chicago. I then went to graduate school near Seattle for a master's, became a therapist, and practiced therapy for over 17 years. In 2001, I became a coach and an entrepreneur, using skills and training from therapy, law, and other disciplines such as improv and Emotional Freedom Techniques. Although I live in Seattle now, I work virtually with people all over the world.

"Early on in my coaching practice, I started noticing that some clients just couldn't seem to reach their goals. It didn't matter how motivated they were, how capable they were, or how clear they were on the steps they needed to take. The usual accountability-based coaching practices just didn't work for them. When I discovered the power of Emotional Freedom Techniques (aka EFT or Tapping), I began using it with my struggling clients. With Tapping, we quickly uncovered subconscious blocks—internalized rules, beliefs, and fears—that were triggered whenever they tried to go after their dreams. When we tapped on these blocks, they released their grip. It was amazing to see people who had been ready to give up on themselves start taking actions they'd been stalled on, sometimes for years.

"I realized that was my mission: freeing women from their subconscious blocks so they can follow through on *their* missions. Our work together allows my clients to change their parts of the world in the ways they're meant to.

"The mechanics of tapping are simple. While directing your focus, you tap with your fingers on different points on your hands, face, and body, which are some of the same acupoints used in acupuncture and acupressure. When I first started using tapping with clients, there wasn't a lot of research to support it. I wasn't willing to wait though, because I saw the big changes it brought to my clients. Tapping worked faster and more effectively than any other technique I'd found.

"Since then, a fairly large body of research has shown that tapping works, particularly with anxiety disorders like phobias and Post-Traumatic Stress Disorder. It's at least as effective as therapy's "gold-standard" approach: Cognitive Behavioral Therapy.

"As for *how* tapping works, we don't really know. But there are clues in the research. There are studies demonstrating that tapping lowers levels of cortisol (the "stress hormone") and down-regulates the amygdala, which is the part of the brain that appears to regulate emotions.

"Memory Reconsolidation also seems to play a part, leading to lasting results, long after someone stops tapping on themselves. So, if the emotional component of a traumatic memory is changed, which happens with tapping, the memory changes for good.

"While science is starting to explain why tapping is a great way to release PTSD and phobias, it still doesn't explain how tapping releases subconscious blocks—*yet*. I'm waiting for the research to catch up in that area.

"I've seen clients hold themselves back in spite of *consciously* wanting something and knowing how to get it. When we go digging with tapping, up comes a rule or belief the client didn't know they had. Often, they disagree strongly with that rule or belief, but they still feel some kind of pull towards it … Until we tap it away.

"A subconscious belief can absolutely prevent someone from creating the success they know they're capable of. Worse, I've seen subconscious beliefs completely block someone from following through on their purpose in life. That can be totally baffling. I've had clients come to me, knowing that they are called by something bigger than themselves—God, the Universe, their Higher Self, call it what you will. Yet, for years they've been procrastinating. Only taking partial steps. Not meeting their potential. Sometimes it's so frustrating, they are ready to give up.

"When we uncover the messages that have been getting triggered in their subconscious, they finally understand why it has been so hard to follow through on their dreams. And once we've released their subconscious block(s), it suddenly becomes easier to do what they've been trying to do all along.

"Clients often come to me after investing months—or years—and thousands of dollars on training and programs that were meant to help them achieve their dreams. But they've ground to a halt partway through because they weren't able to get around what's in their subconscious. I also have clients who have been successful to a certain extent pursuing their dreams. Still, they've hit a ceiling. They can see the next level, but no matter how hard they try, they can't break through to it. And they don't know why. I've even had some clients who know what their limiting beliefs are and where they come from. They've tried a number of different ways to get past them, with some success. But their progress is just too slow. It takes too much time and energy to fight their subconscious. So, if you don't clear your subconscious as soon as you notice you're blocked, you can waste a lot of time and money.

"In my work with women entrepreneurs, I've seen the same subconscious blocks show up repeatedly, keeping them from making more money, becoming more visible and having as big an impact as they are capable of. I created my MVP framework to enable clients to understand and release those blocks.

- "M" stands for Mindset. Women often subconsciously believe they're not worthy of the success they are capable of. These blocks can cause "Imposter Syndrome"—that sneaking feeling that you've gotten away with it so far, but they're going to figure out you're a fraud any second now. It can also lead to a general feeling of not being good enough that causes procrastination, avoidance or even self-sabotage.

- "V" is for Visibility. So many women hold themselves back from getting their message out in the world in a bigger way because they believe that no one wants to hear what they have to say. Or that they have to have *all* the answers figured out first. Or that they can't record videos until their hair and makeup are perfect—oh, and after they've lost ten pounds.

- "P" is for Profitability. This is probably the biggest collection of subconscious blocks women carry around. They can show up as a money ceiling that limits how much you can make, no matter what you do. They can stop you from raising your rates. They can trigger you to spend rather than save. Profitability blocks have kept huge numbers of women underearning year after year.

"Of course, men can have the same blocks. However, many more women seem to struggle with these blocks and to a much greater extent. Perhaps it comes from our training as young girls that we're supposed to be pretty, not effective. Or from seeing the boys called on in class instead of us. Or messages from parents not to stand out. And our experiences in corporate can be devastating, telling us that no matter how good our work is, a male colleague will get the promotion. Or that we can be harassed by a male boss who will never be punished.

"Finally, there are the old patriarchal rules—ones we've all consciously and strongly rejected—that I've seen holding clients back. Rules like: Men are more valuable than women. It's not safe for a woman to be noticed. Men are the leaders; no one will follow a woman. Women can't make as much money as men. And on and on.

"It's time to change *all* of these blocks.

"I worked with a client I'll call Pam, who was incredibly frustrated when she came to me. She had a decent real estate business, but she knew she should be making more money. A lot more.

"No matter what Pam did, though, she could not seem to get ahead. If her business made more one month, she would spend it on a big training she felt she needed. Or, if she managed to hold onto the money that month, the next two months' revenues would dry up. One year, she got a side job to bring in more money, but her business brought in less than year—by almost exactly the same amount as she made with the job.

"She was tired of the money roller coaster she was on. So, we got to work.

"Pam had a number of subconscious money blocks from her childhood. She had grown up poor. Money was always a struggle, so she had internalized a belief that she would never have enough.

"When we released the there's-never-enough block, we found a belief that she had to work really, really hard for money, just like her parents had. After that block was gone, we uncovered family messages that "only greedy people have money" and "spiritual people have to be poor" and released those. Finally, we raised her money ceiling—the set amount that she was "allowed" to have.

"There was a lot rattling around in Pam's subconscious! But as we released each block, she started to do better. She began marketing consistently. She plugged the spending leak and followed her budget. She reached out to and attracted higher-end clients. And Pam saw changes to the bottom line.

She made the highest commissions she ever had. Her business had its highest month ever. And the next month she made even more money. Now, Pam no longer fights herself to make the changes her business needs. Taking the actions she wants to is just … easy."

• • •

With the next three techniques, I've included the practice within the text of the book, but because tapping requires specific movements, I've found it far easier to go through a sequence with a guide. Join me as Nancy and I guide you through a tapping to release your money blocks and increase profitability and abundance:

You can also find out much more about tapping at Nancy's website: UnblockResults.com.

2. Neuro Linguistic Programming (NLP)

When I set the goal of $1M in business in one year, my coach kept asking if I could get to the $1M on a spreadsheet, to show on paper exactly how we'd make that number in sales by December. I could not get there on a spreadsheet. As I shared previously, I'd started EFT/tapping, and we'd had our first two consecutive $100K months. But there was still a several-hundred-thousand-dollar gap between where I was and the $1M mark. Then a friend said, "You should call Suzanne. She's really good with money goals."

"Maybe I'll work with her next year, when I finish the tapping work," I remember saying.

"She offers a guarantee for whatever goal you set," my friend replied.

I set up a meeting with Suzanne. It turned out that she'd helped many women cross the 7-figure mark. She did indeed offer a guarantee. "As a certified Master NLP Coach & Master NLP Practitioner," she explained, "I'm able to guarantee your results in writing. Plus, I'm stubborn. I will work with you until you reach your goal, as long as you keep taking action."

I sat on the Zoom call, looking at Suzanne's warm, comforting, fairygodmother smile. I realized I could wait and work with Suzanne until the next year, or I could start now and hit the mark faster. "Sign me up," I said.

We hit the million mark three months later.

Not everyone has the availability to work 1-1 with an NLP Master Coach, so I asked Suzanne if she would share about the modality and lead us through an exercise just for readers of this book. I wanted you to hear about NLP in Suzanne's own words and experience her expansive energy. After her explanation of the modality and how it works, I'll walk you through a potent NLP sequence. You can also go through this in real time at the portal

Suzanne Longstreet

I live just north of Toronto in a very pretty, small town called Grand Valley with my husband and our cat Ninja. I've always been fascinated with how people are motivated, how they communicate and how they interact with each other. This fascination is what led me to roles in the corporate world in sales, leadership, HR, learning, talent management and organizational development.

Today, I draw upon all my expertise to inspire and mentor leaders to focus on positivity through my knowledge of Neuro Linguistic Programming (NLP) and Positive Intelligence (PQ), so that clients achieve their goals, get clarity and confidence, to grow their mindset to achieve their goals in their business and life. I have multiple designations and certifications in coaching, including Certified Positive Intelligence Coach, Master NLP Coach and Master Hypnotherapist.

What Got Me Into the Work

I struggled with low self-esteem and low self-worth all my life. I was invincible up until around the age of eight. At that time, I started to doubt myself and to attract friends who were mean to me. This continued into my dating life, and I was more attracted to the guys who kept putting me down rather than the nice guys who liked me for me. This devolved into me choosing my first husband who was verbally, emotionally, mentally, socially, and physically abusive. I was with him for just under three years. Then I made the decision to leave him. I never saw him again. The lawyers handled everything, and I was free. Or so I thought.

My bruises faded, the bumps healed, and my bones mended. But what took the longest was getting his voice out of my head. I continued to hear *his* vicious and demeaning comments in my mind. I was hanging on by a thread and considering suicide. I went into a deep depression.

I reached out to various people for help over the next two decades. During this time, I had no dreams, no goals, no relationships, and no real friends. I was existing, not really living. I wasted years living in fear, swirling, and stuffing down my emotions with food. I kept looking for answers outside of myself and was unable to find any solutions. So, I just kept being invisible. I believed there was something fundamentally flawed in me.

Finally, I discovered the powerful and transformational tools of Neuro Linguistic Programming (NLP). I also discovered that I didn't have PTSD—I had Complex PTSD. (C-PTSD). I was relieved that I knew what was wrong, and I now had the way to solve my challenges. NLP gave me my life back.

A bit more about the modality.

NLP is based on the study of the best practices of psychology, neuroscience, positive psychology, performance, cognitive psychology, quantum theory and hypnosis. Essentially, NLP is how we communicate and how we process the information that comes into us from the world around us. The therapy was originally created as a result of the collaboration of Richard Bandler & John Grinder.

The more they studied the methods and processes of therapists, psychiatrists, and psychologists, they realized there were ways to create a change in the person's behavior by changing the way they process the information in their minds, their self-talk and their behaviors.

NLP works with the conscious mind, the unconscious mind, and physiology. We each have a thought that is usually formed in our minds as a picture. With each beat of your heart, you have a new picture in your mind, which is called an Internal Representation (IR). This thought then sends a signal to all neurotransmitters, which bathe every cell in the body, the physiology. Together, the IR plus the physiology create your emotions.

So, if a person doesn't like the emotion they're feeling at the moment, they need to pay attention to the thought (IR) that they are having. Change the IR, or the thought, and the emotion changes.

The Subconscious and Unconscious Mind

In the world of NLP, we believe that all limits to external success and fulfillment are a result of the decisions that were made in the moment that a negative or significant emotional event occurred in a person's life. At that point, a limiting decision was made, and this programmed the unconscious mind to create a limiting belief that stops the person from fulfilling their dreams and achieving the success they desire. The person may not even remember the event that created the limiting decision that led to the limiting beliefs.

The unconscious mind is programmed to protect us from harm. Even though a person may consciously desire success or wealth or fulfillment, if the unconscious mind believes that it may cause the person harm, it will bring up negative emotions like fear, worry, anxiety, anger, and more to slow the person down and keep them safe. This is why some actions become so challenging to a person. When these unconscious limiting beliefs, values, and attitudes shift, then and only then will the person be able to move easily towards their dreams and goals.

Many of the patterns that women have in society today are due to cultural and familial patterns that have been infused in our consciousness and behavior. In fact, sometimes we aren't even aware of the limiting beliefs and challenges until the goals we set are not realized.

Here are some of the limiting beliefs about women and wealth that I've encountered over the past several years with my clients:

a. I can't make more money than my spouse.

b. My spouse is afraid that if I make more money than he does, I'll leave him.

c. This comes so easily to me; I can't charge more for what I do/know.

d. Doesn't everyone already know how to do what I offer? How can I charge them for what is so easy and such common knowledge?

e. Since I can't afford it, others can't afford it either.

f. Women consistently undercharge for their services and give away more for less money.

I have been fortunate to watch so many women transform their net worth after connecting with their self-worth. It's a joy and an honour to see the transformation of a woman when they have released their unconscious minds from the crippling negative self-talk. Every time their past negative emotions and limiting decisions are removed, they take action differently, with more focus and confidence as they step into their true power and worth.

Together, we women are making an impact and a difference in the world by becoming whole, increasing choice, and taking confident actions. The more women continue to work on their self-worth, the more wealth they will create for themselves, and the more impact we will all have in the world.

You can learn more about NLP Success & Clarity

• • •

NLP Practice

Suzanne created an NLP sequence just for *The Science of Getting Rich – for Women* that you can access here

Or read this out loud to do the sequence here:

Part I

Before you can have a limiting belief, you made a decision. Something happened to you that caused you to believe that you needed to keep yourself safe and protected by not behaving in a certain way. It would have happened when you were very young.

Perhaps you saw your parents fighting about money, and you decided there and then that money causes pain and suffering.

Perhaps you were all excited to buy something that you really wanted, and someone made fun of you for your choice. This may have led you to decide that you would never be put in that position again.

Perhaps you had older siblings who would take your allowance or raid your piggy bank, so you decided to never make enough money to have someone take it from you.

Whatever happened to you in your past caused your unconscious mind to make a decision that has led to the limiting belief or limiting beliefs that you are now running. It is this limiting decision that you made that is causing your limiting belief(s) today.

What limiting beliefs do you have about getting rich?

Do any of the scenarios above remind you of something that happened to you when you were very young?

Write out all the beliefs you have about getting rich.

As you become aware of the limiting beliefs you have about getting rich, think back to the first time you had this belief. What did you decide just before you felt that you weren't worthy of making money, attracting abundance, or creating wealth for yourself?

Once you identify your Limiting Decision, use a clearing statement such as:

I release this limiting decision and any beliefs associated with it in all directions of time, space, reality, conscious, subconscious, genetically and ancestrally. I am now FREE to live a RICH, ABUNDANT LIFE.

Part II

NLP Model of Communication:

Neuro Linguistic Programming is the study of how we communicate with ourselves and others.

As you take in information through all your senses, namely sight, sound, touch, taste and smell, it runs through many filters in your mind. These filters are your version of reality (time, space, matter, and energy), language, memories, decisions, beliefs, attitudes and values.

Every person in existence has different filters that cause them to distort, generalize and delete information as it comes into their mind. You have as well, since the information is coming in at about 11,000,000 bits per second (bps) according to Mihaly Csikszentmihalyi, a psychologist and author.

Therefore, your memory of an event will differ from another person's memory of the exact same event. The memory gets changed based on how you process events that happen to you.

Every thought that you have forms a picture in your mind. With every picture that is formed, your mind sends data to the neurotransmitters that bathe every cell in your body; this creates an emotion.

Your emotions drive your behaviors through strategies.

So, if you don't like the emotion you're feeling, change your thought. Change the picture in your mind. If you don't like the behaviour that you're running, then change the thought in your mind.

Can it really be that simple?

Yes!

Try this.

Ask yourself: When you think of getting rich, do you have a picture?

What image do you have?

Is it a healthy image?

Are you in the picture?

What are you doing?

Who are you with?

What are you hearing?

Is it close or far away?

Make the "big" a positive; see yourself in the picture, make it a bright, vivid, happy image of you getting rich and enjoying your life. Bring it close to you and lock it into place.

Visualize this image of you getting rich with you daily.

3. Hypnosis

My freshman year of college I attended a rush event at a campus sorority. The entertainment at the event was a hypnotist. The man was around forty-five years old and looked to me like a Dickens' character, not one of the good ones. He seemed silky and lecherous. He asked a volunteer to come to the front of the room, and, through a series of antics, he put her into a state of hypnosis. In this suggestible state, the young woman quacked like a duck, held a spoon on her nose and crawled around the room on all fours like a dog.

I left the event before the act finished. I felt disturbed, triggered and violated on behalf of the sophomore who'd volunteered to be part of his act. I took that sorority off my rush list and recoiled from any mention of the word hypnosis for years.

Years later, I experienced a severe trauma, the stillbirth of twin boys after I went into premature labor in my first pregnancy. After coming home from the hospital, I had night terrors, PTSD and I couldn't sleep. My doctor prescribed an anti-anxiety medication that allowed me to sleep, but I wouldn't be able to get pregnant while taking it. I tried meditation and visualization, herbal tea, begging prayers. I could not sleep without the medicine.

One night the idea of hypnosis floated into my mind. *Nope*, I thought. No way.

But desperation is a great motivator, and I decided to research the therapy to find out if there was a kind of safe, professional therapeutic hypnotherapy that might be able to help me. I found Sheila Swenson. In seven sessions, by the time our doctor gave us the green light to try to conceive again, I was off the medication and sleeping most nights.

What surprised me in my work with Sheila was that she didn't focus just on the trauma with our twins. She asked what else I wanted in life, in addition to starting a family. I heard every word she offered during hypnosis. I was fully conscious, fully in control of my body and mind; I simply fell into a very deep, relaxed state and, when I left, things that had been a problem were no longer a problem. Sheila also recorded a general wellbeing hypnosis as a gift for her clients. I listened to it that night and every night for the next five years. The wild thing was that, not only did I start having the best sleep of my life, but I began having positive, expansive dreams and waking up feeling enthusiastic about the day ahead.

I've used hypnosis to clear all types of inner blocks and resistance, as well as install the new beliefs, thoughts, attitude and identity I desire to embody. I found hypnosis so effective that I trained in the modality and now create hypnosis sequences for my clients and for our Thought Leader Academy members.

Recently I met a talented new hypnotherapy expert named McKenzie Buzard. I asked if she would explain hypnosis and give us some of the science that goes into the therapy. McKenzie said: "Hypnosis is a type of meditative state that allows you to directly access your subconscious brain and reprogram it. It does this by altering the brain mechanisms involved in attention, mental absorption, reasoning, beliefs and volition; specifically, the dorsal anterior cingulate, dorsolateral prefrontal cortex, and the default mode network. In this altered state, the brain is very suggestible and therefore, more open to change. This is important, because the subconscious brain is where all of our beliefs, emotions, and habits are formed. By working on this level, we are able to define the root cause of what we are experiencing and shift our beliefs and emotions around it. We do this through neural-reprogramming, which is a type of brain training that uses positive affirmation statements to create and strengthen new neural pathways in our brains. Ultimately, this practice changes the entire way we think and feel about a certain topic.

We all have certain beliefs and habits around money. Depending on how we were raised, we will form certain beliefs on what money is, how easy or hard it is to generate, and who we are in relation to it. If these beliefs were positive, we most likely will have a good relationship with money and will not have issues creating wealth. However, if the beliefs are negative or skewed in some way, then we might be subconsciously sabotaging ourselves with the limiting views that we hold. Hypnosis allows us to find what those limiting beliefs are and change them on the powerful level of the subconscious brain. With this tool, we can retrain our brains to think positively and abundantly about money, or any other subject. Hypnosis allows you to take back control of your own beliefs and begin to create the life that you deeply desire.

• • •

I partnered with McKenzie to create a hypnosis sequence just for *The Science of Getting Rich – for Women* (see below) or go to the portal (below) to relax and I will guide you through each step.

Take three deep, long breaths.
Feel yourself relaxing with each exhale.
Feel a warm gold light spread from your crown to your feet.
This is the light of abundance, of riches, of success.
This light is here to support you in creating the Rich, Abundant Life you are here to live.
As you count back from 5 to 1, you become even more relaxed and filled with this loving light.
5-4-3-2-1
You are now in a deep, wonderful state of relaxation.
As you relax and take in these words, this light will now release any limiting belief, thought, attitude, or idea, and any/all resistance.
You are now free from any false, limiting, scarcity idea or experience.

*You now exclusively live and create and attract from a place of wor-
thiness and alignment with success and abundance.*

You are now a vibrational match to massive financial abundance.

You are worthy of abundance.

You are capable of creating and receiving massive abundance.

You now create and receive massive financial abundance.

You are RICH.

You deserve to be RICH.

It's fun and easy to be RICH.

*You now have ALL the resources, love, connections, support, ideas,
inspiration, creativity you need to be financially successful and free.*

You are Financially Successful NOW.

You are Financially FREE now.

*Feel any resistance to your RICH life now dissolve. Feel it leave your
body. Feel it leave your mind. Feel it leave your subconscious.*

You are free. You are clear.

You are Success & Abundance now.

*SEE yourself living a life of abundance, freedom, health, joy, fun,
connection, inspiration, impact, and SUCCESS.*

Visualize you living this life NOW (for 1-3 minutes).

This is your new reality. This is your life now. It's already done.

Now count back from 5-1.

*When you reach one, you will feel energized, awake, alert and
abundant.*

5-4-3-2-1

4. Clearing Mantras

Our limiting beliefs, thoughts and attitudes can spring up at random moments.
I've found it helpful to have immediate power tools to dissolve these beliefs
when I don't have time to do a full EFT, NLP or hypnosis sequence. Think

of these phrases as waves that, over time, raze mountain into the sea. Many traditions have clearing statements that work their way into the subconscious and release limiting, fear-based thought.

The Hawaiian healing practice of Ho'oponopono has been used for hundreds of years to dissolve resistance, fear, doubt, limited ideas and, recently, through Joe Vitale and Dr. Hue Len, money blocks. If you read Doctor Hue Len's story about healing an entire ward of violent criminals solely by using the Ho'oponopono statements, it will stretch your mind. We can use the same process anytime we sense a limiting thought.

Here is an easy way to use this practice, according to Joe Vitale.

1. Notice the limiting thought, idea or feeling. (You don't even have to know exactly what the limit is; as soon as you feel resistance to taking an action toward prosperity or feel triggered or upset by something internal or external, you can start the process.)

2. Breathing deeply, hold the feeling or thought in your mind and say:

   a. I love you

   b. I'm sorry

   c. Please forgive me

   d. Thank you

Joe Vitale suggests that you don't have to like these statements, believe them or even believe in the process. By simply repeating the phrases, you will begin to dissolve the block. You are not asking the situation or block to forgive you; you are asking your mind or life or the Universe to "forgive" you for having the limiting thought.

I had resistance to this releasing technique because I didn't like that statement, but I stuck with the practice after hearing Dr. Hue Len's incredible story. Within 48 hours, I felt a positive shift and was able to take actions like writing and pitching larger speaking engagements and client projects as a result.

If those four phrases feel cumbersome, Gabby Bernstein has a simpler mantra. In her mega bestselling books, she suggests using phrases such as: "I forgive myself for this thought" or "I choose love instead of this." I experimented with variations of her wording and can sometimes feel the limiting idea or feeling dissolve as soon as I speak the words. For money blocks, my favorite version is, "I forgive myself for this fear; I choose Abundance instead of this."

If neither of these statements feel aligned for you, you can try: "I release this limiting thought, and I choose Abundance instead of this."

I don't have a scientific explanation for the way clearing mantras work. What I do know is that, anytime a limiting idea or fear-based thought arises, you have the power to use them to help you receive more money and create a rich, abundant, amazing life.

I love that clearing statements are free and take only seconds to deploy. They are available to every human in every moment. If you don't believe clearing mantras will work, be a scientist in your own life and try them for a week, or a month. Make note of any positive changes internally and externally. Record any unexpected abundance, love, new opportunity or inner peace that comes to you as a result.

Once you release—and keep releasing as needed—your list of fear, doubt, limitation, lack and resistant thoughts, attitudes and beliefs, you are restored to your true nature: an Abundant, Worthy, Amazing, Powerful Creator. The channel of Abundance is open. You are ready to expand. You are primed for a *rich* life, and you are ready to move on to the next step of the equation.

Bonus Release Method

This practice requires the work of a professional, but if you have the opportunity, neurofeedback is a highly effective therapy that not only helped me clear a layer of limiting beliefs but was the primary solution I found to recover from PTSD.

Diane Grimard Wilson, coach, applied neuroscientist, and author of the award-winning book *Brain Dance*, a memoir of her recovery from a traumatic brain injury, explains, "We most often get what we believe and expect, even if those beliefs are buried deep within us. Limiting beliefs will limit prosperity. They are like magnets moving under a table of iron filaments."

Diane uses a brain state training called Alpha Thetato help her clients release limiting beliefs and create more health, peak performance, financial abundance and success. Here is how neurofeedback works to *Release* limits, in Diane's own words:

> Incurring traumatic brain injury in an auto accident and recovering with a great deal of help from applied neuroscience, made me take an immersive dive into the field.
>
> I have been a psychotherapist, career and executive coach for over 20 years. The accident took me on a path of feeling lost, confused and then, ultimately, better for the whole trip. I spent the next six years recovering, figuring out how to drive again, learning mindfulness and to sing, had a retreat with Thich Nhat Hanh and eventually studying … a lot. My career shifted to a neuroscience-based coaching practice in 2011. That year, I passed the board certification exam in neurofeedback with the Biofeedback Certification International Alliance in the top tier of anyone who had ever taken it.
>
> My own life often feels like one big, amazing miracle. This is what I bring to the dreams and hopes of my clients.

THE SCIENCE: EEG-based Neurofeedback with the Alpha-Theta Protocol

Neurofeedback is biofeedback for the brain. Sensors, also called electrodes by some, are attached to the scalp. These relay EEG (electro-encephalograph) information to the client, providing a real-time stream of data that tells the brain how it's doing. Protocols are designed to reward the brain for increasing specific types of brain waves and decreasing others.

Biofeedback is based on the same principle used in training dolphins at SeaWorld or getting us to remember our password at the ATM. Producing the correct brain wave behavior gets us a reward such as a pleasant sound.

All brain waves are electrical activity identified largely by their speed in cycles per second. Alpha brain waves are neural oscillations with a frequency of 8-12 cycles per second. These accompany the peaceful states, for example, like from doing yoga. Theta brain waves are slower (4-8 cycles per second) and dominate when we feel like we are in "la la" land—unfocused, pre-sleep, preconscious.

Theta waves are considered the doorway to the unconscious and store memories that we have not been able to fully process. Increasing theta will increase deep relaxation and, under the right conditions, surface memories that were too difficult to process at *the* moment they occurred. These can greatly influence our beliefs, behavior and habits.

The interplay between theta and alpha waves serves to go deep and then surface images and sensations to integrate. My experience is that often these unresolved incidents unwind without conscious awareness. ("Diane, it's like a lot of scenes were going through my mind, like bits of movies, but I wasn't really watching.") Or we may recognize the scenarios that surface, such as an accident, without being "in" the scene and certainly having more emotional distance. For people who experienced trauma, this protocol should only be done with a trained mental health professional, after a client is stabilized, and has the coping skills to deal with any unresolved material that may surface.

Alpha Theta training is also used to help people who have not experienced trauma to achieve deeper relaxation, especially those who feel they are not ready to meditate. I have had many clients report significant increases in creativity, cognitive flexibility, improved relationships and self-confidence. Research supports such findings.

I use this training with clients in different ways. One is first creating a script describing themselves as being successful in a particularly challenging situation. I will read their script aloud to seed their unconscious mind with these positive images and beliefs just as they are slipping into a deeply relaxed training state. Seeding can be powerful.

The most interesting thing in doing this training with clients is they often look physically different over time. They look more present, more "with it," even if I thought they were before we started. Many lose excess weight without much stress and families tend to love the outcome since clients are more fun, have a better sense of humor and are more present to them. I have had clients who are very successful in their work and life do this training once or twice a week for more than a year. Their life just seems to get better and better on many fronts.

We most often get what we believe and expect, even if those beliefs are buried deep within us. Limiting beliefs will limit prosperity. They are like magnets moving under a table of iron filaments, they will shape activities and outcomes. I respect that each person has *their* own path to discovering limiting beliefs. Sometimes it's painful and surprising. However, if we increase our consciousness and are open to learning and curating our beliefs, we have more control in shaping our future. If we don't address our limiting beliefs, they are very likely to find a way to sabotage us.

Often a pattern I see is that women don't go after what they deserve. We are mothers, caretakers and people who don't expect the same opportunities and compensation as men do. But noticing the inequities becomes painful and internalized as not being good enough. In working on money and earning issues, addressing the worthiness and recognizing the value of one's contribution helps self-esteem, and higher earnings are the byproduct.

• • •

Tanya came to me with issues of a high level of anxiety and angst about her job, life, and not living up to her potential. A very talented woman of almost 37, the issue of her potential had many tentacles including not feeling heard, exercising her own leadership and better earnings. She had an Ivy League business degree and she believed everyone in her class was doing better than she was. She also had a subtly abusive boyfriend who never missed an opportunity to amplify her vulnerabilities. The pivot point when she reached out happened when she began having anxiety attacks at work. The disorienting panic felt like a heart attack and had a secondary impact: she became anxious about becoming anxious, especially during one of her many business meetings. This is a rather common complaint in my practice.

We began a schedule of bi-weekly coaching and neurofeedback sessions to help her feel more in control of her body and thoughts. Sessions included a check-in on how she was doing that day, owning her power in relationships, setting boundaries and restorative sleep. We tracked sleep on her Fitbit readings with the goal of increasing deep restorative sleep. The sleep data was natural for her with her gift for numbers and gave her a sense of control. We used the data to strategize sleep improvement. Sleep is the bedrock of brain and body function in so many ways. Good sleep will increase resilience, focus, flexibility and so much more.

We also did heart-rate variability training, a biofeedback tool based on breathing, to sync the heart and brain. It helped clear her thinking and reduce the anxiety, offering a pathway in the brain from the primitive reactive amygdala to the prefrontal cortex—home of our executive functions, higher thinking, decision-making and compassion. She could use the breathing training during meetings, before sleep and during tense conversations. We focused on finding her resonance frequency, the breath pattern which was stabilizing for her.

She made steady progress and within 10 weeks her panic attacks were almost entirely gone. Her overall resilience increased. Mood shifts from panic states to calm were much easier. She developed a capacity for using her words and decisions to shape her life situation. We identified triggers, sorting and peeling away her emotional reactivity, refining behavioral strategies to deal with the people around her; she felt more grounded. In this phase, she began to see her own strengths, needs and self more realistically, especially the tremendous value she was creating. Taking "a break" from her boyfriend was a hard decision; but she decided it was something she wanted.

After five months working together, she left the job she had when I met first her and, since her boyfriend worked at the same place, it was easy and natural to leave him too. She had found another opportunity that fit much better for her growing abilities. Her level of self-knowledge and understanding of her own worth allowed her to secure a promotion in the move and a larger salary. She also began to enjoy her life more, joined a running group among other outlets, and lost, without much real effort, 32 pounds in six months. And, in her running group, she found another boyfriend who is so good for her.

It's been a process she could have jumped off of at any point past when the anxiety attacks stopped—three months into our coaching and neurofeedback. Instead, having stabilized, she chose to take a deeper dive into the Alpha Theta training. Now, during the pandemic, she trains remotely in the comfort of her home twice a week. She sends me the graphs, and we meet in a weekly virtual session to monitor how her brain is doing. In the meantime, she got another promotion on the new job and, in her spare time, is investing in a small start-up company for a product idea she created with some friends from her MBA program.

•   •   •

Overall, Dian's income increased by 100 percent since we started working together. She is creating a rich life, with deeper relationships, less stress, fewer resentments about life in general and a great facility for managing her reactions and taking control of her own wants and needs. Best of all, at least for her, earning wasn't the main focus. It was truly a by-product of up-leveling her entire self-awareness, getting past limiting beliefs to value herself and manage and create what she really wanted most.

You can read more stories and find out more about neurofeedback @ www.DianeGwilson.com or www.BrainDanceBook.com

•   •   •

We've gone on a journey through five methods to *Release* any limiting belief, idea, attitude or fear. Which of the strategies appeals to you most? Which will you try first?

The *Release* step of the equation is mysterious, even mystical. With these brain-transforming methods, we become alchemists, turning toxic lead into gold—first energetic gold, and then, when paired with the rest of *Be + (Release) + Do = Have*, actual financial and life prosperity. If you've been reading along and are ready to experiences the techniques- go to the Get Rich book portal and I'll take you through them all here:

It's time for the next step in the equation.

DO

A woman called one day to ask about coaching with me. "I want to write a book, but not yet," she said. "What I really want is to make money."

"Okay," I said.

"My husband hates his job. I want to support us, and I'm a really good coach. My clients love me. They renew with me for years."

"What's the challenge you're facing?" I asked.

The woman replied, "I only have this small pool of people who know me. I work with five clients right now, and I want to be working with fifteen and run group programs too. I want to run retreats and coach a high-end mastermind. Every business coach I've hired says the same thing: Build a funnel, spend $30K a month on Facebook ads and hire a bunch of people that I have to manage and who eat all my profits. It sounds terrible. But I guess that's what I have to do if I want to make a couple hundred thousand dollars a year, right? If I want to scale?"

"I don't," I said.

"Don't what?"

"I don't run Facebook ads, have a huge team or run big funnels."

"How did you get to seven figures, then?"

I gave her my plan. "It's not sexy. I build relationships, develop referral partners, teach lots of free masterclasses and bootcamps and speak in communities of people who want to write books and speak on stages. I hire a few key people only if the mission of our company and the role they will perform "lights them up." I give my best ideas in my free trainings and talks and trust that the people I'm there to serve will want to work with me further. They do."

Her face lit with joy.

We worked on the *Be* step of the equation. She cleared limiting beliefs in step 2, *Release*. At each moment when she became overwhelmed with trying to decide how to launch her next program, or if she should hire an assistant, I asked the *Being* question, "What does the breadwinner of your family do?"

She shrugged. "How do you do it?" she asked.

I walked her into the *Do* step. We tweaked my business plan to align with her business. She quickly broke the $250K mark with a 70 percent profit margin, and her husband started grad school. This year's goal: $1M.

•   •   •

You began to activate the *Do* phase of the process during *Be* phase when we asked, "What would the (insert your vision: multi-millionaire or 7-figure CEO or best-selling author or awesome parent or thought leader TEDx speaker) person do next?" In *Be* we ask this question and in *Do* we take *action* on the answers that come from our deepest self, our intuition, inspiration from the Universe and the version of ourselves (or people who resemble that version of ourselves) who've already accomplished our goal.

I want to get straight into the top four ways I have used for this vital step of our equation—my favorite methods to create financial leaps through actions and make our vision board financial goals our current reality. These four strategies have generated many millions of dollars collectively for my own—and my clients' and colleagues'—businesses.

STRATEGY 1: 50 Ways

Many entrepreneur mentors teach a version of the 50 Ways game. I love calling it a game, because anytime we contextualize something as play, we loosen up, get less attached, open our minds a bit and access creativity.

The 50 Ways game calls upon the Reticular Activating System (the part of the brain that will "go seek" evidence and experiences for whatever you program it to as discussed in a previous chapter). It tells our brain, "Hey, there already *is* a way for me to achieve this goal, so now go fetch the specifics for me. It's almost as if we're asking our brain to remind us (versus make up or solve or figure out) something we previously thought was hard and scary.

Here's how to play.

To start, you can do a version of 50 Ways simply to identify paths to bring in money immediately. This is ideal when you might not know what you want to do for your big vision yet. Or, you do know your big vision but aren't making money at it yet. In Phase I, you play 50 Ways with the sole purpose of creating a cash infusion, of getting money coming in and opening any and all channels of abundance.

In Phase II, you can use 50 Ways to reach a big financial milestone, to hit your quarterly or annual financial goal or to inject immediate abundance into your business and life.

How to Play

Start by writing your financial goal at the top of the page. The results come faster when you use a specific number like $10,000 or $150,000 vs saying "more money." Then, set a timer on your phone for 20 minutes. During that time, shut down all notifications and hang a "do not disturb" sign in your space. Your only task during this time is to write every idea you can conjure up to make that amount of money.

As in brainstorming, there is no censorship, analysis or judgment of the ideas you write. You do not have to be willing or excited to do them. The goal here is to get your subconscious and conscious brain tapping into the already existing multitude of ways you could earn, receive or attract that amount of money.

My aforementioned mentor, Fabienne Frederickson, teaches the 50 Ways Game to her clients too. She makes a very important statement before anyone plays the game: "Remember, the abundance will come to you in the form of *opportunities.*"

Why this distinction?

Sometimes we imagine that money is going to show up like Ed McMahan jumping out of a van with a bouquet of balloons and a giant check made out to your name like in the old Publishers Clearing House commercials. We think we'll envision the money, make a dream board, say some affirmations and then, while we lay back on the couch, the phone will ring, the doorbell will chime, a torrent of internet alerts will flood our inbox with cash. That would be exciting! But what hopefully will, in the end, be even more exciting is to discover that the money you desire—*all* the money you desire—is here for you already, and it will come in through *Be* + *Release* + *Do*, and it will happen *through* you. It may not come in magic cash appearing in your living room, but in the form of opportunities that you will action (*Do*) into cash. And when that happens, you'll not only have the money, you'll know that *you* co-created it with life; you called it into being. You will have confidence and be empowered. You'll know how to create it now and anytime you want more.

Back to the game.

You may be tempted to quit before you write down 50 Ways ... don't! You may write three or sixteen or thirty, then become frustrated and angry at me and this book. You will think there are no more ideas. Keep Going. The juiciest ideas will come when you break through the "first-thought" rational level of your mind. If you want help, get on Zoom or a call with a friend and ideate together. I'll show you in the next strategy how to generate even more actions for your 50 Ways list. For now, trust your creative genius brain that has access to the Universe of possibilities and write, write, write until you get to fifty.

The first time I did this, I wrote down about sixteen, then threw the paper across the room. Not only could I not think of anything else, I didn't really want to do or believe that anything I wrote down would actually produce the abundance I wanted. I didn't even like most of the ideas I wrote or want to do them!

"Participate in a medical drug trial" or "Sell the car I use to get to the grocery store or drive my son to school." Nothing sounded appealing. This is normal. You'll weed out unsavory or unhelpful ideas in the next step. Remember that you're not committing to *do* any of these actions yet; we're just playing a game like Pictionary or Taboo that, to win, requires us to fill those fifty lines on the page with *something*.

The 50 Ways game increases in potency each time you play. My first round generated only two really palatable action steps: Send a heartfelt, authentic "love note" to ten previous clients. Ask how they are doing. Ask their #1 goal for the next three months. Then take one action to support them in achieving that goal, without any expectation of payment or them working with me again. My only intention was generosity—to be of real service.

I offered to introduce them to people in the publishing industry, if that's what they wanted next, to gift them a free ticket to our next retreat, if they needed writing time and support or to promote their book to our community, if they were launching soon.

A few of the ten replied with a quick "thank you." Four made specific requests that were easily to fulfill: Send them a recorded training or a fill-in-the-blank pitch template, so they could book a speaking engagement or favorite podcast. I followed up with a note about the trainings I was offering in the coming month and said I would be honored to gift free tickets to anyone in their network who wanted help booking paid speaking engagements or writing a book. I made no request to them personally. I did not ask them to come back and coach with me. However, three of them replied that they'd been thinking about me, that they'd gotten so much out of the work we'd done and my email made them realize they were ready for a next level—to write another book, to speak at TEDx, to grow their audience by 10x. Three of them hired me for coaching without me asking them for a thing. And because I reached out to people I already deeply loved, the chance to work with them again was an enormous abundance in love, joy, gratitude and fun, in addition to the financial investment they made in the coaching which totaled over $30K in four days. If you have ever worked with clients or helped friends or family for free, you now have an action step to put on your 50 Ways list. You can do exactly what I did. In my experience, every client who took this one action step received an increase of financial abundance, either directly or indirectly. Only 49 to go!

The second time I did 50 Ways, I cheated. I only listed 39. It was similar to running my first marathon. did not train properly and started out way too fast in order to keep up with a girl from my university with whom I wanted to run. The lack of honoring myself made me hit the "wall" hard at mile 21. Those last 5.2 miles were agonizing. As I don't want your 50 Ways game to be me dragging myself across the 26.2 clutching your chest so, here are some prompts that helped me tremendously.

- Use the releasing strategies from the previous CHAPTER if you discover a limiting belief that you can't come up with 50 ways. Bolster yourself with the reminder that even one of your 50 ways could get you an abundance infusion. Remind yourself that the Universe is so generous, and you are so amazing and inspired and resourceful. Your decisions determine your destiny so decide: You are going to come up with 50.

And remember this: Each time I've done 50 Ways, it's gotten richer, more effective and generated more financial abundance—so keep playing!

The first time I played, I was handed a blank piece of paper and told, "Go!" I've found over the years of coaching clients with this strategy that prompts can be tremendously helpful. So here you go. (To access our special 50 Ways game that has been infused with inspiration and creativity from our team, go to the portal.) We've got you!

50 Ways Prompts

What is something you are good at doing that people pay others to do? This does not have to be something you love or want to build a business around. If *anyone* pays *anyone* to do this thing, it can go on the list. Walk through your own life and the lives of people you know. What do you pay for? What do they pay for? Here are just a few from my life and lives of friends I surveyed:

- Accounting services
- Bookkeeping
- House cleaning
- Dog walking
- Food prep

- Errands
- Administrative tasks-personal and professional
- Home organizing
- Travel booking
- Cooking
- Physical training
- Editing
- Social Media posting
- Video editing
- IT support
- Email zero inbox-ing
- Elder care assistance like going to a doctor's appointment or picking up groceries
- Yard cleanup/gardening, raking, weeding
- Life Coaching, Business Coaching, Health Coaching, Relationship Coaching, Parenting Coaching
- Online courses
- Workbooks
- Journals
- Fun products that entertain and educate
- Health and wellness products like medicine, essential oils, meditation apps, food trackers, time trackers, fertility trackers
- Books, e-books, audio books, audio trainings
- and so many more!

If you have a skill that anyone pays for, you can offer that service and create an instant cash infusion.

Passions and Hobbies

I heard a story in a Joe Vitale (yes Joe, again, thank you Joe!) book of a woman who was unable to pay her rent. Joe, a prosperity/law of attraction teacher, asked her what she loved to do and had some skill in doing. She came up with three things:

- Travel & Biking (traveling to cool places and riding her bike around them)
- Raw Food Cooking
- Guitar

Joe asked her a few more questions, and when he got to the guitar she said, "I'm not an expert or anything. I taught myself how to play the guitar in a weekend and just like to mess around."

That caught Joe's attention. "You taught yourself guitar in one weekend?"

She had, it turned out. So, he recommended she start with guitar. She created an easy self-study course that she could record and offer online with a workbook. When she posted the course online, she was transparent about being self-taught and being someone who was still learning, but shared that she found the other classes she'd tried intimidating and complex. Her system was simply the couple steps she used to play her first few songs with ease. This is one of those stories that might sound either annoying or amazing depending on your mood. The woman generated around $10,000 in one month and kept selling!

We may not all instantly make five figures a month through one item on our 50 ways, but the lesson for me in the woman's story was to list my passions, check that I had some skill at them and offer something to people who wanted to learn what I'd learned.

People can learn guitar a jillion different ways—online or in person from established experts or rock stars or celebrities—including for free on YouTube. But some people (many, it turned out) were inspired to learn from a young woman who taught herself in one weekend. It sounded manageable, it sounded fun, it sounded easy. You only need to be the fourth-grader to someone else's third-grader to be able to serve and truly help them. Sometimes your version of teaching or coaching or offering something will be even more appealing than the top experts in that industry.

There's another neat principle at work in this story: People don't pay for information; they pay for the *organization* of information. People want (and will pay for) a *system* that will get them a result they desire in the most efficient and easiest way. People who wanted to learn the guitar fast and have fun doing were willing to pay for the organization of the content. They'd learn to play a G-chord either way, but many felt inspired by this young woman's story, her success, her realness and were happy to pay for the course.

• • •

What passion or hobby could you turn into a simple course, workbook, or service? Do you want to lead a bike tour of Napa (paid vacation!), or teach someone how their family can go vegan without being deprived or cut their dog's hair because you spent 100 hours learning how to do this during Covid quarantine and would enjoy showing off your Edward Scissorhands skills?

You may experience resistance to making money doing things that are not your *vision*—the thing you now want to do full time. My experience, however, is that when money starts coming in, it gives us confidence that we'll be able to fund our vision and we feel empowered and invigorated. You're saying *yes* to Abundance in all its forms, and you can have faith that soon we'll be in Phase II when all the money comes in through your vision.

Honing

Once you have 50 ways on the page, go through your list with a highlighter or colored pen and circle or highlight any actions that resonate with you, for which you feel a spark of excitement. Your gremlins will come in hot here, so don't discount something if you're sure if it will work for you. If you feel excited or empowered, highlight it. Then add any that you feel willing to do.

Cross out anything that is not aligned with your values or would have a large cost to your life (like me selling my car when we didn't live near public transportation.)

Then …

Put those actions in order of your excitement first and willingness second. Prioritize those that would be the easiest to action. For example, if attracting an investor for your company sounds exciting but you've never done it before, put that action further down on the list. However, if coaching the six friends who've begged you to please come organize their closets and garage so they look like a page from *Martha Stewart's Magazine* like yours do, and you actually enjoy organizing people's stuff—and these friends have the resources to pay you $100/hour—do that one first.

Once you've completed the three steps, take one item from the list and take action on it before you go to bed. If everything you wrote down is a large project, break one project into steps and take one step at a time. If you wrote "launch new online class," then your first step may be to outline the modules, or call a friend who knows how to build an online platform and offer to do an exchange—you do something they need and they help you with the tech—to help you get your class up and running.

Note: If you come up with some great ideas but find yourself unable to take an action, go to the *Release* chapter, pick any technique and use it on your resistance. Do this one-to-three times and then check in to see if you're available to move. If you're still not, don't worry—you only need extra support. You can ask a friend or colleague who is working on creating abundance to do it with you and create an accountability partnership. Or, you can work with a tapping or NLP or other professional to help you clear out your resistance and let you fly.

Not taking action does not mean you're lazy, hopeless or a piece of dirt. It means you are scared or have an unconscious agreement or a belief that taking the action and becoming wealthy will hurt you or others or be unsafe in some way. You did not get to this belief by yourself and you're not bad for having it. We're going to clear it right out so you are free to create the life you are here to live!

NEXT LEVEL 50 Ways

In this version of the 50 Ways game, do the exact process I've outlined above, but focus exclusively on ways within your desired vision/business that you will attract and receive the money goal you've set.

A Real Life 50 Ways Story

A couple years ago, I had a big goal to reach $500K in sales by the end of the year. That was double the highest amount I'd ever earned, and by the autumn I was nowhere near the number. The holidays were coming and the pandemic had brought fear and contraction into the economy. I had no speaking engagements scheduled, no book launches, no networking events and I just didn't see how on earth I'd make more than $200,000 in two months. My single team member and I were overworked, and I knew it was essential to hire at least one more person but felt terrified that doing so would eat my profits and not allow me to hit my 6-figure commitment to my husband and family that year.

I lit a fire in my fireplace, threw on a bunch of logs and set my phone timer to 30 minutes. I reached thirty-six ways, then forty but could not think of anything else. I did pushups. I turned on loud music. I made jazz squares around the room. I was able to pull out ten more. Of the fifty total items, seven truly felt exciting. I did not know exactly *how* to do many of the seven exciting ways (attract an investor, offer a combination of keynote plus leadership coaching to a corporation, create an affiliate program for Thought Leader Academy) but they felt aligned, uplifting, empowering. I put them in order of ease of execution.

Two weeks later, a friend invited me to a coaching mastermind that she'd just joined. But I had no intention of being part of a new group. Investing in a new mastermind would *cost* money. However, I really like spending time with my friend, so I attended. I loved the people, the energy, the community. The investment to join the yearlong program was significant, about $15,000. My logical mind said joining would be a stupid decision. My intuition said, "Join." In *The Science of Getting Rich – for Women*, we get to value intuition over logic.

I joined the group.

Between November 1st and December 21st, I connected with incredible women, both in and outside of that new mastermind. People I hadn't spoken to in two years emailed me. Twelve new amazing clients joined our Thought Leader Academy, five of whom came directly from that new group. With the joy of knowing we would get to help all twelve become best-selling authors and speakers who would change lives and our world with their message in the coming months, our company crossed the $500K line.

My point in sharing this experience is that joining a mastermind and getting referrals from colleagues I hadn't spoken with in two years was not on my 50 ways list. Yet, I believe *doing* the 50 ways opened the way for these things to happen.

Why?

Enter: the Processional Effect.

I first heard the term "Processional Effect" from a coach named Eric Lofholm. The Processional Effect states that every action you take towards your vision will return to you in a favorable way. The positive result may not return immediately, in a linear way, or from the channel you expect, but the moment you take action, it's on its way!

So how is this relevant to the 50 Ways game?

That November, I made a list of 50 ways to bring in that last $100,000. I took action on seven of the 50. None of those seven yielded immediate incomes, but the new mastermind and "spontaneous" referrals from my current clients and colleagues did. Were the 50 ways I pursued a waste of time? No! Taking action on all seven of the items opened up the channel of abundance. Taking action gets us into the receiving mode, expands possibility and makes us a magnet for abundance.

The Processional Effect also lets us unhook ourselves from checking our email obsessively. This can happen whenever we take an action or become attached to our abundance that comes through a particular client, organization or opportunity. It says you're in action, you are getting your abundance jump, the money is on the way, so you can relax, give yourself wholeheartedly to your 50 ways actions and *know* the money is coming. Once we take actions, and keep releasing any resistance that arises, we get to have fun, breathe deeply, take breaks, let go. Focus on *action not outcome* is the invitation of the 50 Ways game and is a *fast track* to abundance.

With your 50 Ways list underway, let's move on to Doing strategy 2.

STRATEGY 2: THE SUCCESS MAP

Tony Robbins is famous for saying, "Success leaves clues." It's true. For every vision we have, even innovative ones that are going to change our industry and the world, there is someone (or probably multiple someones) who have done pieces of it and by doing so have left you a roadmap.

If 50 ways is a game, the Success Map is a treasure hunt.

Here's how it works: Identify at least three, and ideally ten, people who have achieved your vision (or a part of your vision) *in a way that inspires you*.

My client I described earlier—who became the primary earner and gave her husband the gift of grad school—used this strategy before she'd officially heard of it. She "interviewed" me about how I was making seven figures doing what I loved in an authentic way, found and used parts of my roadmap to make her next multiple six figures.

To find your Success Map, read articles, blogs and books about the people who've done what you want to do. Listen to their interviews on podcasts.

Watch their YouTube videos. Pull back the curtain on their achievements and watch for the mechanics of *how* they achieved what they did.

Identifying three to ten people who are doing what you want to do, and creating the results you want to make in a way that inspires you, is the game. The *in a way that inspires you* is important.

I had another client who had a desire to create big financial abundance. She wanted to buy a condo on the beach to enjoy with her husband and kids. She wanted to take trips and not think about the cost of the hotels or plane tickets. She wanted to hire a home care worker for her father 'who had a fall and needed more attention than she and her siblings could give him. She wanted to serve more people with the incredible energy work she'd studied and practiced for the past twenty years. But there was a problem. Everyone she knew who had wealth was a workaholic, burned out, materialistic and, well, basically a grade A dick.

These scrooges in her life made it seem as if pursuing wealth turned you rotten, and, naturally, if that was what having money meant, unconsciously she didn't want it. I told her I knew many wealthy people who were fantastic, kind, generous and happy. She didn't believe me, so I asked her to go out and find ten rich people who were awesome, generous, authentic, loving, fun, happy and free. She could talk to them or even read about them, but she had to find ten who were people with whom she shared core values and had the lifestyle she desired. After she identified these ten people and saw the way wealth enriched their lives and allowed them to bring even more joy and integrity to others, we cleared her inner resistance to having money and she had her first 5-figure month.

· · ·

Once you identify your Success List, write down the actions (*Doing*) each person took to achieve that goal. After you've listed the top 5, 10, 20 things you observe that they did/do, go through the lists and highlight commonalities.

The principal again here is: Success leaves clues. If 80 percent or more of the people you research all learned a certain computer program, or got a particular degree, or hired a mentor or lived abroad to give them an edge in their industry, chances are you will benefit from taking similar action. Through the examples of your Success List, you'll have your Success Map. The leaders you identified, simply by sharing their stories in interviews, books, podcasts and their own content, will give you the action plan, time hacks, and shortcuts.

I cringe a bit to share my first experience using the Success Map strategy, because the "plan" I uncovered should have been obvious, and I should have already been doing it. (This is how our inner critic works, right? Beats you up with shame in hopes you'll be motivated to change? My hope is by reading this book, you will let go of this mean voice, and with joy and self-encouragement jump into the strategies!)

Here is what happened.

Since third grade, maybe earlier, I wanted to become a writer. I spent a lot of time going to bookstores, looking at books. I read about writers and I listened to interviews with writers. I got jealous of people I knew who published books. I went on Amazon and imagined my book being there. I thought that to write I needed to be in the right mood. I needed to feel confident. The temperature outside needed to be cheerfully warm. I needed to have the exact right computer case, candle, notebook, pen, aromatherapy oil diffused through the room to put me into optimal creative space.

Instead of writing, I daydreamed, walking down the streets of London, where I lived at that time, fantasizing about my first book launch. I could picture the line at Blackstone's, a favorable review in The Guardian. When I returned to the US, the location of my fantasy book launch moved to the 92nd Street Y and the rave review was in The New York Times. All this visualizing was fine; I could even argue I was future pulling myself. But it could never become anything, because I was only doing the first step of the equation. I wasn't *doing*.

Then, on one of my long walks through the bookstores in my neighborhood, I had the idea for the Success Map. I made a list of my twenty-five favorite authors—I made a big list, because research would take me longer and I'd be able to continue to avoid writing—and I read every interview, podcast transcript, biography and memoir about them I could find.

I read about what they did, how they struggled, how they overcame the struggles and how they produced those magical words on the page. I sopped up their stories, their rituals, their idiosyncrasies but what I highlighted on my list was anything they *all* did in common. What all the writers I researched did was they *wrote*, most of them every day, or at least with great regularity and consistency. This should not have been a shock. It's pretty damn obvious that if you want to crank out books, you need to get your butt in the chair and write a lot of words. But it was powerful to see that every single one of them, without fail, had some kind of very consistent practice.

I could have hypothesized this, of course, but seeing those twenty-five names and next to each one "writes every day/most days" smashed whatever level of denial I was holding that I could be the writer I wanted to be and still walk around all day, watch TV, clean my closets, shop online and read other people's books every night, instead of writing my own.

When the solution presented itself in such stark relief on my page, a willingness (or maybe it was a desperation) sprang up. I truly understood that I needed to write daily or give up the dream.

I began to write.

I kept writing. I made hearts on my calendar on the days I wrote. I stuck a card that said "Writer" on top of my laptop so that every day I'd see what I had committed to and put writing first before emails, or ordering groceries or reading someone else's awesome writing, and thinking that was enough. I worked my way down the list of my Success Plan. I *did* other things those writers do as well: attending literary events, submitting my work, studying the craft, working with a coach and editor and connecting with published writers. The Success Map took me from fantasizing about being a writer to getting an agent, book deal with an advance, being published in *The New York Times*, to being on Oprah and to helping others successfully publish their books.

The Success Plan works for *any* goal.

At another point in my life, when I decided that I'd had enough of being broke, of feeling ashamed, of feeling like a dependent of my husband, of not having choices and freedom that I wanted in my life because I didn't make enough money to do so, when I got tired enough of not going to the writing conferences or flying to see a friend, of not investing in my career and keeping my life financially anorexic, I made a Success Map for my financial goal. I researched five to ten women entrepreneurs, who were also authors and mothers and worked with integrity and were powerfully feminine, and I made my Success Map list.

My absolute wild fantasy at that time was to make six figures ($100,000) in a year. Who had done it? What did they do? I found these leaders on YouTube, I subscribed to podcasts, I read articles in Forbes, and Fast

Company and Entrepreneur. I circled the common denominators and some very simple actions became clear: All of these entrepreneurs were visible in the public eye, at least on social media. I did not have a Facebook account. My excuse was I didn't care what restaurant my high school acquaintances were recommending for breakfast. I didn't want to spend time scrolling people's vacation photos on Instagram when I could be writing. That was valid, except that the people who had successful businesses had found a way to be visible to the world *and* get their books written. There was clearly a way to do both.

I realized quickly that I didn't need to spend time reading anyone else's Facebook posts or use it personally at all. I only needed to give generously to the people who were looking for help writing and publishing a book or speaking on stages—people who wanted, like me, to change lives with their mission.

My business strategy up until that point was to serve whoever showed up. Considering that I did very little to interact with anyone and preferred to write and connect with my intimate group of friends and peers in the city in which I lived, it was no wonder that I was making less than 20,000 a year! In fact, it's incredible I made that amount. *Visibility* was on the top of my new 6-figure Success Map.

The women I identified made videos. I did not want to do this. Wasn't that a benefit of being a writer ... no cameras? But the women who were making six figures in their businesses shared videos—lots of them. So, I made a commitment that every Monday I would send out a video to, at that time, a very small email list, and I would post on social media. I started with one video a week, and now I look forward to making these videos. I receive messages almost every day from people who said the video helped them that week, that they got something published as a result, or they got booked on a podcast or they wrote 1,000 words.

The mistake I'd been making was thinking the actions to make six figures were about *me*. The women I admired knew their work was about *service*, about *giving*, about *loving* not boasting about their lives or trying to create filtered perfect pictures. When I made that vital switch in my motivation and intention, my business and income, increased.

Another item on the Success Map to make six figures was *support*. Not one of the women I studied did everything in their vision by themselves.

They had at least one team member who loved the work and helped them grow. Here again, I hit resistance: Who am I to hire someone? I am barely running a business on my own. I don't want to interview or manage people. What if I f___ it up? Who would want to work with me? (Do these same thoughts come up for you?)

Again, this is *limited thinking*.

I read a study that said women focus most on what an opportunity will *cost* them, while men focus on what an opportunity will *bring* them. This is a great place to employ the divine masculine.

I needed to start focusing on the opportunity, not the cost. I made a list of everything I wanted help with in my business and tracked the hours I was spending on that task. I meditated on what I could do with that same time that would more than pay for the investment in a team member. Without feeling ready (I have not ever felt ready for the next big risk), I hired my first team member. Within six months, my income doubled.

When I'd reached six figures and wanted to take our company to $1M in a year, I made a new Success Map.

One of my mentors often says, "What got you here will not get you there." The actions I took to get to six figures would not get me to seven and beyond. Guess what I discovered? Every one of those women I studied had multiple people working together on their team; they became strong and wonderful leaders; they invested in high-ticket mentors and masterminds; and they networked with others who were several steps ahead of their current level of impact and income.

The Success Map strategy works for each new goal, each threshold. Once I reached $1M in sales, I found ten women who had multi-million-dollar-a-year businesses, who were also generous, fun, great leaders, women who were authentic, got tremendous results for their clients and had great relationships and personal lives. What I found, amongst several common factors, was that every one of them had a sales team. So far, I'd done all the sales meetings with prospective clients. I loved those sessions. I got to know a prospective client, ensured I could truly serve them and help them achieve their vision, poured love and affirmation into them so they'd *know*—even if we didn't work together—that they were worthy, capable. And I had that joyful moment of celebration for those who knew we were a great fit.

These were all great reasons for me to head up sales, but my doing so also created a bottleneck in our company. My calendar was booked out eight weeks at a time, so prospective clients had to wait months to have a meeting. We would not be able to help over 100 new women write best sellers and speak on stages in a year, if I continued to fulfill that role exclusively. Yep, you guessed it. The very next step for our company was to find an amazing, authentic, passionate, brilliant individual, who loved what we did and would love our prospective clients. I had the opportunity to get over my fear, the need to control, my ego belief that I was the best person to have these conversations. I saw in plain sight that every leader I admired had let go of this position in her company. I had to find someone who would do it even *better* than I did.

• • •

The Success Map will always show you the next step. You no longer have to wander around the desert, grabbing at shrubs, scraping your fingers and knees and bleeding into the sand for ten years. You can just plug your desired destination in our Success Map GPS and get on the superhighway.

We could stop here. If you play 50 Ways and make a Success Map for each new financial goal, you will know what to do. *Releasing* any resistance using the release strategies will help you take the actions.

But this is a book about richness, wealth, abundance. You deserve an abundance of strategies to have the financial freedom, success, abundance and riches you desire.

Here then, is …

STRATEGY III. THE ABUNDANCE ACCELERATOR

About halfway through our second year of Thought Leader Academy, I noticed that we'd spent the majority of our coaching time on writing and publishing, speaking and audience building. These are the first three pillars of Thought Leader Academy, and they were the primary reasons clients came to work with me. But pillar 4—creating financial abundance through thought leadership—was vitally important. Our clients knew 50 Ways and how to make a Success Map, but, like I want for you, I desired for them to have even more specific *doing* steps at hand.

To achieve the most efficient path to increased income, I took them through the ABUNDANCE ACCELERATOR.

I'm going to give you the exact accelerator steps our clients use in Thought Leader Academy. You can use this process to make immediate cash infusions or achieve longer-term abundance. Woo-hooo!

You can use the Abundance Accelerator Workbook to do each step in the Accelerator here:

WEEK I

VISION: Set your specific financial goal for the Abundance Accelerator (you can set this goal for one month, two months or 90 days.) Decide what of your 50 ways you want to focus on to bring in this #- the program, product, service you want to deliver.

MINDSET: Identify your current money beliefs and use the *release* strategies in the previous step if you feel doubts, fear, unworthiness or are overwhelmed when you set your goal.

ACTION:

1. Identify 3-10 people who represent the exact kind of person you'd like to serve. Schedule calls/Zooms/meetings with each of them individually to find out what they want most right now and get feedback on your offer/pricing.

   These do not need to be people who will hire you. You are not offering them your services. They don't need to be looking for help or support. To invite them to the short meeting, say that you'd like to support whatever they are currently working on and get feedback about a product/program/service you plan to create. Share that your intention is to learn from an amazing person like them—the kind of person you'd like to serve in your work. Share that your intention is for the conversation to be useful to them and that you're excited to support their vision any way you can.

When you start the meeting ask:

A. What is their #1 goal/vision/dream right now (get specific, let them feel it and share *why* it's important to them)

B. What is their biggest challenge to achieving that goal? What is it costing them not to have attained it?

C. Share your idea/program/product and ask what they think of it. Would they invest in something like this? Why or why not? What would a program/product of this kind need for them to be interested in investing in it? For what rate?

D. Ask what you can do to help them achieve their #1 goal right now and immediately help in any authentic way you can.

E. Invite them to introduce you to anyone who could benefit from what you are doing or could be interested in your new program/service.

BONUS: provide them an easy "done for you" email introduction that they can share with people, so it makes it *easy* for them to share with others who you are and what you do. Send this to them within 24 hours of your meeting along with taking any action you can to support their vision.

Examples of Ways to Support Someone's Vision

We don't have to spend money to support someone else's goals. Find out exactly what they need and ask the Universe how you could authentically help. Here are ways I've supported those I've interviewed:

- Given them a five-star book review on Amazon
- Subscribed to their podcast

- Re-tweeted or shared one of their posts
- Referred a client who needed their service or product
- Sent them an encouraging email about reaching their goal
- Visualized their success every morning for one week
- Introduced them to a guest for their podcast
- Promoted their podcast, book or social media content
- Have them as a guest on my shows/retreats
- Introducing them to a conference organizer who can hire them to speak at the next event
- Sharing information about a networking group that might be a great fit for them to meet new clients

Add some of your own ideas here. Almost everyone is seeking more visibility, so supporting or promoting their work to anyone you know would likely be very welcome.

You can also *do* something personal for them. If they love their dog and the dog starts suffering from anxiety and you know a holistic dog healer, make an introduction.

You can send them a favorite book, a link to a podcast interview or you tube video they might enjoy, if a shared love of art, literature or mystery novels comes up. Listen closely for anything they love and do something that connects them to that thing!

WEEK II

Top 10 Lists

1. Make a list of 10 people or organizations you would love to have refer others to your business/service (individuals who lead or know groups of your ideal client)

2. Make a list of 10 people you would love to work with (direct potential clients)

3. (If you've already been doing your service/offer) Make a list of 10 people you have worked with previously (whom you loved)

The combination of all three groups becomes your "Love List!"

Group 1 becomes your "Relationship Development List"
Groups 2 becomes your "Heart List"
Group 3 becomes your "Connect and Invite List"

THEN USE the 5-5-5 method:

If you want to generate a lot of abundance in a short amount of time,
Once a day Monday-Friday reach out to:

- One person from your Relationships Development List
- One person from your Heart List
- One person from your Connect and Invite List

How to Reach Out

Our Thought Leader Academy group all raised their hands at this step. "What do I say or do when I reach out to the people on these lists?!"

Here's what I do:

For the Relationship & Development List: Do one action/week or month that supports them and helps them achieve their goals (Examples: 5-star review of book or podcast that you take a screenshot of and share with them, comment or like a post, send a gift, contribute to their cause/organization, attend their event, bring others to their event).

For the Heart List: reach out with a resource, "thinking about you" email or video, or do something that helps them achieve their vision and/or authentically affirms their work/contribution. Invite them to an event or call with you. Pour into them. When it feels right, invite them to a conversation to discuss working with you. If they've already expressed interest but have a concern (money, time, etc.) offer a solution + special bonus to start.

For your Connect & Invite List: same as your Heart List (send a "thinking about you" email or video, do something that helps them achieve their vision, and/or authentically affirm their work/contribution. Invite them to an event or call with you. Pour into them. Invite them to a call to ask how they're doing, find out how you could help them next and invite them to introduce you to someone in their world who could benefit from your services).

Story Time

I felt very afraid to reach out to previous clients. I only chose people I adored working with for this list and I respected and valued their time. I worried I would feel pushy or the email would seem like an unwelcome sales pitch versus a genuine love connection. To get over the fear, I decided to create a new service. I wanted the email to be 100 percent authentic and for me that would only happen when I had something real and new to share with them. My email went something like this:

> Hi [insert name of beloved client]
>
> I've been thinking about you and would love to hear how everything is going! Working with you was a highlight of last year and I am so excited (though not surprised!) that your book won the indie book award and that you are now a #1 bestselling author. I'm creating a new VIP coaching program that will help mission driven experts and entrepreneurs write and publish a bestselling book and give a TEDx talk. It's much like what you and I did together but for people that don't have time for a group coaching program but want the big added credibility and visibility to be seen as an industry leader. Because I loved working with you so much, I wanted to share this with you in the event you have other colleagues, clients or friends who would like this special service. Thank you in advance for anyone you feel inspired to introduce, I would be tremendously honored to support anyone in your world make the impact they are here to make. Regardless, I am so happy to have had the opportunity to connect with you and would be thrilled to set up a zoom or call to hear your updates- know you are on fire!!
>
> Much love,
>
> Sara

• • •

I sent that email to ten beloved previous clients on a Monday morning. By Wednesday, one previous client had made a referral. But the thing that shocked me was that three of the ten said they wanted the new VIP service. They wanted to write another book and do a TEDx talk. I had no intention of any of those clients doing more work with me at that time. But something lit a spark. The single action generated an immediate $65K in new income with exponentially more from referrals over the next weeks and months.

What if you don't have previous clients or aren't totally sure what you want to "offer"?

If that is the case, do not fear.

If you have not attracted a new client/customer yet or are not sure if what you are offering is what your ideal client/customer wants, go to step 1 again and make your entire focus having 1-1 interviews with people who fit your ideal client profile.

Follow the steps to make the conversation valuable for them and ask direct questions about anything you're considering offering. Get feedback on the service, the investment cost and what would make it a yes or no for them and why.

Adapt your offer so it 1) matches what they say they want and 2) is authentic for you to provide. Write down or record (*with permission*) their exact words, and use these in your marketing, outreach and conversations moving forward.

Research where the kind of person you want to serve hangs out (online or in person) and become visible at those places.

Once you identify your ideal client and where you can find them, use the 5-5-5 Method to meet with five people a week who are an ideal client for your new service or product. You can offer a substantial "new program/product" discount in exchange for them providing a testimonial and sharing about you to anyone they know who is looking for the service you provide.

•   •   •

If *any* steps of the Abundance Accelerator feel overwhelming, you are not alone. We're playing *big* when we engage in this level of doing and it took me a tremendous amount of support to be able to get clear and then take action on my vision. You can book a time to speak with one of our success coaches if you'd like more hands-on help. You can also join our next *free* group The Science of Getting Rich- for Women Abundance Accelerator and do the game with me:

Repeat action steps from weeks 1 and 2 as is most relevant for your vision as many weeks as you want to "play" the Abundance Accelerator. In Thought Leader Academy, we've done 4-week and 8-week accelerators and some clients formed a pod to continue the accelerator actions ongoing.

The Abundance Accelerator will produce results. I've not yet coached a client who took these actions and did not generate income. Let's do this!

Throughout the weeks you play the Abundance Accelerator, you'll want to add this results-boosting practice.

ABUNDANCE TRACKING

There's a saying in metaphysics: what gets tracked increases. During the Abundance Accelerator, *track* every action you take toward your abundance goals as well as all abundance received. This will (hopefully) work to make this feel fun—like a game—*and* research, and my own experience has shown it will accelerate positive results!

You can use the Abundance Accelerator Workbook in our tracker template here:

What to track

What's been most useful to me is to track the key components to co-creating Abundance. The *yes* is the result, but there are actions we take before we get there that make the *yes* inevitable. We'll track these so we can celebrate *action* (versus only results) and gain clarity on what creates the most Abundance for us now.

On your tracking sheet:

1. Goal: write your Abundance Goal for the next month

2. Mindset: what activity/practice you do each day to support your belief in and alignment with that goal

3. Outreach: each action you take to reach out to a prospective client/customer or referral resource/partner.

4. Conversations: each conversation/meeting you have with prospective client/customer or referral resource/partner

5. Negative Responses: (The action here will be to ask anyone who decides not to say yes now if they will share why and what would have made it a yes for them. This will reveal any adjustments you want to consider in investment rate, offer, benefit explanations or bonus.

6. Positive Responses: YES's! With exact $$$$$$ amount

You can set up this "game board" however you like—handwritten with hearts, digital or a simple spreadsheet or chart.

Example:

In the next month, I am so grateful to receive $100K

ACTION	DESCRIPTION	FIELD NOTES
Mindset	6/23: 6 phase meditation on You Tube, tapping, self-hypnosis	Felt positive and excited
Outreach	6/23: Sent video emails to 3 people on heart list, sent pitches to 3 people for guest speaking engagements and reached out to 5 people on LinkedIn who commented on video about publishing	

Conversations- Offers made	6/23: zoomed with 3 prospective clients	
YES's	6/23: 2 signed up for group program at $10K each	
No's	6/23: 1 person decided she did not have the resources to invest at this time. Said she would have done it now if $3K instead of $10K. She asked to be on email list and said she has a goal to start in the fall. Gave her free ticket to next event. Made a date to talk Sept 1st.	
$ Earned	$20K	
OR YOU CAN TRACK THE WHOLE MONTH WITH #'s		
Mindset	III	
Outreach	IIIIIIIIIIIIIIIIIIIIIIIIIIIIIIIIIIIII III	
Conversations with offer	IIIIIIIIIIIIIIIIIIIII	
No's	II	
Yes's/ $ earned	IIII	

The final component: *Rewarding Action!*

Make a list of 10 things you *love*. Try pleasure bundling—giving yourself one of these treats every time you take the action you committed to that day. By rewarding action vs result, we make the action itself exciting, detach from outcome and reprogram our brains for success.

If you hit inner resistance or inner challenges, go to the Release techniques in the previous CHAPTER and clear each day for five to ten minutes.

If you want to join our next Abundance Accelerator and take these steps with our community, go here:

Another Story Time

After that amazing work, you deserve a story about what you can create by doing the Abundance Accelerator.

Jen was one of our first clients to use the Accelerator. She is a full-time single mom who lost both parents in a short period of time right before the pandemic hit. Although she'd had a successful, thriving business as a coach and consultant for almost 20 years, Jen found herself stuck around finances in the midst of her grief and being overwhelmed by home school and the heartbreak of racial injustices pummeling America and her own community.

"I don't know what to do to start generating business again," she said.

We brought a group of Thought Leader Academy members to try out the process that had worked for me every time I became stuck. Jen took the steps outlined in this chapter. Here's what happened, in Jen's own words:

"In the summer, Q3, I started to get stressed out about not having enough clients and money flow coming in. I was in a doubt/lack mindset; what was I going to do?

I did Sara's Abundance Accelerator training, and it totally shifted everything!

- I wrote and published two books last year

- I began intentionally contacting people and companies daily and weekly

- I did all the challenges from Sara and the calls inspired and fueled me!

- I tracked all my contacts on a spreadsheet and continued to follow up with people, and past clients starting contacting me again for my business. It was like magic!

- We created an abundance pod within Thought Leader Academy for accountability, successes and support to stay in Abundance mindset.

- By the time fall hit in Q4, I had sold $100K in consulting projects and coaching programs (and had proposals out for another 230k).

- This completely made up for the slow business in the rest of the year.

- I trusted myself again and know now I can manifest money if I get intentional, track my progress and have a circle of support!

Gina did the Abundance Accelerator with Jen. When she worked a corporate job, she'd enjoyed great success at Fortune 500 companies, yet had started to feel drained as an executive coach and consultant. After her mother passed away, she realized she needed to reinvigorate her consulting practice to experience the financial abundance she wanted and needed for her health and to support her life. In her words, here is what Gina experienced:

- The accelerator provided accountability specifically around me doing what I said I was going to do. It also inspired me to believe.

- The work we did around abundance in Thought Leader Academy supported a breakthrough in monthly billings of $28,000—the first time I hit that mark in 8 years, and by the end of the year, I had a proposal out for over $110,000 of new business.

- I clearly saw the mindset distinction that my financial abundance is tied to joy and fun. If I am not loving my work *and* life, financial abundance feels like pushing a boulder uphill rather than being in flow, and swimming in a stream of collaboration, fun, and joy.

Doing abundance accelerator work, our Thought Leaders have: doubled incomes, landed new jobs, resurrected flailing offers and services, and pushed through limitation into prosperity. You deserve *all* of this and more! Let's keep going!

STRATEGY IV. COMMUNITY (AKA YOUR NETWORK IS YOUR NET WORTH)

I heard recently that if you put a baby shark in a small tank, the shark will grow to about eight inches long. You put the same shark in the ocean, it will grow to 10-15 *feet*. When we *Be* + (*Release*) + *Do* alone, we will get results. One our own, we may grow eight inches. If we want to grow ten feet, we jump into the ocean and let the community of vibrating life and the vastness of our container stretch us our full, giant, genius, *powerful* potential. Jen and Gina and Donna and Diane and Patty and all the mothers, coaches, experts, activists, entrepreneurs, writers and Thought Leaders who have participated in the Abundance Accelerator experienced growth from doing the actions *together*.

This fourth and final strategy—*Community*—is an abundance producer of itself and is also an amplifier of all the other strategies you choose to use.

The summer I first decided to change my financial destiny and drove around every day listening to Tony Robbins on YouTube, I remember him saying that before Michael Jordan became the best basketball player in the world, he always sought out players who were seven times better than he was. Tony began to research other people who'd reached the level of "best" in their fields of play and found that they too sought out as many opportunities as possible to play with people better than they were. Tennis players, oboe prodigies, chess players, surgeons—the takeaway is that being with people ahead of us in knowledge, skill and performance will exponentially improve our game. Tony and others found this was true about wealth as well. Many experts have demonstrated that our *wealth and success will reflect the five people or groups with whom we spend the most time.*

When I was a writer-coach making $20,000 a year, most of my friends were amazing, creative individuals who also struggled with money. I'd *heard* of women who made six, multiple six or seven figures a year, but I wasn't connected with them; I wasn't in community with them.

Increasing our wealth doesn't mean we ditch people who don't share that goal or haven't achieved it. It may mean, though, that we will benefit greatly from adding connections and communities of others who have created the kind of financial abundance we desire.

Why?

If we continue thinking, feeling and behaving the way we have until now, we will not expand, increase and grow. Being only around people who think, feel, behave and act as we do at our current abundance level will keep us right where we are. While we can absolutely read about, listen to and imagine people who've achieved the financial and impact goals we desire, the fast track is to "get in the room where it happens."

Give yourself the gift and the stretch of valuing yourself enough to join a community and build relationships with people who have achieved or even vastly exceeded your goal. Very quickly, with little effort, you will hear how they think, see what they do, watch how they lead and overcome their own resistance and be able to adopt the same solutions, strategies and techniques they use to create wealth in your own life.

I'd listened to Tony Robbins enough to be convinced that I needed to "be in the room" with women who were earning six figures plus, but where were those women? Remember, the antidote is always within the metaphorical "twelve feet." Within two weeks of my declaration to find people seven steps ahead of me in earning, I received an email to attend an online workshop. I signed up for $200, liked the facilitators and was inspired by their story of financial empowerment and positive impact on the world. I appreciated that they taught ways to increase revenue authentically, with service and integrity first. The experience felt really good in my body. In *The Science of Getting Rich - for Women*, we listen and honor the body in knowing what community, what eco system will nurture, stretch and pull us forward to fulfill our destiny.

I took one of their lists of ten recommended action steps (that's all I could will myself to do since I didn't have the *Release* methods yet) and I made an extra $1,000 that week. I knew one strategy was not going to get me to six figures, and I was beginning to comprehend that trying to do all this work on my own was not a stellar plan. But the cost of joining the community run by these two amazing women was $10,000. I had $10,001 in my savings account. That was all I'd managed to amass over the past few years of working. Investing that amount in a group I'd met online for not even a hot minute did not seem logical or wise. It was a silly decision, an impulsive decision, my brain screamed. I also knew that nothing in my life was going to change if I kept doing what I was doing and being around the same people I was around, so I joined their year-long program.

Suddenly I was living in a magical world of women as committed to financial freedom as to serving the world. I'd burned my one remaining boat and *had* to change. As people in Alcoholics Anonymous say when they first enter the program, "We were as desperate as a drowning woman (they say man) seizing a life preserver." That was me in my first Prosperous, Abundant community. I vowed to do *whatever* the business coaching program curriculum suggested. In eleven weeks, I'd made back the entire investment for the program. By month three, I'd earned more than I'd earned the previous two years combined.

I learned that it wasn't about the money; it was about valuing myself and the work. It was about taking the risk to be visible and to be rejected. It was about friendships and partnerships and collaboration. It turned out that Abundance, Richness and Wealth is a team sport.

I met Rachel, who made over $100,000 a year as a psychotherapist and would go on to sign an annual $350,000 contract with a corporation she loves, working part time. I'd meet Lisa Frahley, a mission-driven lawyer who focused on supporting female entrepreneurs. Lisa crossed the $600,000 mark the year I met her and as far as I know, has now entered multiple-seven figures/year. Women from twenty different countries, women for whom English was a second or third language and yet felt called to serve English-speaking audiences with their gifts and who fought through the beliefs they'd be overlooked or passed over because of it. Women who had PhD's and women who never finished high school, women in their twenties and women in their seventies, women who walked and women in wheelchairs and on crutches. We were in it together, and they showed me that not a single one of my excuses held any weight. The only reason I wasn't creating wealth was because of my limited mindset and actions, and no one there was going to stand for me reaching anything less than my full potential.

I've since participated in almost a dozen different business, entrepreneur, writing, artistic and financial communities. I currently work with two mentors and am members of both their communities. One of my mentors lives in Paris, is an incredible mother, works only one hour a day most days and brings in $3-5M/year. She serves with courage, soul and the absolute belief you can create *richness* and have your life back.

My other mentor is a fiery, passionate leader who makes $35M/year at her company. Yes, that's $35 million. For sure more than seven steps ahead of me. Right now, I don't aspire to run a $35M/year company, but I do want to help several hundred women a year write life-changing, world-changing, best-selling books and transform lives of audiences around the world with their message. I desire to buy a new house for our family, help my son travel around the world and support my husband in his greatest creative endeavors.

I joined my mentor's elite mastermind of multi-seven-figure, *mission-driven* entrepreneurs way before I felt ready to be there, way before I hit that mark. I thought of Michael Jordan—before he was Michael Jordan to the world—looking for a game of pick-up with people seven times better than he was. I humbly showed up, knowing I had much to learn and that, although I was still working towards greater levels of impact and income, I could start serving, giving and supporting every member of that group from the moment I joined. I can thank these communities I've had the privilege to be part of not only for my continued revenue expansion but also for my four closest friends in the world. You'll meet some of these women in the coming pages.

So where do you find your Rich, Abundant, Prosperous destiny stretching community? Thanks to our virtual world, it has never been easier to find a group for anything you desire. If you want to learn about investing, check out Sarah Sullivan (you'll read her story in the second half of this book) and her work empowering women to make substantial passive income through investing in real estate. You can find women and wealth meet-up groups, co-ed/non-binary meet-up groups, financial book clubs or health clubs where high net worth and value-centered people work out. If a membership is currently out of your budget, get a guest pass for the day and start there.

You can join masterminds, coaching groups, referral groups, classes, networking organizations, mentorship programs, take online classes, master-classes and workshops with leaders who will teach you their strategies as a gift. The *key* criteria is that the other members (at least a good number of them) are a few steps ahead of you in your goal and have reached that level in ways that align with your values.

After the shift I've experienced from being in community with women "ahead" of me in wealth, I truly have seen:

YOUR NETWORK = YOUR NET WORTH

By being "in the room where it happens," you'll find yourself in partnership with people you admire, with people who are doing exactly what you hope to do. Your five-year plan will become your one-year plan.

Creating this type of community for our clients was my top priority when we opened Thought Leader Academy. I loved coaching clients 1-1, but if I continued only offering individual coaching, they'd never have to shift and stretch to the extent possible if we came together in a group. I'd been forever changed for the good, thanks to the communities others had generously extended to me, and I vowed to do anything I could to pay this gift forward. I see the magic taking place every week. Joint ventures, collaborative book launches, grants generated for those who don't yet have the investment resources. Members who thought writing a book or making six figures was a pipe dream smashing that goal and setting a new one. Together we get to be the rising tide that raises all ships.

You likely won't feel ready or maybe even worthy to be "in the room" with some of these groups at the start. But enter anyway. Move in before you're ready. Before you have anything figured out. Before you even understand what everyone is talking about (that was me in every group I joined for at least the first six months). After stretching and *releasing* all your gremlins, you'll find that you were always worthy and capable and wanted and loved enough to be there, that you are a gift to that room, even on day one. You'll find it was the room of your destiny all along.

Where to find these rooms? I am asked this question frequently by new clients. The good news is, you're already in one room by reading this book and connecting in the book portal. You are now a beloved part of our Science of Getting Rich – For Women Abundance Accelerator Community! Keep reading and you'll find more than two dozen rooms of the women who share their stories of starting from the ground up and becoming millionaires. You can find more communities through a quick internet search on Google, Facebook, Instagram, Clubhouse, in your city or town or local networking group. The moment you set the intention to find your Abundance Accelerating Community, it will be on its way to you. I've got you! This book has you!

And if you want to join our next Abundance Accelerator and play all these strategies with our community or talk to one of our coaches for support, we are here for you.

HAVE

This chapter will be short. Have is less an action step in the Science of Getting Rich equation and more of a Result.

When we *Be, Release* and *Do* what is in alignment with our vision, our rich life, the money or anything else we desire, the *Have* automatically comes. I always think back to my client who was convinced she could never release weight and have a fit, active lifestyle. She was certain that *how* was impossible. Yet, when she identified the fit, healthy, happy, active woman, cleared out the limiting ideas that she could not change and asked what that woman would do in each moment and did it, she became that person. She found herself having a fit, healthy, happy, active life.

When I asked myself every day for one year: what does a 7-figure CEO do next and *did* that next action, I broke the $1 Million mark in sales.

Neuroscientifically, metaphysically, we cannot *Be (Release)* and *Do* something and not have the desired result. Thoughts, attitudes, beliefs and actions create our reality, our results. Align them with richness and you will be rich.

• • •

The *Have* step is a step of receiving, of allowing and of celebrating!

What has already changed or up leveled for you as a result of participating in this book? When you use the equation consistently, you will change, and you will experience riches.

What—even if it's just the tiniest flash or the first sprout of a shoot through the earth—have you already seen?

In *Have*, we stay awake and alert and in excited appreciation for every sign that our abundance is expanding. When you notice an increase or manifestation of wealth, joy, abundance, peace, wellness, financial freedom—of your *rich life*—document it! Keep a running list on your phone, in a journal or use the page in the Science of Getting Rich Workbook I created for you with this purpose in mind. Each night, before falling asleep, list any and all signs you received that day of increased abundance.

Master Practice

If you want to play the *Have* step at a master level and accelerate your abundance even more, record signs that happen to *anyone* in your atmosphere as well. If you hear about someone else's new $10K or $100K client, celebrate it as your own sign that you now have $10K or $100K clients. If someone hits the best-seller list with her book and you're just starting yours, celebrate her win as your own. In Thought Leader Academy we use the mantra "I am one with that" every time our members see someone achieve what they desire.

Michael Beckwith, founder of Agape and expert teacher in the movie *The Secret*, told me that we can only see something if it also exists within us. We believe in the illusion of separation, but, in reality, we are unified. After talking to Michael, I once had the experience in meditation where an inner wisdom spoke to me directly. *When you see something that another person has created or achieved, it is a mirror to your potential. It's a "coming attraction." You are simply locating your greatness in another and have forgotten that the only reason you're able to see that greatness to begin with is that you already possess it within.*

This may sound esoteric. It is, but try on the idea. Think back to the last time you heard about or saw someone achieve what you desire—some aspect of your *rich* life. What feelings arose then, or now? Jealousy, envy, shame, disappointment, separateness, lack, sadness? Maybe you were really, really happy for the person but felt deflated and defeated because you believe you cannot be, do or have that thing or that amount of richness.

Now, think of seeing or hearing about someone achieving that same financial goal or success and imagine that you are only able to see that success because it's meant for you. It's here for you, you're going to have it and you seeing this post/announcement is an affirmation that it is now going to be in your life.

How do you feel when you say *I am one with that*?

What is possible for you if every sign you receive and any you observe in others are all affirmations that it is happening, that you are worthy, that what you desire is coming to fruition.

You are. It is.

Every sign counts. The Universe is whispering to you every day. Sometimes it is even shouting as it points you to new levels of abundance and greatness.

Our decisions determine our destiny. What are you going to decide now that you have the equation for The Science of Getting Rich—for you?

• • •

Now that you've heard my story and some of the wondrous manifestations of abundance my clients and friends are also experiencing using this equation, you get to meet more amazing women who also started from "nothing" and became millionaires. In the coming pages, you will learn their secrets and add their tools to your Science of Getting Rich – for Women toolbox. They've generously opened their hearts and their strategy playbooks because, in this equation, there is no competition, only collaboration.

Feel the waters shifting and lifting you up. You are part of the community of women making global change on this planet. We are your sisters, friends, peers and, when applicable and desired, guides to your next massive abundance breakthrough.

PART II

25 WOMEN WHO STARTED FROM SCRATCH AND BECAME MILLIONAIRES

MICHELLE ROZA

GLADYS DIAZ

We grew up as first-generation Cuban-Puerto Rican girls to parents who came from completely different sides of the tracks. Our father and his family had been well off in Cuba, the result of having a success-ful shoe store business. Things were great ... until they weren't. When the Cuban Revolution happened and Fidel Castro took power, our family lost everything.

Like many Cubans with the foresight to see that things were not, in fact, going to get better, and with the benefit of having the financial means to do so, our family immigrated to New York in hopes of a new start in the land of promises and opportunity. Once again, things were good ... until they weren't (more about that in a bit).

Our mother, on the other hand, came from a life of poverty and aban-donment. She grew up hungry, raised by those she believed to be family members, unaware that her father was not dead until she was an adult. Our mother's experience of life was difficult, painful, and a struggle, and she came to expect that that was simply the way life was.

Things began to look different when she met our father—a man who was a bit older and a bit better off—and every dream and prayer came true. They fell in love and got married. For the first time in her life, our mother experienced what it was like to be taken care of and provided for. They had us, she was a stay-at-home mother, and things were great ... until our father got sick with cancer and eventually passed away, leaving her a young, single mother of toddler twins, and, once again, struggling to survive.

Eventually, our mom remarried, and things were better for a while. We welcomed our little sister into the family, rented a nice house, had a car, and our mom was able to be a stay-at-home mom who took care of other people's children and cut hair in the house, as well as having side businesses such as Avon, Jafra, and Tupperware. We can't remember a time when Mom wasn't selling something. We never really knew that we were "poor" by other people's standards until we got to middle school and experienced bullying and teasing about our clothes and shoes.

When that marriage ended, our mother married an unstable, alcoholic man who physically abused her. Our financial status changed dramatically, and there was no doubt that we were poor. Although we had a home (until we were evicted), cars, and clothes, there did come a time when we didn't have food or money to even do our laundry. We eventually were evicted; the three of us had to go live with other family members.

Although the two of us got to live with our aunt and uncle, who, in our eyes, had always been "rich" (actually upper middle-class, but rich compared to us), our little sister continued to live in poverty with her father. This was difficult for us because it felt unfair that we were now privileged and had "extra" money, and she did not.

All of these pieces of our history created the story that money is hard to make and even harder to keep because, when you do have it, someone or something can take it away, or you have to feel guilty about having it because others don't. Needless to say, the fears around money, making money, having money, and losing money were real and continued to play themselves out into our adulthood.

We honestly never intended to have a business, much less a million-dollar business!

Our Mission Begins

Michelle:

Our mission started with me going through the experience of heartache and unsuccessful dating after the end of a 12-year marriage. I was excited about dating when I first got divorced because I was very young when I got married and hadn't had the experience of dating very many men. Online dating was new, and it felt like an adventure for me.

However, after five years of dating men who either had addictions or some other kind of drama in their life (ending a relationship, just out of a relationship, or still in a relationship), and hearing time after time what a great woman I was but that the men did not want to be in a committed relationship with me, I was feeling disillusioned, disenchanted, and *done* with dating.

Working with a coach, I uncovered that, aside from addiction and drama, all the men had one thing in common. Those five strangers were all attracted to me, and I was attracted to them. *I* was the common denominator.

Answering the question: "What is it that is attracting all these men to me *and* me to them?" was the key to unlocking the door to my heart, falling in love with myself, and healing the emotional wounds that had been magnetically drawing in men who were a reflection of my biggest fears, rather than my heart's desires.

This led to creating a workshop-style book club with 21 other single women who also wanted to create the happiness, life, and love their hearts desired. As part of that "book club," one of the recommendations I discovered was that every single woman should have a happily married mentor she could go to for support, so I reached out to Gladys to see if she would mentor the group.

Gladys:

What Michelle didn't know was that, while I was honored, I was also a bit horrified, because my marriage was *not* as happy as it seemed on the outside. My husband and I were going through a very rough patch. We were arguing all the time, disrespect was running rampant, and intimacy was at an all-time low. I was starting to question whether I had married the right man and if I wanted to stay in the marriage.

But the invitation to mentor 21 single women sparked something in me that had been dormant for a while. I had been very involved in couple's ministry with my late husband from a very young age and had always been drawn to helping women create stronger, more deeply-connected relationships.

When my first husband died, I doubted that I'd ever love or be loved again. However, four months after I started doing the *HeartWork*™ in my own life, I attracted my second once-in-a-lifetime love. Now, six years into our relationship, with one child and a second on the way, things in our marriage were far from great, and I'd begun to wonder if we were going to make it.

What if this book club was a way to reignite the spark in my own marriage?

I decided then and there that, if I was going to mentor these women, I would practice in my own marriage *everything* we talked about and taught them. I had no idea that this was going to be the key to not only creating a beautiful marriage of my own, but helping women around the world create and keep the love alive in their own marriages!

At the end of three months, five of the women were in new relationships and one of them was engaged to be married. The very natural next question we heard was, "When are you doing this again?"

So, we did another workshop-style book club, and, again, at the end of those three months, more women were in relationships, another woman was engaged, and we were being asked if we could create workshops for girlfriends and wives, now that so many of them were in relationships and getting married.

During all of this, my marriage was getting stronger and more intimate, and my husband, Ric, and I recently celebrated our 22nd wedding anniversary and 23 years together. Michelle attracted Arnie, and they recently celebrated their 11th wedding anniversary over 15 years.

Michelle:

Today, thousands of women around the world are enjoying dating, attracting amazing men into their lives, and learning how to keep the love alive year after year after year!

We eventually created Heart's Desire International, and for several years we held workshops and did relationship coaching at nights and during the weekends because we both had our own careers. We made very good money, and we honestly believed that we could never replace our income doing something that was so much fun, so rewarding, and came so naturally to us.

A Leap of Faith

Gladys:

We kept talking about how much fun it would be to have a business where we got to do this full time. It wasn't until I got laid off in 2011 that I was faced with the reality of never again wanting someone else to determine how much money I made, whether or not I could take care of my family, and what was possible for me.

I came face-to-face with my money fears—the money stories I had made up, as well as those that had been passed down to me—and many of the doubts and insecurities I had in myself and my ability to create, not only a business, but a mission, that would allow me to do work that I loved. To make a real difference in women's lives and generate enough money to have the kind of lifestyle I had become accustomed to and that I wanted to continue expanding.

After making almost no money the year following my lay-off, and being unwilling to work for someone else, I hired a coach way before I could afford her (I was making basically $0 an hour at the time).

Learning the skills and strategies to build a business was not as challenging as continuously working on breaking through the fears and limiting beliefs I had around money and my ability to create it while making a difference.

The constant commitment to breaking through led to me making double what I had made the previous year, doubling that the following year, and continuing to double, and many times surpass that, year after year.

For the first five years after I started coaching full-time, Michelle continued to work at her full-time job. She was experiencing similar fears to the ones I'd had around letting go of the security of her job and wondering if she would be able to replace and exceed her income as a full-time coach.

Michelle:

By this time, however, our company was consistently making multiple 6-figures, and I was incredibly unhappy in my current position. Although I made a great salary, I wasn't willing to sell out on my happiness any longer. We had recently taken a huge leap of faith and participated in a reality show for thought leaders who were willing to face and break through their fears. During that experience, I declared that I would be leaving my job by December of that year.

However, things became increasingly unbearable at my job, and one November afternoon, I called Gladys and asked her, "Did you see any of my text messages?"

She hadn't, but when she looked at her phone, she saw that I had sent several messages letting her know that I was about to submit my resignation letter!

Gladys sent me screenshots of our bank account balance, promised me that she would do everything to make sure this was a safe and positive experience for me, and reminded me of what a powerful, strong woman, coach, and leader I was. The next day I spoke to my boss and gave my two weeks' notice and resignation. Despite being terrified, I took the leap with faith and started working as a full-time coach.

We made more money that year than we ever had before, and our income has exponentially increased every single year since!

Gladys:

I won't lie and say that we never experience fearful thoughts, question whether we'll be able to hit our financial goals, or have a disempowering moment.

What I *can* say is that all the *HeartWork*™ that we did to break through and break free from our past, our fears, and limiting beliefs—the very same work we teach our clients to do so that they are empowered to create the life and the love that their hearts desire—has made us millionaires. More than that, it has made us women who are *certain* that we can make money and make our dreams come true as we support other women around the world in making *their* dreams come true!

The road to becoming millionaires was not "difficult," in the sense that we didn't have any major external obstacles or challenges standing in our way.

Yes, there were times we made a financial investment that, at the time, felt a little unreasonable, beyond our means, or not the right time to make that decision.

Yes, there were times when, if we had trusted the coaching we received, we probably would have hit seven figures a lot sooner than we did.

Yes, if we had left our jobs five years earlier than we did, we probably would have crossed the million-dollar mark a lot sooner.

However, external factors such as capital, time, our families, spouses, jobs, our age, our health, or the health of our family members ... none of that ever really came into play, thank God.

The primary obstacles and barriers we faced were internal.

They consisted of allowing a fearful thought or a limiting belief to make us second-guess our coach or ourselves or not trust ourselves enough to carry out the coaching we were receiving or fearing that we wouldn't/couldn't create the results the strategy promised, which stopped us from moving as quickly as we could have.

Michelle:

That's why we believe so strongly in doing our *HeartWork*™. Circumstances, situations, and the curveballs that life many times throws at us—those things are never *really* what stop us or get in our—or your—way.

What usually stands in the way between you and the goal that you want to achieve is the power you give to the fears, doubts, limiting beliefs, and patterns—all past-based choices and decisions made in moments of heartache, fear, desperation, or disappointment.

What we have found and personally experienced over and over again is that, when you get to the root of the fear, limiting belief, or pattern, break through it, and replace that past-based choice with a new and empowering thought, belief, way of being, and pattern, *everything* changes.

Your emotional state changes.

Your perspective changes.

Your attitudes and ways of being change.

And, consequently, the results you create are 100 percent different from anything that could've been created inside of the old paradigm.

This is what we teach and why we teach it. This is what we practice in our own lives every single day.

And this is what has helped us make millions of dollars as we teach other women to do the same—to create, live, and experience lives and loving relationships that far exceed their wildest dreams.

It's freaking exciting!

There was never a time when we wanted to give up on this journey. This has always been more than a business to us. It truly is a mission and a ministry—what we believe God has called us to do: transform the world through the power of love, one woman, one heart, and one relationship at a time.

And, we never *really* had the goal of becoming millionaires.

I'm not saying that to seem humble or benevolent or down-to-earth.

Gladys:

Did we talk about becoming millionaires?

Yes. In fact, I had declared to my kids four years earlier that we were going to be millionaires, and it didn't happen for the next three years. That was not easy to live with.

Did we dream about being millionaires one day?

Yes. We talked about celebrating on a yacht or in a mansion with our teams and family, and how awesome that would be.

Was being millionaires something that was "a real goal"?

No ... not until it was. Let me explain.

It wasn't until we noticed two months before the end of the year that we were less than 20 sales away from making $1 million that making a million dollars became a "real goal" for us.

And what I mean by a "real goal" is that we had a plan, we took consistent and committed actions every single day, and we tracked our results daily. We were hyper-focused on offering more programs and services to our customers and clients to achieve the mission of making a difference for them and reaching that goal.

When we took those steps, we actually did both in six weeks, instead of the eight we had planned for! And what that demonstrated to us was the power of not only thinking, talking, and dreaming about what was possible inside of our business, but believing that we and our team have what it takes to achieve and exceed the goals we set when we are truly committed to doing so.

What's so interesting about this is that it's exactly what we teach our clients when it comes to manifesting the life and love their hearts desire, and here we were experiencing it in a very real way during the last two months of the year by enrolling ourselves, our team, our friends, and our family in a vision that once had felt impossible and now seemed absolutely doable.

It *still* hits us in waves, even today, how powerful and miraculous those two months were!

Michelle:

Manifesting has been part of our daily experience for over three decades. We have seen how powerful we are and how irrelevant and inconsequential the past is, no matter how much evidence you have to support the limiting beliefs and fears that tell you that you can't do something.

One of the most powerful resources we have used to manifest our dreams and the lives that we are blessed to live is, first and foremost, our faith in God.

When you *truly* believe down to your cells that *anything* is possible with God's help, then *anything* is actually, factually possible for you!

That promise in the Bible didn't come with a disclaimer that it applied to everyone *except you.*

It's a promise available to you and for you.

We've also invested hundreds of thousands of dollars in personal development, spiritual development, learning to speak and sell from the stage, as well as using email and other forms of marketing to share our message.

We've invested in learning how the brain works, the differences between the male and female brain, what makes relationships succeed or fail, how to communicate effectively, how to enroll people in their vision, and how to continue growing to new levels of expansion and breakthroughs in our personal, spiritual, and business lives.

Gladys:

More than anything, except our faith in God, the primary resource that we use on a daily basis is the *HeartWork*™ that we teach.

And that, in and of itself, is something we hope you take away as a golden-nugget lesson from this book:

BE your work.

Don't just teach it.
Don't just tell people about it.
Don't just have it as "an offering" in your business.
People don't ever buy a program or a course or a book.
What they buy is the result they want to create.
What they buy is *the promise* of the program, the course, or the book.

Michelle:

And, when you're living and being your work—day in and day out—there's no question that it works.

There's no question that it creates the results you promise.

And *that's* what makes it *easy* for you to share with people what they can have, create, and experience—beyond your case studies and testimonials.

You become the walking, breathing, talking evidence of what the work you teach provides in the lives of the people that you are blessed, anointed, and appointed to serve.

That, in our opinion, is *the secret* to becoming a millionaire doing what you love!

BE your work!

Gladys:

So many books, videos, podcasts, and resources supported us in doing the inner and outer work that led to us becoming millionaires.

Books like the Bible, *The Secret, The Science of Getting Rich, Think and Grow Rich, Draw the Circle,* and so many other personal and spiritual development books. Our bookshelves, as well as our Kindle Audible libraries, also overflow with books about brain science, neuroplasticity, and transformation. I won't dare to attempt to list every resource here because I'm sure I'll leave something relevant out!

Listening to hypnosis and meditation audios and videos, podcasts, and thought leaders speak and teach have also been helpful.

Immersing ourselves in seminars, courses, and programs focused not only on business strategies but, more importantly, the transformational, leadership, and mindset breakthroughs that create exponential growth has been invaluable.

Bottom line: Surround, engage, and immerse yourself in conversations, experiences, technology, and with people who stretch you, hold you accountable, and who hear and see you as bigger than your past, fears, and limiting beliefs, and who put whatever you learn into practice.

That's another golden-nugget lesson to take with you.

Too many spiritual and non-spiritual entrepreneurs invest so much time and money in getting more information, taking more courses, gaining more certifications, etc., and yet do not achieve the level of success that they want.

The reason isn't that the programs, the information, or the mentors didn't work. It's that they're gaining a lot of *information*, but they're not using that information to create the *transformation* that would make *the difference* in their lives.

So, yes, learn everything that you can from people who have the results that you want.

And then practice, practice, practice until you achieve those results for yourself!

Michelle:

We believe that the biggest obstacle blocking women from creating the wealth, abundance, and loving relationships their hearts desire boils down to two main things:

- They don't really believe they can have it.
- They don't really believe they deserve it.

We can't tell you how many women come to us and say things like, "I need to build my business first, and then I can focus on dating."

Or: "I don't have time to focus on my love life. I'm too busy building my business."

Or: "It's not that I don't want a loving relationship; this 'just isn't the right time."

What many women don't realize is that they are trying to create abundance inside of a scarcity conversation. Any time that you engage in a conversation of "I can either have this OR that ..." you are engaging in a *scarcity conversation*.

And it is *impossible* to create abundance of any kind—wealth, health, love, or anything else—when you are living in a scarcity mindset.

Impossible.

Why?

Because you are simply not an energetic match for attracting everything you want. You're literally declaring and proclaiming over and over that you can't handle more than you already have, that if you were to get more it would be too much for you, and you are subconsciously blocking any increase of love, money, health, or anything else your heart desires from coming to you.

Gladys:

Let's be 100 percent real here. If you're reading this book, you're a successful woman, or you're at least interested in becoming one.

And here's something I can tell you about successful women with absolute certainty:

A successful woman is never not going to be up to something amazing.

There's never going to be a time when you're not working on a project that you are excited and passionate about.

There's never going to be a time when you're not leading others.

There's never going to be a time that you are doing nothing.

So, *why in the world* would you already be telling the universe not to send you any love until you have the time, or the money, or the bandwidth to receive it?

When you do that, you're *literally* blocking the very abundance you're putting an unnecessary number of hours and amount of effort toward creating.

Michelle:

And that's what's so heartbreaking. Because it's not the number of hours or how hard you work that results in you creating the success you want.

It's being open, ready, and receptive to welcoming the life, love, happiness, clients, prosperity, and everything else that you truly desire.

And, at the risk of sounding repetitive, this is why doing the *HeartWork*™ is essential.

Until you break through the fears, doubts, limiting beliefs, and patterns that keep coming up and sabotaging your success in any and all areas of your life, you'll continue believing that your success is a matter of something or someone outside of you—a tool, a resource, an app, a coach—when the truth is that the power to create and manifest and have everything you want is within you. It's simply underneath piles of thoughts and behavior patterns that are destined to stop you.

I'm not saying that having resources and people in your life to support you in hitting your goals is not important.

What I am saying is that those resources and people are *not* the answer. Breaking through your Love Barriers is.

Because once you break through those barriers, *nothing* can stand in the way of you creating a life, business, and love *beyond your wildest dreams*!

So, if we were to coach our younger selves, we'd say:

Absolutely nothing is wrong with you.

Gladys:

Remember that your past and your experiences are informers—*not* predictors—of what is possible for you.

You may have made mistakes in the past, but you are *not* your mistakes, and they don't define you.

Do not allow anyone or anything to convince you that you can't have all the happiness, love, wealth, health, and fun that you desire and deserve.

Growing can sometimes feel painful and uncomfortable. It's not always going to feel good and you're not always going to feel like doing what you know needs to be done. Honor your feelings, but don't live your life by them.

Even the most painful and heartbreaking setbacks can serve as a setup for your next breakthrough, so live every moment as an opportunity to cause, create, and *be* a miracle in your life and in the lives of the people with whom you come in contact.

You are a beautiful, powerful, worthy, loving, and lovable woman, and you deserve every single thing your heart desires. Now go *be* it and create it!

Michelle:

If we had known five years ago what six weeks of consistent, committed action, being coachable, allowing ourselves to be supported, and knowing with 100 percent certainty that we could hit $1 million in that manner, it would have been done in two years!

Our next big goal is to find ways to further leverage our time and efforts so that we can reach even more women with our work. We've learned that we've been growing at the level of our capacity—energetically, in terms of how many people we have on our team, etc.—and it's time to expand, stretch, and grow so that we can do more for the women we have the privilege of serving *and* those we haven't had the privilege of meeting or serving yet.

Gladys:

This is a stretch for us because it's going to mean training past clients and other coaches to be coaches for us, which requires a higher level of trust and surrender and confidence in the people that we choose to represent us to be able to teach—and live—the work as passionately as we do.

As scary as this is, however, it's time. Actually … it's *been* time.

And we know that this is how we get to fulfill our company's mission—to transform the world through the power of love by guiding women to break free from their past so they are able to attract, create, and experience the joy of loving and being loved every single day of their lives—one woman, one heart, and one relationship at a time.

•   •   •

Gladys Diaz and Michelle Roza, a.k.a. *The Love Twins*, are certified dating and relationship coaches, NLP Master Practitioners, and co-founders of Heart's Desire International, whose mission it is to ensure that every single woman has the experience of loving and being loved every single day of her life.

Internationally sought-out speakers, they have appeared in various media and publications such as CNN's Changemakers, CNN Español, Univision, Brickell Magazine, and they were recently named on *Yahoo! Finance's* Top 10 Love Coaches in 2021.

Their unique and introspective approach to attracting love and creating intimacy in relationships teaches women the skills to attract and meet the man of their dreams *and* reignite the love, passion, and romance in relationships they once believed were over.

They help women remove the fears and barriers that have blocked them from having loving, fulfilling relationships so they can effortlessly create the loving, lifelong relationships and live their heart's desires with power, grace, and ease.

FARISSA
KNOX

My first memory of money really isn't about money. I think that, while growing up, the consciousness around money was more around debt and fear than money. The overarching consensus was that we didn't have money. We had debt, and there was a consistent fear of getting in too much of it. So, the focus for my family growing up was never about money, making it, or even having a conversation about it. It was about how to avoid getting into debt by managing the little bit you had appropriately. Those were the thoughts that consumed me my whole life until I started actually making some money of my own. Another thing that comes to mind as I think about my childhood is, I always knew I would have more than what I had then. This caused me to make choices that seemed ridiculous to everyone around me.

I remember back in high school, we were living in Richmond, Virginia at the time, I landed my first or second job at a pretty nice department store. It was called Lehmann's and it sold the types of clothes that most professional grownup women or just women who have places to go would have in their closets. It was the first place where I saw clothes and shoes and accessories that were outside of the world that I resided in. My employee discount allowed me to start buying things that not only felt like the current version of me but also reflected the future me. I would bring them home and my mom would go, "Where on earth do you plan on wearing that? You don't have anywhere to wear that to!" And I would say "Don't worry, one day I will have a place to wear these things to." And then she would say, "Well, how did you afford it? You're gonna waste all of your paycheck on clothes at work." And I would say to her with 100% honesty, "Mom, don't worry. One day I'll be rich and this won't matter."

What was my vision? What's the Why behind making a million dollars? In all honesty, I can't even say I had a vision when I started my first company. That same company, an ad agency, turned 13 years old at the end of 2021. Today we're a full-service, integrated marketing communication and ad firm. I only in the past five years or so really started to focus my efforts on financial growth, transferable value, and building the financial structural foundation to a point where I can exit in a multimillion-dollar way. This process has allowed my company to generate over a million dollars a year.

It has been an interesting journey thus far. I shifted my focus five years ago because that's when it became evident to me that's what I had to do. As a young black woman, I've always felt I was kind of playing this game of life and business with one hand tied behind my back. Without knowing the rules and without having someone who was super excited to share them with me. That means I learned the rules of business and, more importantly, the *game* of business much later than a lot of folks. I am not the only woman or black woman who feels this way. This is very true, and very normal for black women and black-owned businesses, to have to learn it all themselves. There is no roadmap for the majority of us on how to grow a business. We usually have one or two employees if we're lucky. The thought is, *Why should you even be growing your business? What is the point?* So when people ask about my vision and why I started working towards that? It was because of the environment I was in at the time. It was 2008, and we were living through a recession. I was in my late 20s, and, out of chaos, as most of you may know, that's when beauty is formed. I was living in the middle of chaos from an economic, business, and job perspective. Instead of waiting around for the market to level out, I decided to create my own space in it to "see what happens." I figured this was a good interim—until I found, or figured out, what my dream job was. The irony is, I didn't realize I was creating my dream job in the process.

I think for me, it was less about mindset obstacles and more about just knowing what to do. I really truly didn't know, not just the what, but the why of growing a business. Money and wealth have never frightened me or scared me. As I mentioned before, I always knew I would be a person who didn't worry about money. This truth was what allowed me, from a very young age, to keep my mind open as it relates to money, the cost of things, and what it takes to actually make money. Most importantly, I understood what it took to keep money. Even though I had trust and knowledge as a foundation, there were still things I was learning every day. For instance, I learned there is more to money than debt and credit and that having cash leads to having power. I also learned that managing a business's finances on a daily, weekly, monthly, quarterly, and annual basis was vastly different from the art of managing it as an individual or household. The way that a household pays its bills and takes care of its financial responsibilities is not at all the same as how a business should operate. I think that is one of the biggest lessons I've learned as an entrepreneur.

The biggest obstacle I've had to face thus far in the growth of my business and personal finances was not having access to capital. People don't realize the impact of this, and some never do. The way you successfully grow and scale a business in order to generate millions of dollars in revenue is not just by getting clients, closing deals, getting you and your invoices paid. That's how you pay *some* of the expenses of the company. If you're lucky, that's how you pay *all* of the expenses. But the way you actually grow and scale a company is by nurturing it, feeding it, and infusing it with cash from somewhere else. That infusion can come from a variety of different places. Sometimes that looks like an investor. Sometimes it looks like a loan. Sometimes it looks like a line of credit. Sometimes it looks like private equity. When you don't have access to any of that, the growth of your business falls on your own shoulders. You are forced to grow your business organically, and, from every dollar that comes in, you have to figure out how to make payroll, how to make rent, how to afford the software that the company needs, and how to scale.

For a very long time, this was my reality, until I started purposefully making the type of banking relationships I knew I needed. One of our worst years of business was either 2011 or 2012. We were coming off a pretty decent year, but I saw the writing on the wall and could tell the business was going to take a sharp turn in the wrong direction. I had made a connection with whom I sat on a board, who introduced me to a business banker. It was that introduction, and eventual friendship, that enabled me to close my first line of credit and get a business loan. I should be clearer, it was my first "big one," because my first real loan was a $50,000 loan from the stimulus package Obama passed around 2009, shortly after he became president. That was a lifesaver for a company like mine that was just getting started and had so much potential. And then, after a few years of surviving, it was either die or thrive. Without that infusion of credit from that banker relationship, RLM would have died in 2012.

The biggest obstacle that I think any business owner faces is access to additional capital outside of the business—outside of the revenue that the business is generating. When you add lack of relationship, lack of access, racism, and sexism on top of that, you're really looking at a hard battle of getting access to additional capital. But it's doable, and I'm an example of that. It's been hard, but that's how I got to overcome the biggest obstacle that I am still overcoming because we're still in that place of banking relationships. I've just gotten much better at navigating them and getting what we need.

If I'm being honest, there was a point where I wanted to give up on my journey to becoming a multimillionaire, but my goal was never and will never be based on a dollar amount. My goal wasn't to become a multimillionaire. What got me to this point is that my actual goals, when accomplished and when done with high quality, automatically generate wealth. I think that that's an important distinction to make. It's important for me because I think when people, especially business owners, are focused solely on doing it for the money, quality suffers, room for mistakes gets created, greed can surface, and other things come up that can sabotage the journey. Additionally, it can sabotage the end goal itself. What I've had second thoughts about and had thoughts about giving up on wasn't the idea of becoming a multimillionaire. Again, I've always known that I was going to be financially successful. What I have thought about giving up on multiple times are the things that I'm doing to become successful and become wealthy. Just being an entrepreneur, for example, is super tough and super hard. You give of yourself at a level that most people cannot even comprehend. You're building and growing, both you and your future as you peer into it. It's very different and outside the regular realm of reality for normal adults who are waking up going to their jobs, getting a paycheck, and coming home.

There have been many days where I've looked in the mirror or put my head in my hands and thought, whose idea was this? Then I proceed to remind myself it was mine, and I do my best to fall back in love with the thing that I'm doing. When it comes to my ad agency, watching her grow and flourish and triple in size in a year and a half, and then turn into the next version of herself, has been a rewarding thing to be a part of—to witness and call mine in a way that there's no way in hell I'm giving up. Now, after all the work I've done, after I've put in all this blood, sweat, and tears, I want to reap the reward at the end of this journey. Again, that reward will be a multi-million-dollar check … and that is something I will not say no to! The other part lies around the other things I'm doing in my life. I do these because they really bring me joy, confidence, and some level of energy. When things start to get hard, I can remind myself of all the positives, and that motivates me to keep going.

There are a couple of things that I have done, and still do, to make sure that I'm continuously moving in the right direction as it pertains to growing and evolving my business. One is that I do my best to surround myself with communities that are either in the same boat as me or have successfully done the thing I am doing. I'm purposefully surrounding myself with other business owners and CEOs on a regular basis, so that we are feeding into each other, helping each other solve our problems, and talking through potential solutions together. In addition to building that network, I continuously evolve my skills as a leader by completing leadership development training and programs. Even if you are not in the same business, there are things that transcend what type of business you have and allow you to learn from obstacles that other people have faced. I also just try to remind myself that I don't have to be perfect. There will be moments during my continued education and building of community where I don't know the answer to questions or it's not in my wheelhouse to answer, but it might be in the wheelhouse of one of my employees to answer—and that's okay.

At a certain point, whatever you're building or whatever you're charged with being responsible for within your business is going to become bigger than you. Before you know it, you're not going to be able to hold it all in your hands, because if we can hold the entirety of our business in our own two hands, that means it is too small. That means it's never going to scale to the size that you want it to, whether it's for impact or financial reward or whatever it is. So it's really important to just be okay with the idea that you are not going to know everything. If you surround yourself with people who are smarter than you in one way, shape, or form, you can source all that'll you'll need to be successful. Whether that be a mentor, an employee, or just a friend—those who have a skill set you don't have can help breathe that into you.

Honestly, I would say out of all the resources that have helped me grow my business to where it is today, the top three that have been the most useful have been the services we've added that have enabled us to take a more strategic, smart, and focused sales approach when winning new business. If I could only pick one element and resource that has infused the growth of my business, it has been the talent that I have recruited and/or hired in the past two to three years. Without the amazingly talented, smart, empowered people in your organization, you have nothing. It's literally the number one commodity that businesses have. We would not have been able to triple our growth over the past few years without our people. If you don't understand the power of people or know the impact they can have, you're already starting from a losing position as a business owner, no matter how much capital you have behind you. You can have a lot of money and you can have a name brand, but if the people who work for you hate it, aren't talented, or aren't good at what you need them to be good at from a customer-facing perspective, then you will never have a product or service be as good as it can be. No matter how successful you become, you're never as successful as you could be if your people aren't happy, healthy, and taken care of.

There are obviously a lot of books written about business, a lot of podcasts, and a lot of products out there in which people engage and maybe take a few nuggets from. But, as a 27-year-old, young black woman starting my first business, I didn't know about these resources. When I did grow up and find them, none of them actually reflected my reality. That was, and still is, just becoming normal to hear. Solid, amazing business advice from a woman. I think the fact that this book is being written is an amazing testament to where we're headed. It's a compilation of women of all backgrounds in all colors and all races and all orientations sharing their journey to financial success in business. The fact that there is a group of us to even tell our stories is progress.

This is the type of book that I would have loved to have read when I was 30, but it wasn't available. So I did not lean into products or books or other people for a long time. I even hated the word *mentor* because it felt as though all my options were old, straight white men, and that was the furthest thing from the personality type I felt could be helpful to me at that time. Now, today, 13 years into the business and 40 years old, I have the capacity to extract wisdom from wherever the wisdom is coming from. But when you're just getting started and you are part of a marginalized group of people (or multiple groups like me), there are some hurdles that you have to get through before you can even hear the wisdom. And, quite frankly, there's a way of speaking that mentors have and learn to adjust to before they are even qualified to speak to us. So it was a rough coming of age for me. But now, here today, not only can I extract that wisdom for myself, but I can be a contributor for others.

I think the biggest challenge for women in creating wealth and abundance is that we are not taught to do it. It's not drilled into us in the way it's drilled into boys. That's not even a viable, acceptable, fantastical option for us as we grow up. You know, there are still a ton of stereotypes, roles, and responsibilities that are put on us from a gender perspective at a very young age. Building wealth, creating wealth, and being the generator of wealth are not things that are yet prescribed and described to girls and women. So the idea that a woman—a young woman or an older woman or a girl—would be focused on making money would require that it is an innate drive in her or she comes from a family who understands the importance of freeing your child's mind to understand they can go on and do whatever it is that they want to do in life. Whether it's creating a business and selling it for millions of dollars, establishing a nonprofit to help save people's lives, writing books, making movies, or whatever it is, it's not until we as a society start teaching and training our children that the entire world is their oyster no matter if they're born with a vagina or a penis, and they can do whatever they want, including a woman making her own money and wealth, that things will change. And that's okay. It's actually better than okay—it's freedom.

What would I tell my younger self who was just starting out? I don't know. Oh my goodness, I'm kind of stuck. So let's see. Honestly, I would just try to calm her insecurities. I would want her to recognize her power, her strength, her ability, and her amazingness way earlier than she did. Not letting her blackness and her femaleness and her youth stop her—because those three things were things I was self-conscious about, being so young and being a business owner and a CEO. I was 27 years old, and for three years, when people asked me how old I was, I would say "almost 30" instead of simply saying my age. When I was 31/32, I was saying I was almost in my mid-30s. I was trying to make myself sound older in the hopes that people would take me more seriously, respect me, and get beyond my youth and my beauty, quite frankly—along with my blackness and my womanness—and listen to my words. Just listen to my words. I would encourage the younger me to not be insecure about my youth, not to be insecure about being a woman in this man's world. A world these men created for them to win in. Not to be insecure about being black, in America, and all that means with the history and the reality of being black in this country today. I would tell her not to let those things be a source of insecurity, and, instead, to allow them to be exactly what they are—superpowers. If I had been able to walk into my superpowers at an earlier age, it would have garnered me a different result sooner. That's what I would tell my younger self: step into your superpowers and stop thinking there are obstacles, challenges, or things for you to be insecure about.

I think one of the most life-changing things I learned and figured out as it pertains to business that really put me on this path of acceleration, from a wealth and an ownership perspective, was when I was in one of my monthly classes for Vistage. I'm a Vistage member here in the Chicago area, and we had a guest speaker come in and do a full-day webinar series on transferable value—how to determine what the value of your company is today and what someone would potentially pay for it. I walked through those exercises and learned what the actual transferable value was for my business. I learned how businesses are valued and, more importantly, the roadmap to get your business to a place of transferable value so you walk away with the amount of money that you feel is appropriate for the work you've put into the business. It was literally a business love language that was being spoken to me. Here was an idea that was really important to me in this phase of my business life. Here's why it should matter to me, and here's a roadmap to take your business from where it is today to where it has enormous transferable value. I walked out of that class thinking, *"This is what I'm going to spend the next X number of years doing for my business, because otherwise what the hell am I doing? I'm just waking up every day doing the same thing over and over."*

Albert Einstein is often quoted as having said, "The definition of insanity is doing the same thing over and over again and expecting different results." Personally, I would much rather wake up every day and add a little something on purpose to what I am building, so, when I look back, I see something of true value. I wish this was something I had known when I initially started the business. This would have allowed me to create something that was valuable and not just provide a service to people.

My next big goal to be completed in the next three years is to fully transition the day-to-day operations of my business, which I am currently still overseeing, to one of my employees. I've not only identified this goal for myself, but I've also shared it with this person. Once this transition is complete, she can continue to build the transferrable value of the company, as well as the wealth health of the business, so that she can inherit a business that is strong, healthy, and thriving. This will enable me to either sell RLM or plan a financial exit in three years. I fully intend to be in that position in the near future.

Back to my roadmap. I have a roadmap and I follow it to ensure I've not stepped off the path to building true transferable value. In the next couple of years, this will look like RLM expanding geographically to multiple cities. It looks like more new business *and* service growth. It looks like the addition of more talented, amazing people. And it looks like the transferring of the many hats I still wear over to other leaders who can do it in their way and add their flavor on top of what has already been done.

That is my next big goal. It's a stretch for me in that most people in my position can't imagine not running their businesses' daily operations, and I count myself among the lucky few who intend to live this one life we're given to the fullest. I would not be able to call my life fully fulfilled if I died being the CEO of my ad agency. There are other things I want to do and places I want to go. There are other things I want to accomplish. In order to do that, I can't be the CEO of RLM for the rest of my life. It'll be an interesting journey once I get to the point where that is actually real and I can do that … It's very important to me that I do it because I do have other aspirations that are equally important to me as what I've spent the last 13 years of my life doing. It's important that the audience who's watching me gets to see me do all of these things. Because circling all the way back to me not having an example or a mentor, a real-life person that I could touch or even read about, someone who looked like me and faced the same obstacles I was facing but was accomplishing things that I had only seen white men accomplish, would have been a game-changer. I'm here now. Part of the payment that I am glad to pay is allowing people—women, black people, black women, black girls, anybody who needs to see it to be it—to see me doing it.

JESSICA
MEAD

Growing up, I lived with a single mom who worked multiple jobs yet still struggled to provide shelter. Then came along a step-dad who pushed her to switch gears and try various entrepreneurial endeavors. Unfortunately, they couldn't get it right or keep us kids in a house or provide us with stability. As a result, I viewed money as something I had to make steadily in my life and believed that the only pathway to accomplish that was college and a normal career with a guaranteed income.

Now I am partners in a portfolio of 22 companies with my husband of 20 years, and we have been building businesses together for 23. I achieved this through a resilient mindset driven by courage, curiosity, and a lack of fear.

When asked about my vision when I started these different businesses I am in now and the why behind the work that I do, it's hard to answer because they're not the same ones I started with 23 years ago. I can, however, share the process. We live a life of intentional congruence, and we shed what is not serving us. Most of our companies are built on the see-a-need-fill-a-need philosophy. In other words, we build or acquire a company because of a need that another company of ours has. They are symbiotic in nature and most happen organically. There is always a why linked to a need that we feel can't be filled ethically or morally or efficiently by an outside vendor.

One interesting story about my journey in business would be something that happened at the beginning of the pandemic. Early in 2020, I acquired another ad agency, rolled it up into BrandLync, and kept all the employees—mind you, up until now, I did all the hiring so I made sure there was alignment. Now I had what I call a blended family, and it was no longer a company of employees I had hired. I learned so much about myself and what it takes to lead people who have no experience working with you. How to adapt but also instill your vision and culture. Gaining an understanding of these new employees was a big learning experience for me. It was also proof that comfort is an addiction. Continually forcing myself to get uncomfortable has helped me grow, not only in business but as a human being.

Mindset is key, and we all have or had internal obstacles to overcome to get to where we are. I always assumed that everyone knew what I knew, so I didn't utilize my thoughts and knowledge to its fullest extent. Once I understood how unique each human being is and how different we all process ideas and are motivated, I started to use this for growth. I am a 30,000-foot observer, so I tend to see all possibilities and outcomes. I work backwards—start with my desired outcome and navigate all the possible paths or solutions to get there. This helps me tremendously to be proactive instead of reactive. I also use integrity, confidence, courage, and generosity as my guides. One of the greatest gifts we are given in life is the ability to transform. If we allow ourselves, we can—at any point—decide to make a change. Transformation can happen in a dramatic, sudden way or organically over time. To fight it or stay stuck or complacent is a tragedy, for yourself. It's during this transformation or evolution of oneself that we discover our magic, our hidden gems, curiosity starts to bloom, and we become to be free …

Being a female has its challenges, and we women have to work way harder than men do to prove ourselves worthy. One of the hardest things I have learned is, no one stays forever. It's better to help people cycle up and out if that is their path than to hold on so tightly that you suffocate the relationship.

Longevity and loyalty are possible, but they only happen if there is aligned self-interest. Understanding the personal and professional goals of every person you hire, and making sure they align with the job and goals you have for them, is key.

> Once I actually let go of the idea that I had to pick a career with a steady income in order to have a decent life, I don't think I ever had a thought of giving up. See, I grew up in a household with entrepreneurs. Observing them experience a little success and then extreme hardship conditioned me to think smaller—to have dreams and goals that felt attainable and realistic. That thinking crippled me for a long time. When I met my husband, I quickly realized he was a true visionary with enormous ideas. He helped free my mind of those limiting beliefs that had me playing it safe all the time. Once I let them go, I grew into the person I am today, and I can't fathom turning back.

My husband, Matt, saw the sparks in me that I was scared to set free. He encouraged me to take control of my life in a bigger way and showed me I was meant to be more than average. I truly think I would be a traditional 9-5 lady had I not met him, and I am grateful for this life we have built.

My journey didn't happen by accident. Here's how I live a life of intentional design and achieve my goals without fail—and how you can, too.

Don't be afraid of people leaving.

During my chaotic childhood, I became accustomed to people frequently walking out the door. As dismal as that sounds, those experiences had a profoundly empowering effect on me. I learned to make the most out of every interaction—to bring my whole self to every conversation or experience.

Here's the thing, when you're not worried about someone leaving you, you're able to focus on whether you want them to stay. Rather than thinking, "If I don't do this, this person will leave," ask yourself what makes you want this person to stick around. Success is difficult to achieve if you don't have your priorities straight and you allow others to run your life for you. People avoid hard conversations because they are afraid the other party will react badly and exit. This is how toxic employees stay employed for so long and deteriorate a company. I stay laser-focused on those creating real value in my life.

I follow this rule in my marriage. With 20 years of marriage and two kiddos, it is important to check in and ask ourselves if we are solid and still desire to be married. Marriage doesn't equal possession nor is it a guarantee of forever. People take it for granted and they don't speak up when they are unhappy, ultimately doing both parties a disservice.

I'm not afraid to go it alone because I control my universe, so I'm not afraid to have the hard conversations. We take our marriage year by year. On our anniversary, my husband and I go to dinner and, even though we're committed to each other for the long haul, we always pose the following questions:

Why are we here? Are we happy? How did the past year go? What do we have to work on? What are our goals? What is your favorite color? Favorite food? Did your bucket list items change? What did I do to make you proud? What did I do to disappoint you? We listen intensely and openly, and we speak with truth and purpose. Our goal is to make sure we still align because love is not enough. Then, we work like hell for the next 12 months to make sure we like the answers. That's how you pour the foundation of a life you love.

Be ruthless about your time.

I don't waste time—it's the one resource I can't earn back. We only have about 80 trips around the sun, and I believe we have a responsibility to make the most of each one. Effective time management at work ensures that I can accomplish the things I value, which include family dinners, adventures, spontaneous moments, exercise, and self-care. Don't get caught in the trap of multitasking, which, in most cases, kills productivity and creativity. Going through your day with purpose—that is, focusing intently on one task before moving on to the next—can be the difference between where you are right now and a million-dollar career.

Control your own finances.

I mentor women entrepreneurs on how to handle their finances all the time. If you woke up alone tomorrow, would you feel empowered to handle your finances? I'm an optimist by nature and a believer in true love—I've been with my husband for 20 years and love him more every day—but I know that nothing is more crucial than self-sufficiency. If he got injured, died, or woke up one day and decided I wasn't his thing anymore, my children and I would be financially secure. That provides me the peace of mind and confidence to chase my dreams. Women, especially, must be in control of their own earning potential, investments, and know how to protect their wealth.

Make a point to connect with people in meaningful ways and listen.

Some of my biggest business wins have come from meaningful conversations with people I bump into in a store, on a plane, or in a restaurant. These days, it's easy to be head down in a text conversation with people you communicate with daily and miss a million-dollar conversation with the person next to you. I make it a point to talk to everyone I encounter and try to ask them meaningful questions. This applies to executives in the airport and the checkout clerk at the grocery store. Being curious has led me to incredible profit opportunities and incredible new hires. Connecting with people in ways that make them feel noticed and valuable is how you increase your network's net worth.

These four principles are how I've succeeded as an entrepreneur and why I have the freedom to live life exactly how I want to, without fear.

•   •   •

I read *The Birth Order Book: Why You Are the Way You Are* by Dr. Kevin Leman while pregnant with my second child. I was curious about how my daughter's relationship with her soon-to-be baby brother would work. This book opened my mind to how people interact and why they are who they are. It spawned my interest in learning more about how to communicate effectively and meaningfully. It gave me an incredible gift: the tools to get past the awkward beginning of any relationship quickly, be a considerate listener, and engage in fruitful relationships. It changed my approach to professional and personal relationships. I am also a big fan of *The Five Love Languages* by Gary Chapman. Investing in knowledge should be a lifelong endeavor.

If I could choose only one of the resources I have mentioned to help me grow my business and reach my next financial milestone, it would be people. People are the resource I need most. Outside of our minds, people are our greatest asset.

There are many challenges for women when it comes to creating wealth and abundance. One is bias. Bias towards women is a very ugly thing. Some of the usual thoughts are: they get pregnant and need time off, they don't think like a guy and we don't have room for all the emotion, this is a man's industry and toughness is required. I think that, when we look at the attributes a female contributes to our life, we naturally want to make them the caregivers and homemakers. We see them as the family glue versus a good candidate for our company. However, I say the natural instincts women tend to possess are the exact reasons why you need more on your team. Every woman needs to understand the following things about themselves and why they have exactly what any company—and the world—needs.

Women are forced to deal with so many vertices in their life (school, groceries, doctors, extra-curricular activities, etc.). They are well equipped to think fast and very efficiently; they are expert communicators with different personality types and are also excellent at relationship building. They think like a mom and will do anything it takes to get the job done. Crisis management tends to be a strong suit for women. Women tend to be conscious leaders and this is key to business in the future. I think companies that are genuinely in tune with the needs of their clients and the divisions in their company need to approach filling the seats in a different way. They need to think about the area they are hiring for and the current team in place—what is missing or what is the vision and culture of that team? Then they need to think about the ideal candidate based on needs and not gender. Fill that seat with the right human being and don't make the mistake of thinking that, even if the current team is only of men, a male is best suited for the role. In fact, the opposite may very well be true. Hire based on needs and the qualities you are looking for.

Hiring from this approach allows you to bring in different perspectives, enhance collaboration—and possibly the reflection of your customers' needs—and expand the talent pool. Women also struggle with finding investors and invest 40 percent less than men. This is partly because financial professionals treat women differently—it's a man's world and women feel patronized and are less likely to be listened to when it comes to investing ideas. Women find value in many different areas than men do. Soft skills are more important to women (alignment on interests, being treated as an equal, taking ownership of actions, feeling understood as a person and with regard to her specific situation).

Women are not a homogenous group. They may be married or with a partner who is a co-contributor to the household, a sole breadwinner (whether married or single), or a number of other options, each with unique needs. I have seen more women reinvesting their earnings into platforms they believe in and in sound business deals than anything else. According to New York Life Investment Management, 51 percent of personal wealth in the US is controlled by women. Women tend to save more and think about money differently. Along with this investing shift, more companies are realizing the power of the female dollar—70-80 percent of consumer purchases are driven by women either by buying power or influence. This tells us that women are key decision-makers when it comes to financial moves and, in fact, statistics show that 96 percent have primary or shared responsibility for family financial decisions. Female investors bring a different value to the mix. They are natural nurturers and understand the value of establishing relationships, and they are really good at leaning on and learning from other women. They are not afraid to seek guidance or help and ask questions when they don't have the answer. Women are naturally more cautious; therefore, they thoroughly analyze investments and consider all the variables involved.

Five Things I Wish Someone Had Told Me Before I Started my Journey to Millions

Have a bigger vision of your life's potential.

Growing up I tried everything, and I mean everything. I was looking for where I would thrive. I just wanted to succeed and not struggle. It may sound silly, but having kids has taught me that imagination is key. Kiddos just believe with everything they have; they visualize and see it happening, and we lose this as we become adults. Your mind is your best asset—use it—80 percent of how you perform is how you think and feel. Along this journey, I claimed the power to tell my life's story and have continued to work towards the next best version of myself. Because, when you upgrade your story, you upgrade your life. That story is the foundation of the culture you are creating.

(Culture is your story.) The most powerful story you tell is the one you tell yourself. Have a mantra that is personal. Your life is yours and you can change it at any point. Somewhere along the way, I started living a life of intentional design, and it freed me to become the mother, wife, business leader, educator, sister, and friend I am today.

Stop setting goals that keep you in a safe, checklist-based headspace.

Our fears and insecurities cause us to think small and set realistic goals that we are guaranteed to achieve. In some ways, your goals have boundaries and are limiting your potential. Having vision breaks those boundaries. See, I didn't realize this, but I was conditioning myself to be average, to accept less, and not believe greatness was within my grasp. This was safe. I was cheating *myself* out of greatness by doing this, and every day I watch people do the same thing. People will distract themselves from their reality so they don't have to take ownership for being lazy or not functioning at their best. Average conforms to reality but greatness creates a whole new reality.

How to handle failure.

How to handle failure, not just for me but the people who work for me. It's natural for people to distance themselves from it—they make excuses (I didn't have all the information; so and so did the report wrong; my car ran out of gas.) They say it was someone or something else, but they will never learn from their failures that way. Instead, I have learned to take ownership and require it from my team. Change the message (I failed to collect the information; I didn't review the report, etc.) Take *ownership, embrace* it, *learn* from it, and *correct* it. Once we do this, we can course-correct ourselves and our actions, making room for more confidence to execute. This lesson would have saved me much heartache and time.

The efforts we make in other people have a dynamic effect in our business and lives.

People are our greatest asset—take the time to learn what their best working environment is and their learning style(s). Learn to consistently communicate and engage with them in a meaningful way—educate and coach them and value their voice.

Business is run on 3 things: Conscious leadership, numbers, and aligned self-interest

Conscious Leadership

I would observe leaders of other companies and I realized pretty quickly that there are levels to leadership, and conscious leaders go beyond. Conscious leadership to me means being aware of and engaged in all aspects of your company. From the employees to the clients, to the programs/products, to what enhances the movement forward, to who the employees are inside and outside our walls and how to work best with them. They inspire, encourage, take time to educate, they know and believe in the mission or goal so hard that they approach from a place of abundance and not scarcity; it changes everything. Conscious leaders are curious and open, willing to listen on a different level, see through all the lenses, and don't control with a chokehold. I am always thinking about these three things: truth, trust, and transparency, and maintaining these as my guiding light keeps me in complete awareness and authentic to who I am. This is Integrity.

I try to lead in the solution and not the problem at hand. This ensures I am not reactionary by nature. The better you understand yourself, what ignites your fire, creates your sparks, brings joy, triggers your negative emotions, motivates you—the more self-aware you become—the greater a leader you will naturally be.

Numbers

Numbers tell you everything—if you don't know your numbers, get out of the game. The numbers will tell you everything you need to know to ensure the business will thrive or end up insolvent. People end up in bad positions because they run on hope and emotion; that is all good, but without knowing your numbers you are in trouble.

Aligned Self-interest

Understanding the personal and financial goals of every person you hire and making sure they align with the job and goals you envision for them is key. Otherwise, you are hiring temporary people to fill a role until the next best job comes along. To me, aligned self-interest is only possible if you encourage a growth mindset atmosphere—it sends the message that you are aware of their personal and professional future and you want them to reach it.

So what's next for me and my businesses? I wrote a book called *Firework Humans*, and I hope to get the messages in it out to as many people as I can. I want to help people discover their sparks and become the best versions of themselves. If I could travel the world making meaningful connections with no timeline, I would be fulfilled in my journey.

●   ●   ●

Jessica Mead is an entrepreneur, passionate educator, loving mother and wife, and fearless businesswoman. She is the CEO of BrandLync, a 30-million-dollar marketing agency that focuses on building/developing high-touch digital and traditional marketing strategies. Jessica is the co-founder of another 20 companies, sits on the board of several companies, and is an angel investor—all while homeschooling her two children and traveling the world. She is a sought-after speaker on how to align business and family goals and values with success.

You can follow Jessica's work online at:

Website: https://jessicamead.com/
Instagram: @_jessicamead_
Facebook: https://www.facebook.com/jessicameadofficial
Twitter: @Jessica_Mead
LinkedIn: https://www.linkedin.com/in/jessicameadofficial/

MICHELLE SEILER TUCKER

If you took a look at my childhood and my early family life from the outside, I'm certain you wouldn't say that making money was in the stars for that little girl.

My brothers and I grew up pretty poor. We lived in an average-sized home in California. My father was from a family of twelve siblings, and he decided in a split second that he wanted to move away from his brothers and sisters. My father basically uprooted us and we moved in the middle of the night to a small farm near Austin, Texas. My brothers were older and moved out on their own. My parents and I then moved to a trailer park in Austin, and a few years later they purchased land and a trailer and we moved to a small town an hour from San Antonio, leaving all of my friends in Austin. That was a very tough move for me, especially not having my brothers around.

My early experiences with money were negative—they were defeatist, gloomy, dismal, and discouraging. I would not have used this language then, but now I know they came from a scarcity mindset that could easily have led me toward a very different life than the one that's turning out for me.

My father was prone to pithy money-negative declarations like, *You have a champagne appetite on a beer pocketbook,* and *Money isn't everything.* My father sure threw his money down the drain drinking all the beer he did … the more he drank, the more negative he was about money.

There was some element of truth in many of his pronouncements. No sensible person would argue with any number of ways my father phrased his common claim that, "Money isn't everything." Of course, it isn't. And of course, *it didn't grow on trees.*

But it wasn't long before I began to realize that if money *did* grow on trees, I'm pretty sure my father probably would have gone into the patch of grass outside of our trailer home on a daily basis and picked it like apples.

I was raised Jehovah's Witness, so I think some of my father's attitudes toward money came from religious thinking that time and effort focused on making money indicated a kind of lack of faith in the belief that Jehovah could be counted on to provide.

"Money is the source of all evil," he often said.

It soon became clear, though, that as much as my father was inclined to take a stance against the value of money, he sure did bring it up a lot.

His language and habits about money were always negative. He really kept saying, "Money doesn't matter. Money is the root of all evil." Every negative phrase that you can possibly associate with money came from my father's mouth.

My mother was less public about her views toward money. My father could preach against the value of money until he was blue in the face, but as a woman, and as the mother of my brothers and me, she knew something about what it took to run a household—a trailer, that is. But my father's views toward money had a negative effect on her as well. Money was a topic better to be strayed from when it came to dealing with my father.

We shopped at Goodwill for my clothes. When we selected and purchased them, my mother hid them from my father in the trunk of her car, after cutting the price tags from them and stuffing them in a pile so they looked like old laundry. She pulled them out and allowed us to wear them only when we could do so in the stealthiest of ways, to keep from alerting my father's attention. She never wanted my father to know what she was spending.

Nothing about money was positively reinforced. And, to give you a further sense of how easily the negative aspects of money can be passed on, to this day, I'm still affected by my mother's secretive behaviors. When I walk into the house after shopping, I'll downplay the costs of the things I've bought or even try to hide them from my husband. However, I am conscious about my behavior and am making sure I work on these negative habits so they don't affect my daughter.

I consistently earn seven figures now, and I'm capable of lying about the price of a pair of shoes.

But who knows? Maybe my attitudes about money were somehow shaped by my parents' attitudes toward it. Maybe living in trailer homes and shopping at the Goodwill and hearing all about the evils of money—all the secrecy and negativity—played a part in how I felt about success from the time I was a child.

Even at seven or eight years old, I wasn't your typical kid. I didn't play with toys. I walked around with a notebook and pencil stopping strangers at the bank, the grocery store, the post office, and even the Goodwill, to interview them.

Who are you? I would ask. *What do you do for work? How did you get started?*

I knew way back then that I had a better life in store for myself. I would be an entrepreneur. I didn't know that word at the time, but I did know I wasn't going to get a *job*. It wasn't quite a four-letter word, but it was close. I knew I was going to be my own boss. I was going to create my own economy. I was going to create my own future!

I have a soft spot in my heart for Goodwill stores, but I knew I wasn't going to have to shop at Goodwill when I grew up—at least not out of necessity. I was going to shop at high-end department stores. I was going to be in charge of my destiny.

And maybe it was out of some kind of heartbreak for my mother that I told her way back then that I would never work for anyone. I had a massive vision that I would head my own empire.

And now I do.

From my youngest girlhood, I knew I would be an entrepreneur. I always knew I could make money. I always see an opportunity where others may not. I'm extremely solution-oriented. I see a problem and I'm quick to find a solution or to invent one if a solution isn't already there. I figure it out and I make money.

I own a medical marketing business, medical clinics, a graphics company, and a marketing and acquisitions (M&A) firm that specializes in buying, fixing, growing, and selling companies. In twenty years, I have sold more than 500 companies, and my firm has sold even more.

I also partner with business owners to build their companies to *Exit Rich* within 3-5 years. We have implemented the "Road to Exit Rich" program, through which we help owners build their businesses to sell for their desired sales price.

I've been featured and interviewed on ABC, NBC, CNN, CBS, Fox Business, Forbes, Inc., and Entrepreneur.

What is Your Why?

People ask me all the time: "Michelle, when are *you* going to exit?"

I get it; my books are titled *Sell Your Business for More Than It's Worth* and *Exit Rich*. On the surface, it may appear that I'm all about *getting out* of business, but, as it is with books, so it is with people, so it is with businesses—the old adage rings true here: *Don't judge a book by the cover.* Look at the story beneath the story.

When people ask me when *I* am going to create my own exit strategy, sometimes I respond by talking about small exits that happen from time to time. When I buy a business, I fix it, I build it, I grow it, and maybe I exit it by selling it—but my primary business is to save businesses from going out of business. I love entrepreneurship and will continue to practice Mergers and Acquisitions (M&A) until I don't, but, even then, I don't know if I'll think of leaving M&A as an exit.

More and more, though, when people ask me about my own exit strategy, I think about the more important question—the question that trembles beneath so many of the questions we have. The question that I find critical, especially for women in business.

And that is: What is your *Why?*

•   •   •

In 2013, when I was doing research for my first book, *Sell Your Business for More Than It's Worth*, startups were risky business, to say the least: 98 percent of newly established businesses crashed in the first five years. Only 2 percent of businesses lasted beyond the first five years!

When I wrote *Exit Rich* just six years later and revisited the exact same research, I was astounded to learn that the business landscape had shifted dramatically. In 2019, only 30 percent of startups faced the risk of crashing in the first five years.

That is still a significant portion of businesses at risk, but in that short span of time entrepreneurs and their startups went from having a 2 percent chance of survival to a 70 percent chance of success beyond the first five years.

Things were looking much better for new companies, but things weren't nearly as rosy for older companies. In that short span of time, the risk had shifted to companies that had been in business for ten years or longer. Now, a full 70 percent of the 27.6 million mature companies in the U.S. faced the very real risk of going out of business.

To the ordinary citizen outside of the business world, this shift in the risky business of small business may appear simply as a *wash*—a canceling out of risk—but to a country that depends on small businesses for its spinal column, a 70 percent loss of mature, employee-rich companies is a devastating statistic.

When we lose small, mature businesses we lose jobs, we lose taxes, we lose spending power, and the American economy tanks.

Steve Forbes, the CEO of Forbes Media, LLC, who endorsed *Exit Rich*, (a WSJ & USA Today Best Seller) states that 80 percent of businesses on the market will never sell. That translates into a simple fact: the lion's share of businesses on the market are going *out of business*, selling for pennies on the dollar, closing their doors for good, and, even worse, filing for bankruptcy.

So, on a national level, my books, *Exit Rich* and *Sell Your Business for More Than It's Worth,* are written for business owners who are in danger of exiting poor, and even those who are not at great risk, as it's imperative to continue to grow your business using the "ST 6P Method". Yes, I most certainly am dedicated to helping business owners exit rich, but, at the same time, helping them to exit rich hints at a far more global benefit of the work I do. Helping business owners exit rich means *improving* their companies; it means evaluating them, assessing them, fixing them, growing them, building them, selling them, and sometimes even buying them. But mostly it means keeping companies alive!

I like to think that I'm helping to save the American economy by saving one business at a time.

That's my *Why?* That's why I do what I do. That's how I make meaning in my working life. That's what wakes me up in the morning and what helps me sleep at night.

Your *Why?* is the meaning-making that serves as the foundation of what you do. It's your passion, your mission. And one way to test if you've found your *Why?* is to ask yourself, *Would you do what you do if you didn't get paid?*

My answer is *Yes!* A thousand times *Yes!* I love entrepreneurship. I love the creativity and problem-solving that are part and parcel of entrepreneurship. My every waking moment is filled with them. I eat entrepreneurship for breakfast, lunch, and dinner, and I go back for seconds every time.

Don't get me wrong, the money is great, but nothing inspires me like saving businesses. I'm helping business owners and entrepreneurs afford the lifestyle that they've always dreamed of and that they deserve for their efforts. More importantly, I'm playing the critical (and often underappreciated) role of helping to save the American economy.

Obstacles to Success

Let's face it, there are obstacles, stumbling blocks, hindrances, and challenges for everyone in business. But it's inarguably tougher for women in business.

When I entered the M&A industry, it was 99.9 percent male. I flew in late to my first M&A conference at a hotel in Vegas. I've been to more than my fair share of conferences, and I've presented at many more. The vast majority of them are hosted at hotels are hosted at hotels where conferences for other industries are taking place—educational and religious conferences, medical and dental conferences, sports management, psychology, trucking, and automotive conferences. So it may surprise you to know that of all the hundreds of conferences that I have seen next door to my conferences, I remember that my first M&A conference took place at a hotel in Las Vegas right next to a dermatology conference.

And the reason I remember it is that, when I walked into the M&A conference, there were more than a thousand men who all looked the same—bellies and bald heads—sitting there. They all seemed to turn my way at the same time, and I can't tell you how many of them made the same old tired and condescending comment that the dermatology conference was down the hall.

The only thing that changed from big belly to big belly was whether they called me *doll, darling, sweetheart, or honey.*

And every one of them got the same response from me.

"I'm here for mergers and acquisitions," I said. I nodded at their shiny heads and said, "Maybe you need to be at the dermatology conference."

The preponderance of men was only a challenge insofar as it's a challenge to women in any industry. It's an annoyance you have to deal with, but it's not really a challenge. I suppose it could be a challenge or a struggle for some women, but I don't look at things as struggles or challenges, I see them as opportunities.

One of the biggest external obstacles for me occurred when I decided to transition into Mergers and Acquisitions over twenty years ago. Though I've always thought of myself as an entrepreneur, and I always told my mother that I would own a business empire and that I would never get a job, I did get one.

Xerox recruited me to be a high-volume manager, and I took the job. They recognized all of those qualities I possessed, from evaluating, analyzing, and solving problems to managing employees. I was making six figures, had great benefits, and they soon discovered I was everything they hoped I would be. Within six months, they promoted me to Regional Vice President, and I was overseeing 75 to 100 salespeople.

But it didn't take long for me to realize I hated it.

I was right when I told my mother I wasn't the job type. I didn't want a job. I didn't want to work for anyone else. I transitioned out of Xerox and started my own franchise consulting, development, and sales business. I did that for a few years.

But buyer after buyer after buyer kept asking me, "Michelle, what about you? Do you have any existing businesses?"

It was so clear to them that I had the skills and the know-how to run any kind of business. But it wasn't what I was doing.

"No," I would say. "That's not what we do."

We were a startup franchise. We helped franchisees sell their franchise and start a new location. And we helped with franchise consulting and development. I was an area developer for many franchises.

But I'm a big law-of-attraction girl, and I believe in the universe. Positive thoughts bring positive results, and time after time, when I recognized that my clients also saw in me what I had long recognized in myself, I knew I had to stop saying no.

So, I woke up one day and said, Yes!

And soon after I started my M&A company, Seiler-Tucker, I ran into one of the biggest obstacles I had to overcome.

As I mentioned, I grew up poor. I grew up in trailer homes and trailer parks. And I grew up as the only daughter in a family led by parents who, at best, sent mixed messages about money. On one hand, they spoke of money as unimportant, and, on the other hand, they imbued it with the weight of all evils. On the one hand, they said it didn't deserve our attention, and, on the other hand, they never stopped talking about it.

It was no surprise, then, that my biggest obstacle was not how to make money, but how to manage it.

I'm not sure I can express to you my utter astonishment when I received my first 7-figure check. My hope for you is that, one day, you face this obstacle. have this obstacle.

The check I received was for $1.5 million. That's a lot of numbers on one check. I went from watching my mother clip the price tags from shirts and skirts that sometimes cost less than $1 and hiding them from my father to figuring out what to do with a check for $1.5 million.

Through the years, I learned how to manage money. There are people out there for whom managing money is a passion. They study it. They live it. They breathe it. My soundest piece of advice for you, once you start making money, is to find one of them you trust. Find one who eats money management for breakfast, lunch, and dinner, like I eat entrepreneurship.

One of the greatest challenges for entrepreneurial women is funding. There isn't as much funding for women as there is for men who are starting and building their businesses. There's not as much working capital available, and it's much tougher for women to get financing.

Another challenge is that women are expected to do it all. We're expected to keep the house clean, have food on the table, take care of the kids, run the household. I think that's very difficult. Women just have to realize that we do the best we can. I wish there was a greater way to have a balanced life, but I don't believe there's really a true balance.

One thing I try to do to encourage women to handle the imbalance is to keep a 30-day calendar—more as a way to manage *energy* than to manage *time*. We get stretched so thin that we run out of energy. So again, it's not about time management, it's about energy management.

I tell them, set aside thirty days—the *next* thirty days—and write down *everything* you do from the minute you get up to the minute you go to bed and then compartmentalize these behaviors and activities. Put them into three different buckets: your A bucket, your B bucket, your C bucket.

Your A bucket holds all those things that only you can do that nobody else can. I'll give you an example.

I have my own podcast, *Exit Rich*. I've been interviewed on over 300 podcasts as a guest, and I know that there are a lot of people who know how to host podcasts and to host them well.

And I've had some significant guests on my podcast, but I am the only person who can host the *Exit Rich* podcast.

Only I can do that. Only I can really write my books.

Now, maybe you can get a ghostwriter and you can use other resources, but for me, what works best is that only I can write my books.

And only I can be my daughter's mother.

I'm the only one on my team who can negotiate these $100 million dollar deals. I can do it better than anyone on my team.

Those things are examples of the items in my A bucket. Your A bucket contains those things that you do better than anyone else.

Your B bucket holds those things that you are really good at. They are your core competencies, too, but you can delegate them. For me, that would be business evaluations. We have an analyst team that does our evaluations and writes prospectuses and a marketing team that does all of our marketing. All of these things I *can* do, and I'm good at them, but I delegate them because I want to work *on* my business, not *in* it.

The C bucket has all the energy sappers. These are things that just zap your energy completely and leave you with no energy to do the big things that you want to do to grow your business and spend quality time with your family.

The C bucket also holds those things that you need to get done for your family. Things like cleaning your house, going to the grocery store, ordering things online, going to the dry cleaners, mowing the lawn, and trimming the hedges. You can delegate these things. You *need* to delegate these things because they're energy sappers.

You need to take stock, look at your life, and ask yourself: what is my time worth an hour? Is it worth $500? Is it worth $1000 an hour or even $5000 an hour? Figure out what your time is worth and pay to delegate the C-bucket tasks that you're wasting your energy on.

These hands that help you take care of the items in the B bucket and the C bucket are part of your team, and it's imperative that you build a great team not only for your business but for your home life, as well.

Coaches and Mentors

Here's one of the biggest secrets to success that is tough for so many people to wrap their heads around. Get a coach/mentor. I always tell my clients, "It's hard to read the label from the inside of a bottle; you need an outsider's perspective to read the warning signs and keep you out of the danger zone!"

I've been to conferences of every kind imaginable. I belong to masterminds, but I discovered the biggest tool for my business's growth in 2011 when I finally made the decision to hire my first mentor. I had never hired a mentor before, and it was eye-opening and life-changing.

I'm half kidding when I call it the biggest secret, but the fact of the matter is that it takes many of us a long time to understand the enormous value of a good coach. It's the best, most important kind of continuing education. And it's hard to understand because we're inclined to think that people who are successful are often in the business of coaching and mentoring everyone else. Why would Elon Musk need a coach? Why would Oprah Winfrey need a mentor? Why would Michelle Seiler Tucker need a coach? (*These* names are placeholders for me and, perhaps, Sara. I'm sure you've got other more fitting names to take their place.)

Well, it's a different answer for every one of them.

For me, it's like having the best therapist in the world. The good ones can open your eyes to things that you can't see because you're just too close to them.

My mentors helped me to see that I needed to write a book. They helped me to see that *I* was the best-kept secret. Of course, I was living my own life, and I was living it rather successfully. There was no difficulty finding the work I was doing, and I was successful at helping business owners exit rich, so I didn't think of myself as a secret.

But nobody wanted to talk about it. Very often, the sellers wanted to keep the *sale* of their business confidential because they still owned a percentage of the company, or because the seller was financing the sale, so the buyers didn't want to alert everyone in their orbit that there was a new owner.

Sell Your Business for More Than It's Worth was a game-changer. I got huge recognition from it, and it propelled me to my first intro into *Inc.*, and for a time it was our number one lead generator. It generated more leads than I ever imagined. Now, I get leads every time I am featured in *Inc.* And none of it might have ever happened if I hadn't sought out a mentor.

Affirmations

I've always been a pretty motivated, determined, persevering individual. I'm my biggest cheerleader. Some of my affirmations are the best negotiators. Xerox used to call me The Closer. When anyone else struggled to close a deal, someone would tell them, "Call Michelle. She's The Closer."

And I remind myself of that.

"I'm The Closer," I say. "I'm a great negotiator. I'm a tremendous problem solver. I'm an amazing leader."

I do that with my daughter, too. I think it's very important and quite timely that I'm talking about this right now because the legendary Bob Proctor died today.

I drive my eleven-year-old daughter to school, and, for a while, she tortured me daily with mindless songs with inane lyrics that have no positive impact on anyone's growth. One day I had enough, though, and I said, "Nope. None of that music today. We're going to listen to Bob Proctor."

And so began our everyday habit of listening to Bob Proctor. He's all about the law of attraction, improving upon your mental faculties, and achieving greatness

It's a huge asset listening to good motivational tapes and podcasts. I love Joyce Meyer and her lessons about enjoying the ordinary events of life.

And Tony Robbins. As far as affirmations go, Tony Robbins' material has been the most significant for me and the growth of my business.

I think of these people as another kind of continuing education. They coach and mentor me in ways that don't require face time.

If I could only equip myself with one resource, I would make that resource a coach or a mentor. If you want to go from 5 figures to 6, if you want to go from 7 figures to 8 figures, you need to hire a coach. You need to hire a different mentor. What got you there won't get you here. What got you here won't get you there. The biggest thing I would do is look for somebody that I think would be the best mentor to get me where I want to be.

And books serve my need to continually grow, as well. Napoleon Hill's *Think and Grow Rich* and the book he co-authored with Sharon Lecter, *Outwitting the Devil*, my co-author of *Exit Rich*, are two of my favorites. I also love Robert Kiyosaki, the author of *Rich Dad Poor Dad*, or *The ONE Thing* by Gary Keller.

Entrepreneurs are like *squirrel, squirrel, squirrel.* We get distracted easily. It's called the Shiny Penny syndrome. I love that Keller's book has you focus on one thing, get that done, and then move on to the next. Entrepreneurs are inclined to do everything at once. But the only way to eat an elephant is one bite at a time.

The Question of Balance

Maybe it's easier for men to find a balance in their lives, but, as I say, I don't know if it's possible for women.

I will tell you this: I know how to unplug. I'm good at it. I go on four or five vacations a year. I spend time with my daughter. She's my everything. She's at the top of my A bucket, and when I spend time with her, I unplug completely. No cell phone, no TV, no computer.

I'm all about what she wants to do. We'll play tennis. We'll go do something that she wants to do. I help her practice and watch her compete in all of her gymnastic meets. I never miss a meet, even if I have to cancel a business deal. Money, you can always make. Time, you can never get back. We enjoy swimming, biking, playing basketball, and I love teaching my daughter all about entrepreneurship. We've got to have this family time.

We've got to make our family a priority. We've got to make God a priority. But you have to give them your all. You can't go into business half-ass, and you can't do God and family half-ass. You've got to focus on what you're doing at that time. If there's a way to achieve balance in your work and life, it doesn't happen without unplugging at those important times.

Notes to My Younger Self

As difficult as it may have been from time to time, I don't think I would change much about my experience as a young girl. I've always been a dreamer. I've always been a visionary. I've always had glorious and beautiful visions of what I could do and what I could accomplish. I don't have a reverse mirror, as I only look forward, not backward.

Those platitudes about the evils of money that came out of my father's mouth, those shopping days at the Goodwill and garage sales, the money-adjacent secrets my mother kept from my father—all of them may have been as necessary for my success as anything. An important lesson my mother taught me was about the value of a dollar! She would go to a garage sale or Goodwill and get 20 items for 5-10 dollars. I remember one day asking her for some money to go to the mall with my girlfriends. Their moms gave them anywhere between $50-$100. My mom gave me $20 and she told me to maximize every penny. They bought 1-2 items … I went to the sales rack and bought 8 items with my $20. Now, that was twenty years ago, but my mom taught me how to look for bargains. Just because something costs less doesn't mean it's worthless—sometimes less is more, like how I ended up with so much more than my friends who had more money.

The one thing I would tell myself as a younger woman would be to get a mentor earlier on. I'm extremely successful, but I think I would be even more successful if I'd had a mentor early on, and not just any mentor. There are a lot of stage speakers who claim that they're the best, and they're multi-millionaires, and all of that. Then you do a little research, and you find they're not all they're cracked up to be. It's important that they share major elements of your worldview. You want to make sure that you select someone who's been down the road you want to travel. And just because they're a great mentor for some people, doesn't mean they'll be a great mentor for you.

Learn from Other People's Mistakes

I'm a big fan of learning from your mistakes, but the final piece of advice I have for women (and for everyone, for that matter) is to learn from *other* people's mistakes. Regardless of your history as a mistake maker, the people in your orbit, collectively, have made many more mistakes than you have. They've already paid the costs of those mistakes, and if you can learn from them without paying the costs, it will shorten your learning curve and your path to success dramatically.

I never gave up on my journey to become a multi-millionaire. I have aspirations, still, to be a billionaire. But there have been times when I've stopped and thought, *Oh, my gosh,* and I ask my husband, "Why am I doing this? Why do I keep torturing myself?" Because M&A is one of the most difficult industries you can possibly be in. It has a 98 percent failure rate. There are objections and rejections everywhere. You can get all the way to the finish line and not close. It's a demanding and extremely difficult industry. There have been times when I thought there just has to be an easier way. And then I go back to that *Why?* I spoke about above.

I don't know *exactly* what the future holds, and I know that some things are out of our control, but I do know that the girl who lived in that trailer home and shopped at the Goodwill still has hopes and goals and dreams. She knows how to pursue them, and now, in the midst of this crazy world, she has one additional hope: that you never let go of your own hopes and dreams. It is never too late to pursue them.

SARAH SULLIVAN

"Don't pay someone for something you can do yourself."

"Save the good wine for when people come to visit."

"Put money into an IRA for your retirement."

"Don't spend money on that."

"Get straight A's and then a steady job—it's the best way to be able to retire by 65."

"*Do not* talk about money!"

"Your most important resource is your brain—always invest in education."

These are all the things I heard over and over from my parents growing up, which created in me a reserved mind around money. A scarcity mindset. A gripping mindset. A bubble of ignorance in which I operated.

Wealthy people *do* talk about money. All day long. Not to show off, but because money is a reflection of the value you create in this world. Money allows you family experiences, a certain lifestyle, etc. Money is more than numbers, and we need to talk about it all the time!

One day, as I was putting my two- and four-year-old daughters to bed, I had an out-of-body experience. As if I were a spirit on the ceiling, I was watching myself.

That day, like most days, I had woken up at 6 am and gotten my children up and out the door to be the first ones at daycare. As usual, there was lots of yelling and threats of "Hurry up, or else!"

I got them to the daycare just as the doors were opening, rushed them inside, gave them a kiss and ran off while they were running after me, asking for another kiss and another hug. Little two-year-old Avalon even escaped the daycare worker and ran down the street after my car as I drove off.

I watched her through my rear-view mirror in annoyance.

I sat in the car, in traffic, for an hour.

I arrived at work to sit at a desk for ten hours. I got yelled at by my boss, as usual.

I got back in the car to sit in traffic for an hour.

I arrived at daycare to find the lights out, doors locked, and a daycare worker standing outside the door with my daughters. I was the late mommy, as usual.

We got home and I prepared dinner while doing work on my phone and telling the girls to get out of my way so I could get things done faster.

When I put them to bed 90 minutes after we arrived home, they kept running out of the room, asking for one more kiss, one more huggy.

I had a big presentation the next morning. I needed to prepare. They were being *so* annoying. Why were they being so needy?

After about 20 minutes of them repeatedly running out of their room, I squeezed them, releasing all my day's frustrations onto their little shoulders, yelled at them, releasing even more of my day's anxiety, threw them in bed, yelled some more, ran out of the room, and locked the door behind me.

That was going to leave marks.

They ran to the door and clawed at it, crying at the top of their lungs for Mommy.

I fell to my knees on the other side of the door, sobbing into my hands.

As mentioned, I had a view of the scene as if I were a spirit on the ceiling. I was *so* ashamed of who I had become. If anyone had seen what was happening, I would have been *so* embarrassed. It was wrong on so many levels. I dedicated more of my soul to my boss who yelled *at* me than my baby daughters who yelled *for* me.

Those babies saw Mommy for 90 unpleasant minutes a day.

I sobbed for a while (I'm sobbing right now as I relive this moment) and then I went to my husband and said that we *had* to change our lives, *drastically*. We sat down together and set a goal that in four years I would be financially independent. At that point, I didn't know how it was going to happen, but it *was* going to happen. By the time my elder daughter was eight, I would be a multimillionaire *not* working for anyone else. I would be a calm and present mother for my daughters. Why eight years old? 3rd grade. Mean girl stuff starts. Hormones. It was so important to me that I would be able to be the mother they needed.

That was my original why, my original vision.

Fast forward to when my daughter was eight and I turned 40. I wrote an email to all my clients, thanking them for helping me achieve my goal and letting them know I planned to scale back now that I had reached my goal and "retired" from my 9-5 job via real estate investing. I felt financially safe, peaceful and comfortable. In return, I received over 100 emails from clients letting me know I had changed their lives, how they too were retiring earlier than they'd expected, that they were also able to live more luxuriously than they'd previously thought they could due to investing with me. Again, I broke down crying, this time happy tears. I was so touched.

I caught a new vision.

I get to share my gift and help others invest and grow their wealth and feel peace in their lives as a result.

Many people have asked me if I had to overcome any mindset obstacles in order to reach the place of consistently earning a million dollars or more a year. I'm always working on this one.

I keep reinventing my vision to be outward-focused. I constantly update my vision of who I get to serve. Okay, so I retired. Now what? Who else in my life, on my client list, am I able to help retire?

When I broke up with my second fiancé (not my husband), he said that I was extremely selfish.

I resented that ... until I realized that I was indeed very self-focused. Being a self-serving person can help you focus and will get you to a certain level of success. However, shifting that focus to the success of others, on serving others, enables you to experience hockey-stick growth and success—the sudden and extremely rapid growth that often happens after a long period of linear growth. Focusing on the success of others was the key to my growth and success.

Another critical success factor (although not a block to overcome) that created a massive shift in my business was partnerships. When I tried to do everything on my own, I got nowhere. I couldn't get my business off the ground. Then I started asking people who were already successful in my industry what they needed to grow. When I found folks who mentioned my specialty, we partnered together to explode and create that hockey stick growth!

"Don't pay someone to do something you can do yourself."

Remember that phrase I heard all the time from my mom? It was in the back of my mind every day as I grew my company. I didn't want to hire someone to do what I could do myself. That meant I worked *a lot*. This resulted in fatigue, and still does. I'm constantly working on delegating and building a team.

How did I overcome this? By surrounding myself with entrepreneurs who did well where I did not. By reading books like *A CEO Only Does Three Things* by my friend Trey Taylor. By joining groups and masterminds like Board of Advisors where entrepreneurs help each other overcome gaps and obstacles in their business. By realizing that the voice in the back of my mind came from someone who was not growing a business, so it didn't apply to me anymore.

I hired a housecleaner. I hired an assistant. I hired and fired and continued to learn. I read, took courses, focused on improving the skill of delegation that will be the key to the sustainability of my company's growth.

Was there ever a point I wanted to give up on my journey to becoming a multimillionaire? I did give up when my *why* was weak.

At 28 years old, I graduated with my MBA (which was supposed to be my key to becoming a millionaire). The economy was crap. I got a "job," but I was so bored! I took a right turn, forgot about climbing the corporate ladder, and we moved to England.

On my 30th birthday, my husband put me on a train from London to Bristol, England. I had applied to, tried out for, and was accepted to circus school!

I trained Monday to Friday, 8-5, with 16- to 18-year-olds who aspired to be in Cirque du Soleil and travel the world performing on cruise ships. It was *fabulously* fun! They lived six to a small apartment, sharing beds and dumpster diving for dinner. I, luckily, was still being supported by my husband, to whom I went home on weekends. I performed trapeze, partner acrobatics, and had so much energy loving life. I thought it was perfect and decided to be a performer, not giving a care to money. Then one day I saw a pair of checkered Vans in the front window of a secondhand shop. They looked brand new, so I bought them for three pounds for my extremely acrobatic friend for his birthday. When I gave them to him, he cried. He didn't remember ever having such nice shoes. This was wakeup call number one. Did I really want to be poor, but have fun?

That year the Olympics were in London, so a bunch of us tried out to be in the group of traveling performers who promoted the event throughout the city. I made it through tryout round two, but in round three (group dance number), I accidentally kicked one of the judges in the face. Yes. My foot, their face. I was (understandably) disqualified.

Soon after, I got pregnant, my husband was laid off from his job, and we returned home from England pregnant, homeless, jobless, and without much left in our savings.

We had family to crash with, so we weren't living on the streets, but we were poor. At that point, I reset my goal to being wealthy. That meant back to corporate work for me, because that was the path I knew at the time.

Fast forward to the opening story with my kids.

Once I set the goal to be financially free so I could be there for my daughters—so I could be a different mom—I *never* wanted to quit. At times I was physically exhausted and I wanted to sleep and not do what I needed to do. But I never wanted to give up.

Ever since my *why* became external, I have never wanted to quit.

What were the most important resources, tools, affirmations, mindset strategies or practices that I used to build my business to where it is today? Simply summarized, the most important catalyst I used to build my business to where it is today is listening to people who are where I *want* to be, not those who are where I *am*.

This seems simple, but sometimes it's difficult in practice because those who are where you are, are all around you.

Remember that saying I heard repeatedly from my dad? "Your most important resource and investment is your brain."

I've invested heavily in my brain. I've spent hundreds of thousands of dollars on coaching and education.

I always have a mentor or coach. Always. Do it. Pay for speed and efficiency.

If I only had one resource that would help me grow my business and reach my next financial milestone, it would be tenured business partners.

Early on in my wealth-building journey, I attended the first 10X Ladies conference in Vegas put on by Cardone Enterprises.

Danelle Delgado got on the stage, told her story, and shared her biggest tool for success: A simple 90-day goal setting and planning worksheet. This helped me go from ideas into action into results, which has consistently helped me and the clients in my inner circle reach goals over the years.

On a sheet of paper, create a table like the one below. In the "What" column, write in three goals. Requirements: 1) They can be completed in the next 90 days. 2) They are bigger than anything you have done in the past. 3) If completed, they will create the shift and progress in your life that you have been working towards.

In the "When" column, put an actual date or number of days from your start. Don't wait the full 90 days to do everything. If you have intermediate milestones, list those.

In the "Why" column, make this relevant. It must hurt or be really exciting. If not, don't bother with it because it's probably not a game changer for you.

In the "Who" column, list the people you need to tell about this goal or whose participation you need in order to complete it. Adding a professional to your team? Expanding your network? Asking a mentor, coach, or accountability partner? Once I told my friends I couldn't hang out for 30 days because I was in crunch time with a new business strategy.

In the "Sacrifice" column, list what you are willing to give up or forgo in order to complete this amazing, life-changing goal. I've given up drinking wine for 90 days. Sometimes I'll sacrifice sleep and health, but note that it's for a very short time. Also list out what you are *not* willing to sacrifice such as your health or time with your kids.

Finally, the "Reward". This should be something exciting and meaningful to you that you don't normally get. The results should be as specific as possible with numbers or dates.

Good luck! And thank you Danelle Delgado!

WHAT	WHEN	WHY	WHO	SACRIFICE	REWARD / RESULT
1. Hire a strong real estate CPA	14 days - make a list of 4 CPAs to interview 30 days - complete all 4 interviews 40 days - sign engagement letter with chosen CPA 90 days - complete tax strategy for the year with chosen CPA	I'm bleeding $$$ because I haven't implemented a tax strategy for my estate	Husband. And ask my network for recommendations. Multiple CPAs	Their fee The fear of looking clueless in front of an intelligent professional	Get a babysitter and do a 50-mile bike ride along the coast with my husband. A strong ROI with my tax return! Actual results: paid $3500 CPA fees, saved $56k in taxes.
2.					
3.					

The greatest challenge for women in creating wealth and abundance, at least in my socio-economic circle and generation, is that women don't talk enough about money. I didn't know how much income anyone made or what I should have expected to make. I didn't know how much life cost … until I got out there on my own.

And we don't talk about investing. It's not enough to talk about how much money comes in the door; we need to talk about how we can keep more of it and how to grow more of it.

The advice I would give someone feeling blocked by a mindset obstacle is to surround yourself with wealthy women. Ask specific questions. Get to know your numbers. Normalize talk about revenue, profit and investing.

If I could coach my younger self just setting out with a dream or an idea, I would tell her to think outside the box. Get to know yourself as best you can and build a business around your strengths. Ignore your weaknesses!

My next big goal is to hire a CEO to run my company. I have my eye on the next company I want to run.

My good friend, who is brilliant, created a machine that pumps out diamonds. Pretty awesome. Someone else now runs that company.

His newest invention is a sustainable, clean, community-based energy source. Partnering with him to launch this company could allow me the biggest possible impact on this planet and enable me to contribute to a healthy life for my daughters and my grandchildren. I feel honored that I've been able to affect the financial success of so many individuals thus far. Creating a cleaner planet would be an even bigger honor!

• • •

Sarah Sullivan is the founder and owner of SuGo Capital, an investment company that connects investors to strong passive income via real estate. SuGo Capital consistently offers hands-off investment opportunities for both accredited and non-accredited investors. Sarah's passion in life is sharing her knowledge around real estate, all the options that are out there to make money, and helping people advance on their path to building wealth. Sarah is the host of the Confident Investor series and the Women's Wealth Show. SuGo Capital currently has 1800 units and over $180M worth of assets under management.

RECHELLE
BALANZAT

The stories we choose to tell have an impact.

Growing up, I wanted to be a person of substance. I wanted to accomplish great things, do good work, and give back to my community. When I looked for role models, I found them, but few looked like me or represented where I came from—my gender, my socioeconomic background, my diaspora.

It's hard to be something you can't see, but I didn't let that stop me. I set out to become category leader in laundry and dry cleaning—a big dream, I know. But it's *my* dream. Should who I am, or where I come from, dictate how big I'm allowed to dream?

I successfully launched my company in 2014, and it was an immediate hit. I quickly grew my team to meet the demand. At the same time, I tried to raise funds to scale growth. 2014, '15, '16, '17, '18 ... the years went by, but I never raised the capital. Lots of money doesn't necessarily equate with success—success is possible through other means. But it does take money to make money. And for my story, not raising the capital meant my path was longer and harder—with more sacrifices.

Seven years went by before I received my first outside investment. Seven years alone, believing in a dream and a vision that only I saw. I paid a hefty price and made sacrifices that would drive anyone mad. Others would've given up. But I never did. It's tough to beat someone who never gives up.

Like many immigrants, I grew up in a humble home. My mother was a single parent who juggled three jobs to provide for me. Early on, I understood the value of sacrifices and creative problem solving. That experience instilled in me a unique way of thinking, although there are many more like me. My story is part of a larger collective.

I just released my first book, *JULIETTE*, a highly personal retrospective of my entrepreneurial journey, tracing the evolution from ideation to execution. To be successful, first you must believe you can be successful. Think it. Manifest it. Repeat it, over and over. In *JULIETTE*, I invite readers into my world, chronicling the improbable odyssey of founding, building, and scaling a company without outside capital. I share my process and how following my dreams helped me find myself.

Back in 2013, I had this great idea for a company—an app that would pick up, clean, and deliver your clothes in 24 hours. I thought it was genius! But there was one big problem—how did I build a company from scratch?

As the saying goes, "Where there's a will, there's a way."

Resourcefulness. Relationships. Resilience.

I forged my way by being resourceful, leveraging my relationships, and remaining resilient through it all.

Here are the three things I did to get my company off the ground.

1. Before I launched my company, I worked at another tech startup where I had great relationships with the engineers. I approached the best one, pitched him my idea, and asked if he would consider building it for me in his free time, but charge me one year later. He said yes.

2. I cold called laundromats and cleaners throughout New York City. This may sound weird, but I actually love cold calling. There's something powerful about picking up the phone and talking to someone. You can learn so much in those first few minutes. I cold called

different cleaners to see if anyone would be interested in partnering with me. It took some time and convincing, but eventually one cleaner opened his doors to me. I worked for him for free—sweeping the floors, cleaning clothes, running the machines. I did as much as possible to soak up everything I could about the cleaning business. After a while, I earned his trust, and he gave me the keys to his place. That was how I was able to get space and equipment without the initial startup cost.

3. I didn't have a marketing or advertising budget, so I approached a large real estate developer I had worked with in the past. I asked if they would let me pilot my business in a few of their buildings. They agreed and allowed me to put up flyers in the elevators, a display in their lobby, and they announced my service through an email blast to their residents. And that's how I got my first customers. I'm so proud to say that, seven years later, those initial buildings and customers still use *JULIETTE!*

So, while it's true that you need money to make money, don't forget that you also have the ability to create something from nothing, and that is far more valuable.

I could tell you lots of interesting stories about things that have happened since I began leading my company, but we don't wash and tell ...

"Drop Your Pants Here." I smiled as I glanced at the Etsy-made sign. Like any hip, modern laundry and dry-cleaning service, the sign was ... clear? Yes. Creative? Sure. I didn't, however, realize how specific this instruction was. On another day, doing someone else's laundry, I was up and at 'em early. If not me, who? The dryers were rumbling with separate loads, and I let them fill the silence as I pressed another client's pants. Then the bell above the door rang.

"Good morning," my regular said. "Do you hem?"

"Yes!" I smiled and nodded. His slacks were grey and a bit baggy. He dropped his pants just as I was about to continue the conversation. Yes, literally. Then he calmly picked them up and handed them over. No need to use the *JULIETTE* app to schedule a pickup—he went straight to it. I took the inside-out pants with caution. "Ummm." I clutched the pants. "I'll mark them and fit them for you, but not right now," I said awkwardly, but my awkwardness didn't match the situation.

He held up his hands. "No issue. I can just..." He looked around, as if slowly realizing he was naked. "O-Okay."

I didn't expect him to stay like that, although I'm not sure where I thought he would go. "Here." I pulled up a chair. "Take a seat."

There I was—just me, loads of laundry, and a pants-less customer.

I've gathered many more stories for my repertoire since then!

Before I launched my company, I would sit in the laundromat and time everything. I timed how long it took to sort through a bag. I timed how long it took to wash clothes, dry clothes, fold clothes, and pack clothes.

I tried to understand the operations of a laundromat minute by minute. It wasn't funny then, but it's funny to me now. It's funny to think I was naive enough to believe I could control every minute of a business.

I would sit in front of the washers and dryers with my notebook and count everything. How many bags came through, how many pounds were washed, how long everything took. I wrote everything down in my notebook and I probably looked crazy. One day the owner of the laundromat told me something I'll never forget. He told me not to be so "smart" about it. He told me that so much of business is just common sense, and that I can't control everything. I still carry that lesson with me today.

No is a powerful word.

When I decided to become an entrepreneur, I had no clue what lay ahead. My idea was all I had. It made perfect sense to me. Who wouldn't want to be a part of this amazing business? I jumped right in, frantically calling cleaners and laundromats. I got many "nos." To be honest, being an entrepreneur means hearing "no" a lot.

"We will not invest in your firm."

"No, we won't lend you money."

"We won't partner with you."

"We don't think your business plan will work."

And so on ...

But here's a secret: *no* is very powerful. It forced me to learn new survival skills, which sharpened me and improved my performance. It taught me which leads are worth following up on and which are not. It taught me which ideas are worth pursuing and which are a waste of time. Most importantly, it has helped me develop a part of my brain that is aware of who might want to listen to me. The odds are stacked against aspiring business owners. Most startups fail in the first five years. Knowing the distinctions is crucial, so be prepared, but keep your vision. Work hard. There is no wrong way to be an entrepreneur. This journey is entirely yours. So be yourself. Be sure of your abilities, and never give up on your dreams.

In 2013, I was on the ground floor of social media marketing. I founded my own agency and was scaling tech startups' followings from zero to a million, six months at a time. But in my notebooks, I had the idea for something greater: A service I knew New Yorkers would line up to use, powered by technology that could flip an industry on its head—with the potential for implementation in every major city across the globe.

But where to begin? I had zero experience building applications and no familiarity with the laundry industry I was attempting to reinvent. Putting pen to paper is one thing, but leaving behind a burgeoning career in digital marketing to pursue an intersection of industries in which you have no experience is another. It wasn't an easy decision, but I figured that, in order to fly, first I had to jump. My mother thought I was crazy and had good reason. After putting down my social media business to focus on building *JULIETTE* full-time, I became friendly with Mr. Kim, a local laundromat owner I met over a cold call. As our relationship developed, I began working for him free of charge.

Every day at 6:00 a.m., I would arrive at the laundromat and, between sweeping the floors and switching loads, I would take meticulous notes until I left at 6:00 p.m. I did this for one year. From the outside, it seemed ludicrous. But, in my gut, I knew I was on the right path. I learned everything there was to know about the backend operations of laundry that first year. I tabled the lobbies and put up flyers in the elevators, and, when the launch finally came, *JULIETTE* had a user base on day one.

$1.2B has been invested in laundry and dry-cleaning technology. I have received $0 in institutional investing. Since 2013, I have been hustling, grinding, and sacrificing. While my counterparts went on to raise (and lose) millions of dollars, my path was longer and far more difficult. If I had to sum it up in a sentence, it feels like working ten times as hard to get half as far. But hard work never scared me away. I stayed focused. I single-handedly built, grew, and scaled my company. I doubled my revenue each year for three consecutive years until the COVID-19 pandemic hit. When COVID wiped out 90 percent of my business, I not only rebuilt my revenue and client base in six months, I redesigned my entire technological infrastructure. A month after releasing the hybrid AI text solution, we introduced GPS and ETA tracking on all orders. I did all this without outside investment. But the truth is, I could do so much more with the proper support and resources—and I know I'm not the only one.

. . .

I launched *JULIETTE* in 2014, struggling to find any funding. It takes money to make money and, boy, was I looking high and low for something to come my way. Still, I remained focused. I needed to stay focused. *JULIETTE's* roots can be found in Tom Ford branding. I fell in love with his chic, sexy black aesthetic. The way the white words stood out on top of a black background is what I aimed to replicate. Something about it yelled confidence, and I needed to be heard.

In 2015, I still had no luck with fundraising. I struggled, but I couldn't let my faith waver. When you find something you love to do and you have the determination to do it, you should never let your faith waver. In November 2019, on a Sunday afternoon, I got a text message from a friend: My friend Alex wants to invest in you. My friend told me to send over documents, a contract, and an application. On a Wednesday, the funds I needed were put into my bank account. No document was done, no contract was signed, and no application was filled out. Was this guy my saving grace? You're damn right he was. And my saving grace's name is Alex Cunha. Oh, and it turns out he's a spokesmodel for Tom Ford. I spent days focusing—manifesting—on the brand. Everyone's path to what they need or desire is different, but the power of my thoughts translated into energy, opening up this door of opportunity.

Think about it: Isn't it easier to achieve something when you make yourself *believe* you can achieve it?

If you ask Alex why he invested in a business whose owner he'd never met, he'll tell you: "I don't know." But followed by that "I don't know," he'll say that something in him just knew it was the right move.

He could have chosen to invest in a number of other businesses, but, after pondering on it, he made the decision that translated into a life-changing moment for me. At this point, we hadn't even directly spoken. We met after the fact. I felt as though I was finally heard.

And here we are now, about two years later, and *JULIETTE* is beating its 2019 revenue numbers. You could believe in faith or you could believe in coincidence, but no matter what you believe in, there will always be a blessing heading your way when you're committed, dedicated, and passionate.

•   •   •

Steve Jobs: The Exclusive Biography by Walter Isaacson fascinated me the first time I read it. I had to read it two more times over the years to get the full effect. I admire Steve's ability to convince and inspire people to build great products. Perhaps he wasn't known for his charm or his grace, but I respect his ability to get things done.

The 48 Laws of Power by Robert Greene is a practical guide on ambition. It opened my eyes to the psychology of those who want power.

How to Win Friends and Influence People by Dale Carnegie is another great resource that has helped me on my entrepreneurial journey. Warren Buffet took Dale Carnegie's class, and to this day has his diploma hanging in his office. Read the book. Enough said.

However, if I only had one resource that would help me grow my business and reach my next financial milestone, it would be my commitment to continuing to listen to my inner voice, work hard, and never give up. *JULIETTE* is the dry cleaning and laundry company of the future. Our technology is cutting-edge, and our clients enjoy a seamless experience with the tap of a button or one-word text response and our GPS feature. *JULIETTE* is everywhere without being anywhere.

"Nearly eight in ten investors say that multicultural and female entrepreneurs receive the right amount, or more, of capital than their business models deserve, yet these same investors dramatically underinvest in this population."[1] Women receive 2 percent of all venture capital funding. Less than 0.2 percent goes to women of color. Why? My hope is that, in sharing my story, I shed light on the other stories that aren't getting told.

No matter how dark and lonely the nights become, the sun will always rise. Every day is a new chance. It's not about obstacles or setbacks. It's

---

[1] "The Growing Market Investors Are Missing ," Morgan Stanley, lat modified, 2018, https://www.morganstanley.com/pub/content/dam/msdotcom/mcil/growing-market-investors-are-missing.pdf

about never giving up. It's about believing in yourself when no one else does. Defending those dreams. Standing up for yourself.

It's a scary place to be. But, I assure you, it's the most powerful place. All obstacles and challenges make you stronger, wiser, and sharper.

5 things I wish someone had told me before I started my entrepreneurial journey.

1. Good is good enough.

    When I first started, I was such a perfectionist and agonized over every little detail that it slowed me down. When I was designing the app, I kept changing the layout and appearance. This only delayed our launch and ultimately cost me more money. In the end, what mattered most was that people knew how to use our service and not necessarily the shape or color of a button.

2. Talk about your idea.

    In the beginning, I was so protective of my idea. I thought that if I shared it, someone would steal it. The reality is that so much thought, work, and execution go into launching a business idea. Ideas are a dime a dozen. People who implement them are priceless. By keeping my business idea to myself, I missed out on conversations from other people who could've given me great feedback and insights. When I finally did start talking about my idea, others wanted to contribute and help me figure things out, which is the opposite of what I thought would happen.

3. Profitability.

    Have a clear path to profitability. Launching a new business venture can get expensive very quickly. If you aren't careful, you could easily go into debt chasing a passion. Be honest and realistic about the financial feasibility of your business plan.

4. Don't be emotional.

    As entrepreneurs, it's difficult to detach our sense of self-worth from our business. Perhaps we get defensive from someone's feedback. Your gut and intuition can be great guides when having to make difficult decisions. After all, you know your business best. But don't let emotional attachment blind you from an opportunity. For example, if someone offers a comment, gives feedback, or makes a proposition that strikes the wrong chord with you, take a minute to think through why it's upsetting you, then ask yourself if it's only that your ego is bruised or if the feedback is valid.

5. Exit plan.

Have an exit plan. Unless you foresee taking your business into old age with you, consider what an exit plan might look like. Do you want to sell to a competitor? Do you wish to be acquired? Do you want to pass the business on to a family member? Knowing your destination will help guide you in what roads to take. For example, if you know that you would like to be acquired, then consider the things that would make your company a valuable acquisition. Once you have that information, you can build your company towards those goals.

Our goal at *JULIETTE* has always been to become a category leader in laundry and dry cleaning. We believe we can accomplish this through our technology and our branding. Our unique approach allows us to be everywhere without being anywhere. We want to be the first recognizable brand in laundry and dry cleaning.

JULIETTE is the future of laundry and dry cleaning.

•   •   •

Rechelle Balanzat is the CEO and Founder of *JULIETTE*. Born in the Philippines, she immigrated to the United States where she earned a degree in philosophy from Fordham University and graduated with honors. With a background in finance, technology, and public relations, Balanzat is a serial entrepreneur. With *JULIETTE*, her third venture, she aims to become a market leader in laundry and dry cleaning by reinventing the experience through branding and technology.

You can visit us at:

https://www.juliettecleaners.com
https://www.whoisjuliette.com

NICOLE
BARKER

Shiny wall-to-wall winding pipes reached all the way to the warehouse ceilings. "Wow!" my little brother exclaimed from behind a face smudged with a touch of grease. "Look at all that copper! We should buy it. We could make a fortune at the scrap yard."

The concept of profit and loss was lost on my five-year-old brother as we wandered through the corridors of Home Depot with my stepdad. A mechanic's hands are rough, but my dad has an incredible sparkle in the corner of his eye that instantly washes away any grime or grit. He smiles from ear to ear as we all relentlessly tell that story 30 years later at every family get-together to poke fun at my wide-eyed little brother, who now owns multi-family rental properties that my cousin manages while my brother is off flying Black Hawks. We grew up in a trash pile—quite literally. Our mother took over her parents' company in her mid-twenties after my grandmother died, so our family owned the local trash company. We played in heaps of cardboard piled to the sky. We rode forklifts and I was running accounts payable by the age of 14.

When a big national chain company came knocking to buy our mom-and-pop operation, my mom ever so politely told them where they could shove their lowball offer. Instead, she doubled down on the business and invested in a piece of equipment that would tighten our profit lines by twenty percent and keep us in the game for another three years, despite the noose tightening as the goliath operation threatened to squeeze us out. As the only female owner in the nation, she held her own in a male-dominated industry, even though she was younger than I am now. My stepdad managed the fleet of misfit, tattered truck drivers. They balanced 14-hour days with managing to get us to school and carting me to gymnastics and my brother to football. As well, my mom cared for her younger brother who has Down Syndrome and lived with us after their mother died.

We worked hard for our money. That was the story and it was true and it served us well. I grew up with a better work ethic than my brother but a much more rebellious spirit. Money came fast when I took my first restaurant job. Although my parents surely would have supported me, I wanted to work. I wanted my own money, my own car, my own freedom. When my mom finally sold the company for millions, instead of the initial $50,000 they had tried to force her out with, I had just graduated high school and was on my way to a world of trouble. The service industry taught me that I could make as much money as I wanted. All I had to do was show up to work and really connect. Tips were limitless, and when my mom gifted me $11,000 when the company sold, I was gone. I thought I was invincible. Selling less than legal substances came fast and easy, as I was able to buy in lump sums and was a natural. From the start, money was a game. And I wasn't only determined to win, I wanted to beat everyone else. Fiercely competitive, I dove headfirst into the game. Like my ambitious mother, I wasn't interested in anyone else's rules.

Although the product I now sell is 100 percent legal, taxable, and above board, I carry a lot of my core money values from the time I spent learning the tricks of the trade in the hospitality industry. I know a lot of people want to tell Ivy League tales filled with accolades and anecdotes, but I have never been that girl. I believe that the people who do the best work get the best rewards. Creating the very best marketing system, the very best online course, the very best coaching calls was actually instilled in me from years spent behind the bar. I had to earn the best shifts. Earn the best regulars. Earn the best titles in cocktail competitions and bartender events.

And earn I did.

This perfectionism, coupled with my work ethic, drove me to do wonderful things—admittedly, for the wrong reasons at first. I just wanted to win. Just wanted to beat the competition. Just wanted to be better than the rest so that I could prove my self-worth. Battling launch after launch in the online coaching industry, I immediately produced five-figure months—a feat that generally takes most coaches years to achieve and that I accomplished in my second month. I achieved my first six-figure month in my eighth month. Climbing high and climbing fast, I was changing the game. I didn't do things like the other coaches. I didn't listen. I was defiant and headstrong and determined to win. But then, *she* came along. A sparkling shimmer of a human. You might think that it was one of my clients who changed me, but it wasn't. It was a reflection in my own mirror.

• • •

One day, in between client calls, I caught a glimpse of myself in the mirror and I saw something foreign. A smile. A real smile. My best friend will tell you that, ever since I left the bar world and immersed myself into truly helping people do more than get wasted, I'd had a real smile. Not the fake one that I put on to people-please and go along to get along behind the stick. A smile that came from my soul. It snuck up on me. I didn't even know it was happening. Most people will tell you a line or two about serving others, but the truth is, I have been serving others my whole life. In that moment, in that mirror, I realized that, for the first time, I was finally serving myself. And like magic, I was happy! Fulfilled. Alive. It was absolute magic. I knew I was never going back to the bar. I finally felt as though I belonged.

It wasn't all sunshine, unicorns, and rainbows, of course. Turning 5-figure months into 5-figure days is a stretch of epic proportions in how you view yourself. Self-doubt knocks on the door relentlessly as common sense and well-meaning "friends" warn you about the evils of making money too fast. It's hard to break free from the bartender mentality—the inclination to sit and endlessly complain as we so often do in a frenzy of commiseration. Leaving behind the only life I knew and trading it for a bunch of strangers on the internet was challenging, to say the least. I felt like a crazy person some days as thousands of dollars entered my bank account in glittering lump sums. People didn't believe me. They called me a liar and shamed me for talking about money so openly on social media. Once again, I was alone in an income bracket that simply didn't compute for my friends and family. Some people asked for money. Others shook their heads in disapproval, telling me it wouldn't last and I should get a real job that was more practical. Most of them just faded into the distance … or maybe I did, as I traded the barstool for a Zoom call and whiskey for water.

It's lonely at the top, as the familiar adage goes. And for me, it was at first. Shaking off the shackles of who I used to be, accepting and claiming my new identity, was the challenge. Bartender to Bentley-owning millionaire was quite the shift in only one year. Letting go of the girl who hated herself and stepping into everyday elation might seem easy from the outside, but old habits die hard, and the familiar snag of self-sabotage was a daily tug on my sleeve. Old thoughts, old patterns, old people who I thought cared about me—they all had to go in order for me to become the woman that I am now.

It's a steep learning curve—taxes, LLCs, people seeking to take advantage of newly expanding mindsets and bank accounts. Learning to trust myself to invest in big decisions was a challenge. Every single internet entrepreneur was after me. I received cold DMs to the moon from people offering me their thing after sharply twisting into my pain points. I gave into the dire warnings of more experienced, didactic wolves that had been in the game much longer than I had been. I bought things I certainly didn't need, trying desperately to quell the fear swelling inside me as I looked around the room, searching for the adult, hoping to God that it wasn't me. Old suits could smell fresh blood, and I fell for it hard once, spending $15,000 on snake oil. It was a rookie mistake. The more money you make, the more expensive the mistakes become. The stakes are just higher. I still struggle to see in what and in whom I truly need to invest, foolishly believing that other business owners all operate in the same line of integrity with which I sped up the mountain.

These days, I have a wonderful team that does the vetting for me. Learning how to outsource decisions that I don't have time to make properly has saved me tens of thousands and has made me hundreds of thousands. Surrounding myself with the right people has proved invaluable, not only for my growing net worth, but also for my sanity. The pressure of big-money decisions was a burden that kept me up at night. Money is supposed to give you security and the belief that everything will be okay when the sun comes up, but I soon learned that the feeling of solidity doesn't come from seven figures staring back at you on your bank home screen, but from a deep dark corner inside your core values and sense of self. Having been the biological daughter of a monster, abandonment was a familiar sentiment. I spent a good deal of time worrying that, like everything else, the money would up and leave me in the middle of the night. I now have a daily ritual of allowing more trust and building more and more belief in my ability to safely receive money and wealth.

The road was steep and the walls were high, and where others often turn back, I am just getting started. I know I'm supposed to tell the hero's journey of triumph over that day I almost quit on myself, but the truth is, that story had already happened long before this business came along. So, there wasn't a moment of surrender in my business journey because there is no longer any quit in me. I don't care how difficult the task, how impossible the goal, I'm here for it. Because not that long ago, I was in a constant state of not wanting to wake up. That hard-working bartender was plagued by the endless merry-go-round of malicious thoughts of hoping that she just wouldn't wake up the next day. Tear-stained pillows pressed into my face as I wondered if it was possible to suffocate myself. I consciously chose not to drive with my kids in the car because I couldn't trust myself to willingly stay on the road.

Depression didn't quite cover it. The sleepless anxiety, the agoraphobia, the desire to rip my skin off and run naked out into the wild never to return—I simply didn't want to be me anymore. Booze was my only solace, and while so many people told me that I had a drinking problem, that wasn't true. I had a living problem. I didn't want to be alive, and Jameson was the only thing that could take the edge off of the particularly long and relentlessly dull pain that ached inside of every cell in my body. A decade of bargaining with myself. Just wait until after Christmas. Can't do it in the same month as her birthday. Will my son survive having two dead parents? Suck it up. You have to. Keep going. Only two more weeks and then you can do it. This was the soundtrack that played on repeat in my head like an old Toyota pickup truck with a CD stuck in the deck. Over and over again. It's a wonder that I made it out. I wish I had some triumphant moment of declaration to share, but I don't. It was a Tuesday like any other when I decided I didn't want to do this anymore. And just like that, instead of thinking about killing myself, I started thinking about what I would do instead. That was the day I quit drinking, quit smoking, quit doing cocaine and quit sleeping with random men. I didn't want to live like that anymore. So, I didn't. Things got a whole lot worse before they got better, but they did in fact get better.

•   •   •

My life changed on a beach. I was standing there in Bali, staring out into the sunset-soaked water, the waves gently splashing over my feet as I surrendered to the feeling of worthlessness. I allowed it to wash over me for the first time, finally admitting exactly how much I hated myself. I let that feeling spill into a single flower and then set it free out to sea. I watched it drift away, carrying with it the emptiness, the suffering, and the self-sabotage. I decided that never again would I tell myself that I was worthless. And I didn't. Instead, I started to write a new story. One that would lead to a world full of wonder. A magical tale of the Seven Layer Transformation, which is the cornerstone practice in my client attraction program. It is a tool that I now use daily to help me shift my emotions through a practice of neutrality that allows me to choose how I feel in each and every moment. We get to create our reality based on our perception of ourselves. When we create fulfillment, success can't help but follow, and when we learn to feel those sensations, we can't help but invite more of the same. It seems like magic, but really, it is very ordinary. When we feel good, we do good, and when we do good, we feel better. And when we feel better, we do better, and so the cycle continues until we are wandering up a spiral staircase of limitless success.

The truth is that the only resource we truly need to grow and reach our goals is belief. Believing is seeing, not the other way around. When we commit to believing in ourselves a little bit more each day, every goal becomes attainable, every milestone a stepping stone for the next. Before we know it, we are already the people we had once wished we could be. It doesn't take time, it only takes intention, because we can change any belief fully and completely at any time. You may have spent your whole life believing that unicorns aren't real, but if one walked into your living room right now, you would certainly change your tune. And then you would be the crazy person raving about a white, horned beast for the rest of your life, right? Belief is a powerful tool, and we are the ones wielding the sword.

I'm sure there are zillions of resources out there to change your life. Books, podcasts, articles, online courses, all of the things. But for me, it wasn't a self-help or a how-to that really did it. Sure, I invest in online coaching, and

I have learned boat loads from industry greats like Dan Henry and Dino Gomez, but honestly, the book that changed my life was *Memnoch the Devil* by Anne Rice. I think I read it for the first time in fifth grade. Anne Rice died this year, and a little piece of me died with her as I watched all of her characters disappear forever. Her ability to articulate character taught me how to not only read stories, but also read people. My obsession with detail and seeing beyond the thinly veiled expression on someone's face comes from her writing, her stories, and her ability to show the truth in the most terribly beautiful of ways. I will be forever grateful for her mind, her presence, and the collective knowing that she shares with all of us even after her death.

•   •   •

As women of wealth, we face a challenge that many act as if it is external—the belief that it's a man's world and it's somehow harder to be successful if you are a woman. That's a popular opinion, but I don't believe it. Having lived through rapes and sexual harassment and unfair treatment, I can tell you that the only reason someone isn't as successful as they say they want to be is because they don't believe they can be. It doesn't matter what your gender is or isn't; it only matters how you view yourself. You can choose to let the garden between your legs end in a fall from grace or you can choose to believe it is your greatest strength. Either way, you will be right. The only real obstacle is the one you face in battling the perception you maintain of yourself inside your own mind.

People often ask me what I would say to my younger self, that girl who was needlessly suffering all alone in the darkness of her own thoughts. But I can tell you, it wouldn't matter what I said; I know for a fact that I was screaming at her. My future self is likely screaming at me right now, but I can't hear her, and I couldn't hear myself back then, either. The lessons present themselves when we are ready and willing to create the shifts in our lives. The only feeling worth sharing with my former self is the sensation that I have won. That is my past self's only currency.

Whether five years ago or five hundred years ago, it doesn't matter. I am and always have been exactly where I need to be to learn what I need to know to get where I want to go. Time is simply a measure we use to count the days to mark the age we register in the mirror. Maybe if we didn't count the days, the crow's feet would disappear. Every single thing that you want is obtainable right now, in this moment. It's only a matter of choice. Had I known the power of choice when I was younger, I likely still would have wasted it, as I did. But knowing what I know now, millions later, if I had the opportunity to sit with the younger version of myself, I don't think that I would talk. I would just listen. I would want to hear her hopes and dreams. I would want to make sure that I am living up to her standards. I don't think she needs to learn from me, but I would relish the opportunity to learn from her. In her eyes, sad and tortured, she was longing for something. She must have done literally everything right for me to be where I am now, 37 years old, making millions, serving incredible clients, loving every day of my life with my two amazing children and my loving fiancé who sees me for me. If I could tell her anything, I would simply say thank you. She is the one who got me where I am now.

Million-dollar virtual retreats are on the horizon. I am stretching my mindset, my energy, and my belief a little bit more each day to become the person capable of tripling her existing revenue goal. More strategies are being employed now. I am growing my audience and actively amplifying my voice, stepping into bigger circles, seeking to swim with bigger fish. I know that my message converts. I know that people want the results that I have and that I help them to achieve them with my programs. My clients' results are rippling beyond the edge of what I ever dreamt to be possible for myself, let alone them. I am ready to expand. I am ready to become the next version of myself so that in five years someone can ask me these same questions and I can reflect back to this moment, thanking myself for the work I am doing right now. It was the exact thing I needed to do to catapult me to the next level of success and fulfillment.

·   ·   ·

Nicole Cherie Barker, CEO of Wonder Women Client Attraction, has helped thousands of women-owned businesses by teaching them to stay authentic in order to attract true clients with ease and without cold outreach.

Nicole has an inspiring story and the background of a true survivor and fighter. She has overcome abuse, loss and grief, and today she is helping others to do what she does: believe in themselves and make a living out of personal authenticity. Nicole has been featured on NBC, CBS and FOX among other publications.

NEL
SHELBY

I grew up in Colorado in a supportive community. I was raised as a Christian Scientist with a deep, deep faith. I am the first of three girls in my family, so from a young age I felt very responsible for everything and everyone. I remember leaving a note on my father's pillow that said, *Dad, please be happy.* I wanted everyone to be happy. I wanted all to be peaceful, and I worked hard to keep things under control. Except that things were not completely under control. My father had a pretty intense temper, and he was set off mostly due to money. My mother would sneak us to the shopping mall, spend a lot of money on expensive clothing, and then try and hide it from him. He would find out, lose his temper, and then a day later apologize and say, "I'm sorry I lost my temper."

I was never completely clear if we had enough money in our family or if it was tight. I typically got everything I wanted, but it felt as if it was at a cost. I remember asking my dad if I could go to dance camp, which cost exactly $5000, one summer during college. Given his reaction, I gathered it was not possible. The next day he called me and said, "Sorry I got upset; I can make it work." I never knew if he actually had the money or not, so the situation was confusing and unknown. One of my very clear memories is of my mother and father creating the envelope system. My mom kept envelopes of money in her car, and each envelope was labeled gas, clothing etc. My mom could not spend beyond this envelope. The system didn't last very long, but I remember feeling worried, like what if the money in the envelope runs out, then what? Since my family had a strong faith in God, the undertone was that God always provided. God did always provide, even though it felt hard at times.

I have been a dancer my whole life—tap, jazz, ballet, dance competitions. I also sang and acted and loved it so much. When I was 19, I traveled around the world performing in a group called Up with People. I sang and danced, and it was one of the best years of my life. Performing was very important to me. I ended up going to college to get my BFA in dance with a double major in broadcast media. After I finished school, I had this dream to dance and sing on a cruise ship, which would combine my love of travel and my love for performing. When it came time to send the audition video, the video I made was of me singing "Life is a Cabaret" from *Cabaret*, the musical. The video was terrible. I looked so tiny in my pink sparkly dress, and you could barely hear me. As I look back, this was my deciding moment. I was determined not to let this happen to others. I want to make sure dance is captured beautifully so that performers may continue to show what they do, get work, and expand their career. This is why I film and edit dance as my career, and this is why I founded my video production company. By the way, I had no idea I could create so much financial abundance from this work.

I had so many obstacles to overcome. When I began working with a business coach in 2008, I thought I would be getting some great marketing ideas. As we talked, I realized we weren't discussing marketing ideas, we were working through mindset stuff. I didn't truly feel I could make money doing something I loved. The poverty mentality runs through the performing arts field but mostly the dance industry. If this mindset was prevalent and a big part of the field, how would I ever get paid for my work?

Video professionals are typically men. As a woman, you walk in with a camera—especially twenty years ago—and people may not take you seriously. That was tough for me to work through. Over fifteen years ago, I was filming in a theater in New Jersey, and I brought my husband with me to help. I asked for a sound feed for my camera. When I plugged in the cable, it didn't work. I told the sound person, and he looked at me and then went behind my camera and started playing around with the settings. My husband was shocked. If I was a man doing this work, this guy would never have touched my camera. After that experience, I was clued into what was going on, and I put my big girl pants on and just moved forward. I discuss this issue openly, and I train the younger women on my team how to handle this. However, I did not want that attitude to hold me back. I feel this was a pivotal moment in my story of "I can do this!"

Countless times I wanted to give up. I really did not set out to make a million dollars. I am a dance videographer at my core, and how could a videographer who films dance make a million dollars? In 2020, as the pandemic set in, all my jobs were canceled, theaters closed up, shows were canceled, I had nothing. I laid off my team, I cried, I grieved. As I sat on my couch day after day meditating, praying, and writing, I kept writing *God, please show me how I can be of service during this time.* At that point, my company was making over half a million dollars, and, to me, to make any money again would have made me happy. However, the question of how I could be of service kept me alive. A few months later, I got a call to do a virtual convocation for a college, which they wanted me to produce on Zoom. At first I thought, *It isn't dance, why would I do this?* And then I remembered the question: *How can I be of service?* I felt this was a message from God to pivot and do this. My client was so happy, and from there, business took off. I mapped out how to get to a million during a pandemic, and here we are two years later. This is only one example of getting through a panic point. I have had many others, and how I do it is I take the next right step and trust.

Complete trust in God is the most important tool I have used to build my business to where it is today. I have a very deep spiritual practice. It has not always been perfect—I go in and out at times—but it never leaves me. I study the Bible and a book called *Science and Health with Key to the Scriptures* by Mary Baker Eddy. These two books have changed my life and continually open up blessings. While this has always been a practice in my life, in the past eight years I have deepened my meditation practice. Every day I meditate and sit down and pray, read, and write what I hear from God. I feel very vulnerable sharing this, but as I get older and as the world becomes more spiritual, I think it is important to share that I pray. When I was young, I couldn't share that I was a Christian Scientist or that I prayed, as people would think I was a bit crazy. Now I am so grateful I can openly share.

If I only had one resource that would help me grow my business and reach my next financial milestone, it would be my deep commitment to prayer and taking the next right step.

I studied and practiced Vedic meditation for a long time, which really helped me. I listen to a lot of Esther Hicks and Eckart Tolle. I know this sounds funny, but I love spreadsheets, and I map out so much in spreadsheets. I mapped out how to get to a million on a spreadsheet, and that clarity is so healing and helpful to me. Then the books—oh my goodness, there are so many. *Atomic Habits, Ask and it is Given, The Big Leap, The New Earth*. It really is all mindset. I listen to what others say to me, and then I go grab the book. I must admit sometimes I read the first 15 pages and get what I need and then move on. I have tried to be better about being okay with that and not thinking I should read the whole thing. Oh, and for a long time I loved the podcast "How I built This" with Guy Raz. I haven't listened to it for a while, but it really helped me to hear about how others created their empire. A life changer for me was Tony Robbins' book, *Money: Master the Game*. When my mother-in-law passed in 2018, my husband was sure we would inherit a big sum of money. Well, we did not; his mother gave pretty much all of it to his sister, since she was concerned about her well-being. It was very sad, but the blessing in this was my newfound love for being completely financially independent. My husband and I both listened to Tony Robbins' book. I started reading Barbara Stanny's books, and then I spoke to her, and she said, "You can do this." I also read *Profit First*, and from there so much shifted financially. I believe we are on even better footing now than if we had inherited a huge sum of money.

I feel the biggest challenge for women in creating abundance and wealth is feeling that we don't deserve it. I notice this with myself and so many women. Who do I think I am that I can make a million dollars? Am I worth it? I am not the kind of person who can do this. Even now, this comes up with me. Recently I was working with a coach on my obstacles, and she said "Nel, you don't feel loveable, do you?"

Oh my gosh. I just burst into tears and said, "No, I don't feel loveable." So here we are, 20 years in business, so much opportunity and success, and

I am a ball of moosh. This coach and I are working on it, but it still creeps up. When it does, I say to myself, "Be not afraid." This is from the Bible, and God said this to Mary before she had Jesus. Mary had Jesus in such tough circumstances, and God said be not afraid, so, if Mary can do it, so can I. I also continue to say, "I am not concerned about anything; wonderful things are happening." We have a choice, and I think of this often. We can keep going down the pity road or, when we notice it, we can give ourselves grace, lift our chin, and repeat *be not afraid*. So much easier said than done, but it works!

I am very ambitious and always have been, so, quite honestly, I would tell my younger self to worry less and enjoy the ride. Even two years ago, I wish I had bought into the idea that I did not have to work so hard to earn good money. About ten years ago, a friend was sitting next to me in a spiritual retreat, and he said, "Nel, what if, instead of working so hard, you worked less and spent three hours a day praying? Can you imagine what you would accomplish?" At the time I thought, *No way, that is too much time to sit and pray; I need to hustle.* Now, at the age of forty-four, I get it. Meditative, thoughtful, prayer time is what creates the space for abundance. I am getting better each day at truly knowing this and practicing this.

•   •   •

I will be completely honest: Last year is the year I hit over a million dollars, and it was so exciting. Not necessarily the money and what I could do with it, but the idea that this could happen in the work I do. My next big goal is to continue to create this massive abundance and keep my team doing work they love as well as continuing to do work I love. The pandemic has opened a whole new channel in terms of how we deliver and what we create, so I am ready to do big productions, livestream dance all over the world, be of service to the dance field on what is next, and keep producing high-quality digital programming. My team is so talented and my love of directing cameras has increased in a huge way, so I want to do big productions, big documentaries, tell people's stories, help dance shine. I have been a lot more vocal about how I create success, especially with my colleagues and my team, which has really helped them in their lives to think bigger. I pivoted in a huge way during the pandemic. Many witnessed this pivot, and they would tell me it gave them hope. Sometimes, I feel I am doing this for others to see what is possible, and I say this with humility and love for humanity. If I could think really big with you right now, I would love to produce and direct a dance documentary for Netflix or Amazon Prime. They would fund the whole project, and I could bring my team with me.

• • •

Nel Shelby preserves and promotes dance by documenting live performances, producing livestreams and virtual programs, and creating marketing videos and documentary films. Nel Shelby Productions serves a diverse list of dance clients, and the entire team has training in movement. Nel is Producer/Director of NY Emmy-nominated documentary PS DANCE! a documentary about dance education in NYC's public schools, and she is Video Producer for Jacob's Pillow and Vail Dance Festival. She lives in New York City with her husband, dance photographer Christopher Duggan, and their two kids.

View Nel Shelby's work at www.nelshelby.com or on Instagram at @ nelshelby.

LISA
LANE

I was born and raised in Edison, New Jersey. Neither of my parents had the privilege of attending college, but their goal, from day one, was to save their hard-earned money to be able to send my two sisters and me one day. Thanks to their hard work and conservative lifestyle, I was able to attend the University of Delaware, but my parents didn't foot my entire bill.

I got a job as a resident assistant to help pay for room and board, and I still graduated with college loans. Knowing that I needed to pay them back motivated me to look for work right away, and I landed a job as a pharmaceutical sales rep when I graduated.

I grew up in a modest three-bedroom, one-and-a-half bath home. My parents owned one car between them and shared it. They were hard workers, and they were smart. They scrimped and saved to accomplish their goals, and I learned to do the same from their example. We went out to eat only on occasion. A typical family vacation was a road trip to Florida during summer months, but it was by no means an annual trip.

I learned a lot about money during my childhood years. Most important-ly, I learned that you could have fun and save money at the same time. From day one of my first job, I saved. Over time, my savings grew enough for me to be able to self-fund my entrepreneurial endeavor, but it wasn't easy. Even when I realized that my idea had potential, I still worked nights and weekends to help make it happen.

I learned early on that most people who do well financially in life are either salespeople or owners of their own businesses. Like many of us, I always dreamed that I might invent something big one day. It wasn't until I acciden-tally had that ah-ha moment that the opportunity arose, and when it hit me, I immediately sprang into action.

I knew that I had a great idea in my head, and I did all in my power to get it right. I taught myself everything that I needed to know, which included market analysis, prototyping, sourcing, and e-commerce success strategies.

After a couple of years of research, I ordered product and then sat back and waited, praying that something magical would happen. I was optimis-tic and scared at the same time, but was willing to risk everything. In my head that was okay. I convinced myself that the risk was worth the potential reward, and with a bit of luck my plan paid off.

Today, two-and-a-half-years post launch, we are scaling the business and are adding line extensions in the pet and bath space. We have plans to sell in more brick-and-mortar stores as well as internationally. Our goal is to reinvent the way we rinse, clean, and bathe, and we are well on our way to achieving that.

•   •   •

I knew that I had a great problem-solving product in my head. Deep down, I knew that it might have mass-market appeal, but I never imagined that my light bulb moment would grow into what it has become. At most, I was eager to be able to quit my job and work for myself, but this has blos-somed into an inventor's biggest fantasy. Sometimes I have to pinch myself to see if I am dreaming.

When I first launched, I found that 10,000 Rinseroo units had been improperly assembled. The only solution was to open every box, remove the contents, re-assemble, and retape every box. It was extremely stressful because I had no staff to help and had to recruit my husband and family. That mistake was time-consuming and *not fun!* Thankfully, we persevered and learned a lot.

I believe that the most important traits any entrepreneur can possess are confidence and an undying commitment to making their dream a reality. Also important is a sales personality, a creative mind, and a willingness to take a risk. Someone once said that you have to go out on a limb because that is where the best fruit is, and I believe in that very much.

I think the biggest obstacle is coming up with the idea itself. I feel as though I happened to luck out. As I mentioned, I wasn't on a mission to be an inventor.

Once I had my idea, I wanted to find out what else was out there—mainly to see if my idea was patentable—but I also wanted to improve upon what was currently available. My goal was never to compete as a copycat product, as that only drives down profits. I wanted to create a better mousetrap and figure out a way to sell it to the masses. When you come up with something that is a true game changer, it sells. The bigger the market, the better.

I envisioned seeing a Rinseroo in every household in America, and I still have faith in that becoming a reality one day soon.

The problem in today's competitive e-commerce space is that great products get copied and knocked off frequently. With Rinseroo, this happened almost immediately. Other sellers popped up all over the place, using our copyrighted images. They used photos of me and my dog and that was infuriating to see after all the hard work and time that I had invested.

Thankfully, we had intellectual property protection, and we immediately took action. We hired an outside company to be our watchdog, and they helped to remove the infringers. We have gotten good at policing our brand and that is so important. Without protection, it just becomes a race to the bottom; profits go away, and brand reputation suffers, too.

There was never a point where I wanted to give up my journey to becoming a multimillionaire. Once I realized that I had something worth pursuing, it only fueled my desire to grow it. I was on a mission, and nothing could stop me. That's not to say that there haven't been bumps in the road. Thankfully, the bumps have not been too significant, and I have yet to have a panic attack.

•   •   •

None of us can achieve success without some help along the way. I am so grateful for one of my lifelong college best friends, Carolyn Favorito, Esq., who helped me get to where I am today. We met our freshman year while attending the University of Delaware. She also happens to be my patent attorney.

When others told me that they didn't think I could get a patent, she told me I could and encouraged me to pursue it. I hired her and she fought for my patent as if it were her own. If it wasn't for her, I may have given up. She was my biggest cheerleader and motivator.

When it comes to the most important resources, tools, affirmations, mindset strategies, and practices that I used to build my business to where it is today, there are too many good resources to list. But the key, in my mind, was to do my homework and learn everything I could to help better my odds of success.

I also hired my son to work for me, not only because he needed a job at the time, but because I knew that he would be committed to my goal of growing the business. I compensate him well and am generous with his time off. My goal is to keep him around for a long time, and that is more likely to happen if he is happy working for Rinseroo.

•   •   •

My ah-ha moment was pure luck and probably the easiest part of the journey. The difficult part for me was being able to answer the "Now what?" question. I was excited to have an idea but had no idea where to go from there. The thought of going from concept to fruition baffled me. At that point, I decided I needed to figure it out, and I took to the internet and to books to learn how to make it happen.

One book in particular, *The Mom Inventors Handbook: How to Turn Your Great Idea into the Next Big Thing* by Tamara Monosoff, was especially helpful. It taught me just about everything that I needed to know, and I have recommended it to many.

I have come to the realization that no human is able to learn and master everything. There are talented people out there who can do certain things much better than I ever could. No doubt, smart, dedicated people are the best resource to grow and scale a business. As long as we all have the same mission, teamwork is the ultimate key to success.

I'll admit that I never felt like being a woman was an obstacle to my success. The great news is that women are making serious strides in entrepreneurship, and a lot of that is because it's easier than ever to build a business from home. Women can truly do it all. We can be moms, we can raise families, and we can be the breadwinners.

I believe that the only thing that might hold women back is our innate desire to sometimes be moms rather than business owners, and I get that. I chose to be a mom first, too, and if I could do it the same way all over again, I would. There is no better time spent than with your kids, and if that means having less income, that's okay. My kids were grown when I started on my entrepreneurial journey.

•   •   •

Here are five things I wish someone had told me before I started my journey to becoming a multimillionaire.

1. Building a business doesn't happen overnight. It takes planning, dedication, and a good amount of luck. In my case, it took approximately three years to go from idea to having a product in hand. I don't think it's a good idea to rush the process. Taking the time to tweak, learn, and plan is a great strategy.

2. Bringing a product to market or starting a business will likely cost more than you expect. The Rinseroo was not high tech, didn't have any intricate parts, and I didn't have huge mold costs, but everything added up. Try to estimate your costs before starting out and add at least 25 percent. Prototypes, samples, drawings, patent and copyright, etc. were just a few of my startup costs.

3. Regardless of how successful your product or business venture is, be prepared to not make a cent during the startup phase. If you can't afford to not make money, know that you are trekking out on a difficult path.

4. Half of bringing a product or business to market is development. The other equally important part is marketing. My life prior to starting this endeavor was in sales, and that experience has helped tremendously on this journey. If you are only a maker and not a marketer, you may need a partner who is, or you may need to hire one.

5. The most successful products check all these boxes: It is demonstrable, it solves a problem, it is an improvement over what is currently available, and it appeals to the masses. When I started, I knew that the Rinseroo left no box unchecked, and that gave me the confidence to move forward.

My dream of creating and bringing a product to market has become a reality. I am proud of myself for accomplishing that, but I have only just begun. My goal now is to scale and build the Rinseroo into a household brand. We are in the process of adding line extensions in the pet and cleaning spaces, and I am thankful that many of our ideas were generated by feedback from our customers. They are constantly reaching out to let us know what they would like to see next. I think they will be thrilled with what we have in the pipeline.

•   •   •

Lisa Lane is the inventor of the Rinseroo, a patented slip-on shower attachment hose that she brought from concept to store shelves. Her company is Lane Innovations, based in New Jersey. Her recent success story is one that all started in the bathroom at her Jersey shore home. She claims that she was standing in a tub when she realized that her idea had mass-market appeal.

Lisa launched the Rinseroo on her own website, as well as on others, just over two years ago. Since then, her brand has become a top seller on Amazon Launchpad, and it also sits atop their "most wished for" list. She is currently at work scaling the brand into thousands of retail stores nationwide and is in the process of adding line extensions in the cleaning and bathroom space. She hopes to re-invent the way we rinse, clean and bathe, and she is well on her way to seeing her dream come to fruition.

The best way to keep in touch with Lisa is to visit Rinseroo.com or follow her on social media.

Tik-tok: Rinseroo
Instagram: OfficialRinseroo
Facebook: https://www.facebook.com/GetRinseroo/
YouTube: https://www.youtube.com/watch?v=F6jY-1Yxn4E
LinkedIn: https://www.linkedin.com/in/lanelisa/

SPARKZ

I grew up in an average, middle-class, low-income household with my mother and five siblings. Financial hardships and struggles were no strangers to my family, but, as children, we never fully knew what all my mother dealt with. My mother always kept a smile on her face. I never saw her cry, and she always made sure my siblings and I kept one another close and protected. We played together, my siblings were my best friends, and home seemed normal for us. As kids, our "normal" was so disjointed because, in reality, some of the situations we were in were anything but normal. We spent time in shelters, we stayed in homes without utilities connected, and we got dressed for school in the dark numerous times with smiles on our faces.

I grew into my adulthood still facing financial challenges and homelessness. As an adult, I had gotten a gym membership many times just to be able to shower while I was living out of my car and/or storage, staying in hotels when possible, and working multiple jobs for warmth during the cold winter months when hotels weren't an option. I'm no stranger to the struggle. After spending the majority of my life in poverty, I knew I didn't want to bring children into the same cycle, so I couldn't live that way forever. I knew from a young age I would take control of my life in ways I had never seen up close.

When I was growing up, money and nicer things were not readily accessible to me, so I learned at a very early age how to appreciate the things that I did have and not complain about what I didn't. As my mother was a single mom, there wasn't any extra money floating around to even fathom the "wants." The idea of being financially responsible simply meant being able to maintain the bills. We didn't have supplemental funds to do extracurricular activities, so we did little to none. Life wasn't hard to understand—you did what you could afford to do. There were a few common sayings in my household, one being "live above your means" and the other "trying to keep up with the Jones" and I knew not to try and do either! To me, those phrases meant that we shouldn't try to do what everyone else was doing just because they had access to more resources than we did. If my mother had a list of things to do and a certain amount of dollars, she would prioritize what needed to be paid for and disregard any wants because the only thing that was important was that we had all of our *needs* met. She often put us kids before herself, so my take from that was that it's okay to go without as far as luxuries and unnecessary wants go, as long as I was able to have a roof over my head, food in my stomach, and clothes on my back. As a child, I grew up in survival mode and thought that was how life was meant to be: full of challenges, sacrifices, and check-to-check living. Thankfully, I was just ignorant, and life had other plans.

Sparkz is primarily a nail care provider, famously known for my work with celebrities, but my services don't stop there. I wake up every day and make women feel more beautiful inside and out while getting paid to do so! I've always espoused uplifting women. I've been an advocate for sisterhood since early childhood. My current success comes from being one of the best nail techs in the city of Houston, servicing and partnering with the majority of the female artists local to the area.

Working with celebrities pays pretty well, but the networking opportunities I am granted with each new contract is what helps keep revenue and exposure rising. My work speaks for itself. Although it was a hidden talent I didn't know I had in me, it's opened so many doors I would never have imagined I'd walk through. If you visit Sparkz Styling Studio for the nail services, you're likely to leave with a new outfit, skincare, hair or hair accessories, or, if nothing else, a positive attitude and inspired mind. I take the time to listen to my clients and ensure they are *in love* with the results of our creations and the warm hugs after each service. That's what I love about reconditioning them regularly. I never feel as though I'm getting up and going to work—I feel as though I'm going to see my friends, visits that happen to pay for the luxury lifestyle I maintain. By simply being true to myself and my passion, I've flown all around the world and met A-list celebrities wanting to work with me and advocate for my brand. Seeing me today, you'd never know that three years ago I was homeless. I thank my business for that regularly.

·   ·   ·

My business started off primarily as a nail company, established solely for the purpose of trying to pay for hotels to sleep in because at the time I was living out of my car. When I started doing nails, I had no clue I would take it this far. I actually had no license or certificates to provide the services I was offering, nor did I aspire to obtain any, because it was just a hustle I came across that could help my husband and me eat and sleep comfortably. It was a transitional gig, that was all.

Little did I know that God had bigger and better plans for me.

I did a few sets of nails out of the hotel room I was staying in, and before I knew it, I looked up and had three or four nail salons reaching out to me to work in their shop. They *loved* my work. Because I didn't have the proper credentials to back me, legally I was unable to accept any of the offers. Luckily for me, my uncle and big cousin owned a local barber shop where they let me rent a booth to work from for $50 a week. I was extremely appreciative of the opportunity they allowed me, but the environment wasn't ideal for women to come and relax in, so it was hard to keep consistent clientele, even being the most affordable in the city. I could barely afford my $50 booth rent and supplies, let alone have any extra dollars for my day-to-day life. Still, at that point I had already seen the potential and what I could obtain by taking the craft more seriously. I took it upon myself to get licensed for nails, and from there I was able to work in my first actual nail salon. Seeing clients coming in regularly, my name ringing bells, and people driving from other cities to sit in my chair and be serviced by me was all the motivation I needed.

·   ·   ·

As I accomplished goals faster than I set them, my vision became greater by the day. I aspired to run my own salon and have other nail techs working under me so we could handle my overflow of clients. Being the empathetic, genuine, and loving person that I am, I built a nice rapport with almost everyone who sat in my chair. We had authentic conversations in which I encouraged them to go after their personal goals and shared the story of my journey to help inspire them to achieve whatever they wanted.

I continued working, pushing my brand, and marketing on social media, and that's how I began getting celebrity clients. I signed a few celebrities to be ambassadors for my brand, and it grew what seemed like overnight. To this day, I still provide luxury nail services to women and motivate them while encouraging them. While servicing women regularly and getting to know them personally, I also learned a lot about their needs as far as physical maintenance is concerned. From there, I created my own skincare line, luxury hair brand, and luxury fashion line to coexist with my nail brand, SPARKZ ONNA SET, that are all doing well. Just one idea bouncing off another and expanding as time allows.

•   •   •

One of the most interesting times I had while building my brand was one that I felt was a test from God but also a breakthrough for me personally. The very first set of nails I made for a celebrity was for a well-known artist, and I was supposed to meet her at one of her shows here in Houston to exchange the nails. Now, typically, clubs are not my scene, so I hardly go, but occasionally my friends would drag me out with them. I asked all my friends, who know I don't normally club, to come with me that night. If they didn't, I would have to go alone because I had to be there for business purposes. None of my friends were able to join me, so, determined to get my first set out there, I went alone. The evening started off fine, but before I knew it some guy stole the nails from me and another started swinging at me out of nowhere. I got robbed and beaten up by two men that night. I had gone there feeling so confident and beautiful, excited to meet the artist, and left feeling completely discouraged about whether or not this was the line of work I should be in. I wondered if I should even leave the house again when I didn't have the support system I needed and felt as though I couldn't do much alone.

I stopped working for four months after that, for obvious reasons—discouragement being the biggest one. One day, I finally logged back into my social media account to see that Crystal Smith, Monaleo, and Big Jade were all interested in working with me. I had to decide at that point whether I was going to let my past continue to block my future and all that I had worked so hard for, or if I would take the moment and learn from it. Clearly, in writing this, I chose to learn from the experience. I'm so glad I did because, had I stopped then and there, I wouldn't be nearly as successful as I am today. Getting robbed and beaten up showed me who I shouldn't bring along the journey because, when I needed them, they left me alone and vulnerable. Dropping the dead weight allowed me to prosper in ways I wasn't aware I was being held back from. Everything can be a teachable moment if you're willing to learn.

•   •   •

The silliest mistake I made as an entrepreneur was relying on family and friends to be my biggest support system, including hiring family to work for me, thinking I was paving the way for everyone to become successful.

Granted, family and friends will generally be supportive, but they are often looking for something in return—discounts or free services. I found myself constantly working and tired yet still unable to afford things I wanted, even just a meal or a nice, twenty-five-dollar shirt. What I learned from that was I can't stoop to people's expectations of me and succeed at the same time. I didn't have to provide services for little to nothing to get people to choose my services because, when people truly support you, they will pay your price and tip and not ask for discounts. Of course, when I started charging everyone the same price and setting standards and expectations for my brand, I lost some of the people I was hoping would support me the most. That did show me that business will succeed outside of "my people" better than it would if I broke my back to cater to their needs. People will use you for what's beneficial if you allow them. Don't ever sell yourself short simply because boundaries are uncomfortable. None of my decisions meant that I didn't love my people personally, only that they weren't the clients I needed to serve. I learned not to be afraid of change and growth.

•   •   •

One of the many mindset obstacles I had to overcome in order to reach the place my business is in today is discipline, discipline, and more discipline! Many of us have lots of money coming in throughout the year and can never account for where it goes. I had to teach myself discipline with spending habits, time management, and prioritizing tasks. My first year working for myself, I was making $250 daily *easily*, yet, whenever I wanted to do something, I didn't have the money for it. I had been so used to going without that, when the money started to come in, I would blow through it on meals or lend it to people who wouldn't repay me. I helped people I knew wouldn't help me if I needed it just because it was uncomfortable for me to say *no*. I bought drinks and bottles every time I was out with somebody and picked up tabs to show people a good time, regardless of what was expected of me. I was so frustrated because I felt as if I was in a position to help people and I wanted to do that, but I ended up being taken advantage of at every possible opportunity. The first thing I needed to learn was how to tell people, including myself, *no* without feeling bad about it. The next challenge to overcome was to do everything with purpose, on purpose. I created a work schedule for myself and spaced my tasks out evenly so I had a normal workday and could have a personal life outside of my occupation. Learning these two important tactics gave me a sense of peace.

•   •   •

The hardest external obstacle I had to overcome was money issues. In the beginning, I had so many plans for my business, but I barely had enough money to maintain what I was already doing, let alone try to expand. Right as I was launching my brand, COVID-19 came about and shut the world down. That was more than enough reason to give up on my business, since my salon was mandated to close. Eventually, I decided to start offering mobile services to serve people in a safe manner, meet my financial goals, and maintain life post-pandemic. To overcome the tribulations of COVID-19, I became a traveling nail tech and still provide those services for clients who fell in love with the option to have luxury brought to them in the comfort of their own homes. That grew my clientele base almost two and a half times, solely because commercial salons shut down and I kept going.

I've faced many panic points on this journey, but one thing about me is that giving up was never an option! As mentioned before, after I got robbed and beat up, I was extremely discouraged, but even then, in the back of my head, I knew that this was the best move for me and my future. I can't see myself ever entering corporate America again, clocking in for somebody else, making them money while receiving the bare minimum. I believe life is all about perspective, and if you allow room for doubt and see reasons not to perform at your very best, those negative thoughts will consume your mind and focus. As far as I am concerned, there will always be a way for my brand to succeed. Regardless of what obstacles come up, I have to find the best way to maneuver around them to reach said success!

·   ·   ·

I'd like to humbly thank my husband. I'm forever grateful to him for always believing in me and for working so hard to allow me to put all of my efforts into my business. In the start-up phases, we oftentimes had less than twenty dollars and needed to figure out how we could both eat and put gas in the car. I was spending all the money on my business, and it wasn't bringing in earnings as fast as we would have liked, but he never gave up on me. He always encouraged me when I felt discouraged, as has every person who has sat in my chair, stopped by my location, or supported me in any way, shape or form.

The Bible has been and always will be the most important resource in my life, as it guides me to be a blessing to others and carry myself in ways in which I'm susceptible to receiving the blessings that were created just for me. To match my faith, it was important to have a "grind mode" that complemented in effort my thoughts, wishes, and goals. I affirmed daily that my small business would be a big business, and not only talked about it but came up with different tactics to gain more exposure for my brand and solidify what my faith had already assured me. I go through life with the mindset to be kind to everyone and not miss an opportunity to speak, because you never know to whom you may be speaking and in what ways you can help each other grow. There's no room for negative thoughts in my mind. I focus on the positive because it's always a "glass half full" situation. Being a positive person naturally makes other people want to be around you, and it attracts you to other positive people, which only allows more room for growth and healthy bonds.

The social media app, Clubhouse, came out at the end of 2020 and was actually a pretty big aid for me. Different groups were always talking about various business endeavors, tactics, and strategies. At the same time, they had chat rooms with my target audience (celebrities) freely speaking, which allowed me a platform to connect with people I might never have had the chance to through mainstream social media outlets. Clubhouse and the information I learned there helped me step by step when it came to legitimizing my brand and obtaining the proper licensing and paperwork.

I would say that the most beneficial resource in achieving my next financial milestone is networking in general. There are so many educated people in the world for me to connect with—many who are further than me on their journey and can offer advice on strategies to learn in order to improve as a business owner so I can broadcast further and secure more clients. It's the most personal means of social media communication because everyone communicates in person at the same time, with no back-and-forth text messages or emails leading to misunderstandings or poor communication. Networking at events taught me about HARO, which is how I landed so much media coverage for my business, resulting in more revenue.

Being a woman is such a huge challenge when trying to create wealth and abundance because we are always the underdog. Women can be viewed as weak because we are naturally emotional creatures, so it can be more difficult to be taken seriously. Also, women usually have so many other people they need to tend to—children, a partner, family, or friends. Being needed by our loved ones is bittersweet because we're always glad to do what we can for them, but it can become too overwhelming to focus on ourselves. I know moms sometimes look up and realize they haven't combed their hair in three days, but the kids are cute every day, so they're happy with that. We as women have to take control over the narratives of our lives. My advice to you all is to look at how much you do for others with no pay or reward other than an occasional "thank you." Realize what that same drive can get you when put into your own life and go for it! We can be successful, and we deserve luxury. We need to remember the importance of putting as much energy into ourselves as we put into the people we love the most.

•   •   •

Here are Five Things I Wish Someone Had Told Me Before I Started my Wealth-Building Journey.

1. It may feel lonely—that doesn't mean you're alone. When you are tired of achieving the same results, you'll start to outgrow certain behaviors and release anything that's not beneficial to your growth. Because those things might've been around for a while, you may be uncomfortable without them. But once you accept your new reality, you'll start to flourish because you've dropped the dead weight and bad energies that were holding you back.

2. Be resourceful. It's not always about what you know but who you know. Connecting and networking can help a great deal as well.

3. Walk by faith. Nobody outside of you is going to see your vision until it comes to fruition. You have to decide for yourself exactly what you want out of life and make a step-by-step plan on how you're going to achieve it, then stick to it! If the plan is solid and you stick to it, you'll see it start to unfold, and then you won't have to tell people to convince them of what it will be; they'll be able to see what it is and try to become a part of the legacy.

4. Embrace your journey. Like J. Cole said, "There's beauty in the struggle." Some of my happiest moments in life happened when I was homeless. Financially, things weren't the best, but I didn't have to question the loyalty of anyone around me. Having people in your life that you can trust is something we sometimes take for granted.

5. Consistency is key! I know you've heard that one before, but it's one of those things you won't understand until you live it. Consistency is the quality that separates those who "succeed" and those who don't prosper.

I'd like to see myself on the red carpet for one of the Galas, nationally recognized as an amazing nail tech. I aspire to be the "Arrogant Tae" of nails and want *every* celebrity and women in general when they come through Houston to know exactly where to go to book. I've landed several celebrity clients already, and I have created nails for two album covers, so the attention is already on me. I use epitome accessories and rare techniques that add a different touch to each project. Everyone loves authenticity, and I bring it to the table every time, so the red carpet is well on its way.

I'm also working with ladies under the same engineer as Cardi B, so I hope to meet her one day soon to enjoy drinks and laugh. Although I'm on my way to achieving these goals, they are a stretch for me because most celebrities in the industry already have a set team and aren't frequently looking for new people to fill roles. Still, my work can change their minds; I know it! When I make it to the red carpet, it will represent for me and all the little girls who come from where I did that really, no matter what your past, anything is possible. And you don't have to be a doctor or lawyer or do sports to be Main-Street successful; you can do what you like!

•   •   •

To learn more about my brand, you can follow me on Instagram@Sparkz. Sensationz where booking site and catalogs are listed, or you can shop online at www.sparkzonnaset.bigcartel.com.

Sparkz is a serial entrepreneur, including founder and CEO of Sparkz Styling Studio and Sparkz Onna Set. Sparkz Styling Studio is a business created to provide women with epitome quality fashion and to empower everyone to look and feel their best, with the understanding that when you feel your best, you perform your best! The goal is to assist in confidence-boosting and serve motivational purposes for all women. Sparkz also advocates for Suicide Awareness and donates annually to local barber/beauty shops during the back-to-school season so they can spend time with younger, less fortunate children in the community and inspire them to take more from life than what is given. You may know Sparkz from Sparkz Onna Set, a luxury magnate most notable for her work with high-profile celebrities.

DR. SONJA STRIBLING

I am from the small town of Wilson, Arkansas, where working in the nearby cotton gin or factory was the job to have. As the 12th child (yes, twelve kids), my mother was a housekeeper with a third-grade education, and my father was a farmhand with a second-grade education. I have very few memories of my dad being around because he and my mother separated when I was a baby.

My mother worked hard to provide for my older sibling and me. I can remember my mother keeping cash in a box under her mattress, saying she didn't trust the banks with her hard-earned money.

Truthfully, I didn't know I was poor until I went to college and almost all my basketball teammates had rooms with phones and cars. I went to bed hungry many nights because my mother could only afford to send me $25 a month.

When I first started my business, I was just retiring from the United States Army, where I had spent twenty-one years working seven days a week, eighteen or more hours a day most times. My thought and goal was to make $10,000 monthly, which would replace my military income. (Funny story: I used to sit in the boardroom and share with senior leaders that one day I work from 12 pm-1 pm and make more money in that one hour than I did in one month's pay. They all would laugh out loud because that is unheard of for those of us who only thought that one should work for someone else and then retire with 50 percent of that income.)

My overall thought was to help other women win in life, although I had no concept that it would be to this extreme.

Like other entrepreneurs, I struggled at the beginning with imposter syndrome. Because of my past, I didn't think I was deserving of the lifestyle I dreamt of having. I have to remind myself I deserve to be happy, even to this day. I deserve to be wealthy. I deserve to lead other women to their 6-Figure and Beyond Legacy ... I can do this!

I would say the first external obstacle I had to face was having to do it alone—not having a spouse to lean on and having to make all business decisions myself. Another obstacle was the finances; in the beginning, I had to trust to invest in myself. When I started my coaching empire, the investment was $25K (money I didn't have in my bank account or anywhere else in sight). I knew I needed to offer the highest level of coaching and couldn't afford to walk away because of not having the funds to invest. So, I gave the deposit, which was everything I had in my account ($2,200). This was my rent money, car payment, and money for my son's high school football sports fee. Then, I sold everything I had to make the remaining amount for the investment. Within seven days, an unexpected check came in the mail that covered the outstanding balance. Within 90 days, I generated $250K in one 24-hour period. I truly believe that, when we set intentions, God and the Universe will call in the things we need to be successful.

Was there ever a point I wanted to give up on my journey to becoming a multimillionaire? Absolutely. For me, it wasn't moving as fast as I wanted. One of the hardest things that occurred was losing friends because I didn't have the time I did before starting my business. I was changing, I would say for the better. I realized that not everyone could go with you on your journey to greatness. You may have to go at it alone without the people you thought would be there.

Long before I became a millionaire, I saw it clearly. It happened in my mind before it took form in my bank account. I expected to be great at this gift I was given. I also worked diligently to control my thoughts. Every morning before my feet hit the ground, I would say, *Lord, who do I need to serve today?* I pay close attention to my emotions. I am 95 percent high-energy and great spirits. The other 5 percent of the time, when I am not, I do a self-check on why and what happened to make me feel the way I do. Did I read something? Did I hear something to change my thoughts? I address this immediately by asking: Can I control the problem or control my thoughts?

That one resource to help me grow my business and reach my next financial milestone has been coaching, consulting, and mentorship from some of the top coaches I work with regularly. They helped me see that success was out there for me and that there were one thousand and one ways to be successful. The most important resource was a guild with fellow members who could see and understand my blind spots. Training was helpful, but a coach/guide was the game-changer for me and my "journey to millionaire."

The books below also changed the game for me. Each one paved the way for me to think differently, walk with authority and take up space in the coaching, speaking and self-development space for women.

- *Think and Grow Rich* by Napoleon Hill
- *Secrets of the Millionaire Mind* by T. Harv Eker
- *The Richest Man Who Ever Lived* by Steven K. Scott
- *Becoming a Millionaire God's Way* by Dr. C. Thomas Anderson
- *The One Minute Millionaire* by Mark Victor Hansen and Robert G. Allen

What I have seen over the last few years is that many women I serve—helping them build their coaching and speaking business—are challenged by the following:

1. Balance (work-life) – One thing that isn't taught much in business building is discipline. Many just want the techniques, but the principles and mindset work needed isn't a priority. Success is 90 percent mindset work and 10 percent skill and technique.

2. Imposter syndrome – They believe they aren't worthy of wealth and abundance.

3. Understanding their worth – 61 percent of women would rather talk about their death and funeral than talk about money or ask to be paid what they are worth.[2]

4. Having a safe space to grow mentally, spiritually, and financially – As women, we need a safe place to grow in these areas and not feel judged.

If I could, I would share and coach my younger self through the process of trusting myself, trusting my decisions. And to not be so bothered by what other people say or feel guilty for desiring more for my life! Finally, I would remind myself that my mistakes are not a death sentence.

As a mother of three boys and a divorcée after 18 years of marriage, I know all too well the mindset of a woman who wanted more but didn't know what that more was or how to get it.

My life journey includes:

- Having a child at 15 years old
- Being raped and left for dead at 17 years old
- Joining the military and retiring after serving my country for twenty-one years
- Being a combat veteran (serving three combat tours, one in Iraq for fifteen months)
- Being married for eighteen years and going through a divorce that took three years to finalize
- Losing houses and cars
- Being clinically depressed (partially losing my natural mind)

Yes, I know all that sounds so traumatic. My point in sharing this information is to show you that, although we may experience tragedy in our lives,

---

[2] 61% of Women Would Rather Talk About Their Own Death Than Money, Nasdaq, last modified MAY 22, 2018 May 22, 2018, https://www.nasdaq.com/articles/61-women-would-rather-talk-about-their-own-death-money-2018-05-2

we can still muster up courage and strength and use the negative energy to create the life we deserve and desire. But it takes an inner power that many find challenging to discover.

• • •

Five years ago, I wish I had trusted the process more—specifically, the process and the power of Facebook and YouTube ads. I was so nervous about my business and adding social media ads because I didn't understand how they worked. I started with $2-$3K a month and was so nervous that I would lose what I had invested if it didn't work. Over time, I got more comfortable with the process and began to invest more—to the point where I have invested 6-figures that yielded a return three times that.

My next big goal is to generate 7-figures and beyond monthly—to $1M in 72 hours with over 500 clients—helping them become the first millionaire in their family. Why? I never thought it was possible for someone that was a mom at 15 years old and left for dead at seventeen. This was not something I could even conceive. Now it's not only about the money—it's the authority and credibility it brings to share, knowing what is possible.

• • •

Sonja Stribling, Ph.D., is a U.S Army Major and combat veteran, recipient of the Barack Obama Presidential Lifetime Achievement Award, and former TV Host on Bravo Network, and has been featured in USA Today, Forbes, NBC, Fox, TV One, The Word Network. She now uses this training and experience to lead thousands to their victory in dominating their space and using their inner *power* to ascend to their *Next Level* life and business.

Having overcome a series of life-changing experiences at a young age—including being a highly decorated combat veteran with a 21-year military career to going through a harrowing divorce that left her financially and emotionally bankrupt—Dr. Sonja has drawn upon her past pain to connect her closer to her purpose. Her mission is to use her *leadership skills* and *own journey* as a means to help others ignite their inner strength and realize their true potential as human beings, business owners, and world-changers.

As the Chairwoman of the Born to Be Powerful Academy®, her firm's courses, events, and results-based coaching & consulting programs equip emerging and established women, thought leaders, influencers, entrepreneurs, and game changers to find and use their *power* to have a fulfilled life, booming business and living on their own terms.

From her one-on-one coaching and group training events to online seminars, thousands shift their life, career, and business from her teachings. Her core belief is, "Regardless of what the world expects from you … you can do more. Regardless of what they expect, you won't be held back. Regardless of what is expected of you, you can do the impossible! *Shatter expectations!*"

"One of the remarkable surprises, and one that I totally did not expect, was who I became through the process. Pain changes us. It makes us kinder and gentler and more aware. I became all those things. I love the person I am today, and you can love the new you, too. I can help with that."

– Dr. Sonja Stribling

DEANA LA ROSA

Growing up as the baby of seven in Queens, NY, and having a dad who worked two to three jobs all the time really put us on a strict budget. Money didn't come easily, and we always had to be prepared for a rainy day (as my dad would say). We stuck to what was necessary and nothing more: housing, food, clothing, and the minimum. Life as an adult was about work, work, work. My mom stayed home to manage the house and kids. She felt the need to ask my dad for permission (from my viewpoint) to buy anything, whether it was food for the home or even school stuff. The way I was raised, money was not attainable, and, given the conversations related to money, I came to think of money as the root of all evil. Very few people had that lifestyle, and it was more honorable to work hard. If they had a lot of money and life was easy, they were not honorable people; they did not hold integrity.

When I started my business, the vision was to take what I learned and empower others to own a home of their own and even invest in becoming financially abundant: "Work to Live, Not Live to Work" was my mantra. I wanted to pay forward all I had learned from real estate and empower others to do the same. I believe that, when you are given blessings, you should share them.

Some mindset obstacles I had to overcome to reach the place of consistently earning a million dollars a year and more were the doubts that I was worthy, the expectation that it would all crumble because it was too good to be true, and guilt over being successful and having that lifestyle, among others.

I had to handle the peaks and valleys of this journey with *faith* that this was all part of the bigger plan of success, even when I was in the middle of a crisis or failing. My faith and knowing God was with me and that this was part of my plan to give back, empower, and inspire others continues to be my guide. To this day, I still struggle with overcoming obstacles. Each time I feel like *Wow, I made it!* I have to ground myself on the why of it all because the guilt sets in. I think of my dad, who worked so hard at his two or three jobs to make ends meet. He had no time freedom, no financial freedom. He locked down the phone in the house and our thermostat so we didn't change it because he knew the bills had to be to the penny so he could make the payments. I don't think I will ever forget that mindset, but I manage it by grounding myself in my why and trusting in God's plan for me. It will always be a part of me, but it doesn't hold me back anymore, which is the key. I believe it keeps me humble and grateful for every little thing.

Was there ever a point I wanted to give up on my journey to becoming a multimillionaire? Yes! I felt like an imposter if something failed or didn't end up as I wanted. *This is not for me; that is why ...* I would collect evidence that I was not meant for that life and struggling was the *norm*. I remember when 9/11 happened. I had worked seven years at a company, and my stock options were a few months from being fully vested. I had put in all that hard work, and then the market crashed. After getting out of the city that day, I didn't want to go back. My oldest, Meghan, was five months old, and I felt as though I was validating the "see, this is what happens; being wealthy is not for me" mindset. Then, when I moved away from all my family with two little girls to go to Florida for a marriage that didn't work, I ended up getting into real estate, rebuilding my life as a single mom, and building up an amazing business. Then in 2007/8, I had just gotten remarried, we had my daughter Ella, a step-daughter, and I got pregnant with Joey right away.

I was on *top* of the world and then the market crashed again, and I lost it all. My son had health issues and was in the NICU (he was a miracle baby), and I had to choose between focusing on him or giving 100 percent of my time to rebuilding the business. My new husband was going through home and business trials with me too. While this was going on, we were also dealing with our former spouses. At the time, the contention with them was bad, and there was resentment and animosity of both our relationship with each other and our success plaguing us. To ease the stress, I decided to focus on my family while my husband took the lead on the business front. I went back to my mom's old role as a stay-at-home mother, and although I always swore growing up that I would never rely on a man for money or permission, here I was doing it. I had to let go of all my limiting beliefs around relying on someone else to support me.

I started praying and praying and kept researching online for guidance and inspiration. I also had an amazing husband who understood me and supported me, knowing how independent I'd been prior to all this happening. I looked around and saw so many suffering after their financial loss, and I felt so blessed with my husband and our now five kids. My son was home, and even though it would be a long road, he was alive. How could I be anything but grateful? I decided to do whatever I could to get people in my community to focus on gratitude for their health and family, realizing the money would come back. I would create a new business and still build the real estate with my husband, just from home and in the background while I focused on our kids. I became my husband's coach and cheerleader to ensure he stayed focused, empowered, and feeling peace about our family. As I encouraged him, I began to be more encouraged to start again to build—and so I did. That was a turning point where I felt I broke through to a stronger *why*. Others needed my experience, vulnerability, authenticity, and 100 percent possible mindset.

•   •   •

The most important resources, tools, affirmations, mindset strategies, and practices I used to build my business to where it is today were *possibility* and having *hope* that there was more. Next, it was praying and being grateful for the step I was in. Even when the market crashed and my youngest was in the NICU, I realized that I had always been so blessed with my kids and husband. I had so much peace around the knowledge that this was the journey God created for me. Those challenges were an education for a lifetime.

We are our best resource. Having a strong vision of what we're going after and the *why* behind it, tapping into our purpose, is key to the success of any dream.

Coaching, goal setting, and time blocking are also valuable tools that have helped me reach my goals. If I don't control my day, my day controls me and leads to procrastination and overwhelm. Also, praying and realizing that we're not given more than we can handle is crucial for keeping my mindset focused. Finally, the books *The Miracle Morning* by Hal Elrod and *Core Calling* by Shanda Sumpter have been game-changers for me on this journey.

Being a mom and balancing/managing the business/home life can be the greatest challenge for women trying to create wealth and abundance. Guilt and shame creep in—guilt that business is also a priority and shame when you're on a business call when the mom next to you is playing with her child at the park. Women feel that they're the glue that holds everything together, and then in business, they're all in. They don't know how they can be 100 percent in two large areas of their life and think one must take a hit, but really, we get to juggle them both. Letting go of the shame and guilt is hard.

My younger self was super motivated and worked her rear end off, whether it was washing windows or entire houses. I wish I knew back then that life happens *for* you, not *to* you. I would encourage myself to believe in being grateful for who I was and understand the concept of money and how to have a better relationship with it as well as being more grounded in my vision and passions.

My dad's health began declining five years ago, and my husband's father was diagnosed with cancer. I wish I had given myself more grace and focused on developing my leadership skills. If I'd had the leadership skills I have today, I feel as though I would be at a different place now. I also wish I'd put fewer restrictions on myself around asking for support. If I was not as hard on myself, I would have sought support and wouldn't have cared about how others viewed me.

•   •   •

My next big goal is to create a fund/real estate investment portfolio that others can come into to create a retirement fund for those at different financial levels. It would be a way for me to help create wealth for others and coach them along the way, so they have the chance to live an abundant life. That is important to me because it is something that I wish I had during my most challenging times—whether it was losing everything during the market crash or working through my son's medical bills. I want to be a miracle for someone else and help them soar. I am working with county commissioners and local nonprofits to find properties to pinpoint good places to invest. We will build this portfolio that will allow anyone with any income level to begin their investment journey in real estate. Real estate always has been, and always will be, a good investment. This will allow new investors who do not have the experience to get a foot in the door without putting everything at risk. This will be my "pay it forward."

• • •

As a wife, mother, entrepreneur, best-selling author, and family coach Deana La Rosa takes pride in all of her endeavors. After 20+ years as a business owner, Deana has learned a tremendous amount from the highs and lows of the economy and her businesses. Deana has also navigated co-parenting and blending families and coaches other parents going through a separation, divorce, and remarriage/step-parenting.

Although Deana is proud of her professional victories, she has learned that her family and community are the greatest measures of success. Deana lives by the mantra "Live to Give" and sits on the board of Housing 4 All and The La Rosa Foundation, which impacts the lives of thousands of families in need each year. When Deana is not at her office or serving her community, she travels on new adventures with her family.

My parents went through a nasty divorce when I was four years old, and I remember not understanding why Santa didn't leave much of anything for Christmas. Childhood consisted of hand-me-downs that didn't fit properly, being on reduced lunch at school and everyone knowing it, and heading into a new school year with a few chosen outfits put on layaway.

We lived with my grandfather, who grew up during the depression, so meals were stretched as far as they could go. We never went anywhere or spent money on anything outside of necessities. Once I was old enough to understand that not all families lived this way, I started to believe there was something wrong with me and my family. My best friend and her family were always dressed in their Sunday best at church and proudly sat in the front row each week. Because my mother was divorced and we were Catholic, we had to sit in the pews. I don't think I was old enough to articulate the meaning of it, but I do know that it felt inherently shameful, as if we were less than everyone else.

When I first started The Goal Digger Girl, my vision was to give female entrepreneurs simple tools they could implement on social media so they could grow their businesses online. My first few attempts at growing a viable online business failed miserably because I wanted it so badly to work but I couldn't figure out the social media component. Then I invested in my first coach and would implement whatever she taught me immediately and then turn around and teach it to my small audience. I would literally say things such as, "Last week I tried this out and it totally worked! Here's how." My audience loved that I was teaching everything in bite-sized steps and that I wasn't some fancy social media guru, just a budding entrepreneur wanting to share what was working for her.

The *why* behind the work I do is that I have cried myself to sleep more times than I like to admit, wanting to change my family tree and my financial situation. I wanted a different life for myself and for them. Once I cracked the code, I vowed to spend the rest of my life teaching others how.

I had already been working on my mindset in general, but when I did $250,000 my first full year as an entrepreneur, I had spent it all by the end of the year. I realized then that I had to master my money mindset as well, or I would continue to self-sabotage. I focused on being comfortable with talking about money, setting bigger financial goals, and "feeling" wealthy.

As I started to generate more revenue online, I realized that I had to face my demons of not feeling worthy or good enough. I'd struggled with alcohol abuse for about a decade and knew it was holding me back. I worked intensely with a therapist to overcome the strong addictive behavior, and when I finally did in the summer of 2017, my life forever changed. When we have something like that controlling us, we can't step into the person we need to become to achieve everything that we want.

When I decided to move network marketing companies, I experienced massive backlash. Haters sprouted up all over social media, and I felt so attacked. Naturally, doubt crept in. It was a lot to handle emotionally to have close friends turn on you for making a business decision. But I sat with the feelings and asked myself if I'd done anything to hurt anyone, and the answer was no. It was then that I decided to move forward in faith and unapologetically make decisions in my business.

I am a huge fan of vision boards—I make a new one each month on Canva, and I also write out my monthly goals on a dry erase board in my office. I use the ThinkUp app to reprogram my mind based on what it is I am focusing on developing.

If I only had one resource that would help me grow my business and reach my next financial milestone, it would be infrastructure. Once you move beyond a solopreneur, you can't scale without a strong team behind you. My job is to stay in my zone of genius and delegate everything else.

I listen to one book a week on Audible, typically around wealth, mindset, business, and success. I'm always enrolled in several coaching programs, so I actively digest that content and implement it as quickly as possible.

I honestly don't think most women are comfortable talking about wealth and abundance, much less desiring more in their lives. If you look at the last few decades, it's just now becoming mainstream for women to be working and participating in the household finances. I want them to know that it is our birthright to be wealthy because we can do more good in the world with financial resources than without.

If I could coach my younger self just setting out with a dream and an idea, I would tell her that not only is she good and worthy, she is the light to others. She only needs to focus on what she wants and go after it. Don't get distracted by the doubt or the fear or the lack of certainty. Confidence is built through courage. Be courageous and take that next step forward.

•   •   •

Five years ago, I wish I would have known how important audience building is, specifically building a solid email list. I also wish I'd known that you can scale an online course or a group coaching program way faster than random one-off offerings here and there where you constantly reinvent the wheel and have to come up with new things. I also wish I had started running ads a lot sooner!

We recently started our non-profit, Elephant Sisters, where we support women in our community and their families. I want to raise $100,000 this year for that so no sister has to abandon her dream of building a business because life happens. My other big goal this year is to hold our first in-person conference and have at least 1,000 women there. I have a plan in place for all of this and more, and now it's time to implement.

•   •   •

Kimberly Olson is a self-made multi-millionaire and the creator of The Goal Digger Girl, where she serves female entrepreneurs by teaching them simple systems and online strategies in sales and marketing. Through the power of social media, they are equipped to explode their online presence and get real results in their business, genuinely and authentically. She is also the founder of the non-profit, Elephant Sisters.

Kimberly has two PhDs in Natural Health and Holistic Nutrition, is in the top half percent in her current network marketing company globally, is the author of five books including best-sellers, *The Goal Digger*, *Why Balance is B.S.*, and *BOSS It Up, Babe!*, has a top-25 rated podcast in marketing, and travels nationally public speaking. Most recently she has shared the stage with Rachel Hollis, Chalene Johnson, Marina Simone, and Jessica Higdon.

BELLA SCHNEIDER

Growing up, I was the primary breadwinner in a family of holocaust refugees. In addition, my parents were deaf and my brother was blind. Our money consciousness was one of lack. We had to maximize everything, and my father would always proudly tell me how he was able to subsist his entire life on one pair of shoes. I was determined to succeed on my own so that I could support them, not live with a feeling of lack, or be judged by others for what we didn't have.

I opened my full-service spa-salons, LaBelle Day Spas & Salons, as the first of their kind in the San Francisco Bay Area. My spas supply all beauty and relaxation services under one roof including skincare, haircare, nail care, massage, makeup, and med spa services. I formulate my own skincare products that we use in the facial rooms, sell in our boutiques, and retail to spas around the country. My professional wholesale company, Bella Schneider Beauty, sells, distributes, and trains estheticians internationally on clinical esthetic protocols.

I was always attracted to the beauty business. I knew that looking good was a strength, not something to be modest about. Women tend to think that vanity is inappropriate, and I realized I needed to help professional women overcome this self-imposed boundary. I wanted to empower women in the workplace to look and feel good so they could accomplish their personal and professional dreams. Over time, this message has become more accepted by both women and men, which is a sign of the times. Originally, though, I knew that education was essential. Being a woman in the business world in the seventies was not a given. So, I decided to get a business education without knowing what the practical application would be. I worked at a department store for Estée Lauder and realized the market potential for European skincare; there was a real need for clean skin and simplicity rather than using makeup to cover up bad skin.

The most exciting moments come when success is effortless. My first spa took off immediately. Even though I was pregnant and financed the first location with sweat and tears, my appointment books (we had books back then) were completely full. Women drove from an hour away to have our facials. Then my clients begged me to open more locations and offered to help me secure the financing to do so. I've noticed this trend since my spa's inception. When I make choices from my gut, success runs after me. I don't have to force it.

In the beginning, I used to walk door-to-door with my publicist to introduce myself and network. She was old-school and taught me how to be more social in an American way. That automatic friendliness was not part of my upbringing in communist-era Eastern Europe and then war-recurring Israel. I was miserable and would look worn out after our block tours of the neighborhood. I once even had big sweat stains on my dress. Over time, I realized that you need to work hard, but you also need to enjoy what you do. If you're unhappy, it comes off fake and isn't sustainable. I also learned that it's important to be gorgeous yet comfortable—wear clothes that support and don't deter you!

I had to expand to keep up with the needs and demands of my clientele. The spa industry was a buzzword, yet, despite this, my 700-square-foot San Francisco salon was thriving. I wanted to open a more lucrative operation with extensive facilities including massage, hydrotherapy, facials, my brand of products, an entire nail salon, wardrobe consulting, and a skincare boutique, so I decided to add the spa concept to my salon. I needed money to expand and add another location, and getting a loan from a bank was virtually impossible as a woman in the beauty industry. I had to be willing to ask for help. Luckily, one of my clients was a woman who helped me get a loan. Thanks to the help of my strong-willed female clients who were also breaking the glass ceiling in the banking industry, I opened a 3,000-square-foot spa three years after my start. What I learned from this and have consistently applied since is that *it's important to encircle yourself with qualified, trustworthy allies to meet your goals.* I don't do everything myself. I focus on what I excel at, which is creativity, innovation, beauty, and guts. I have a group of managers and employees who focus on what they're best at whether it be accounting or technology. I've had people working for me for over thirty years, and I trust their work ethic. They are a huge part of my success.

Specifically, acquiring funding in a male-dominated society that didn't value beauty or wellness was a challenge. I had to rely on other women who understood these values and were already maneuvering the multi obstacles in the financial and business worlds. Women who had the experience, connections, and know-how to help me acquire funding so I could continue to grow and expand.

• • •

I never looked at my journey as one to becoming a multimillionaire. I always had fun with the process. I am a great gambler. Blackjack is my forte. However, I'm not reckless. I even supported myself at one point playing cards. Success to me has always been about picking challenges that excite me without investing myself in ways that were foolish. I take calculated risks. I don't put money in that I can't afford to lose. Nonetheless, I have had moments where I've been willing to live with very little for the sake of the future. In the beginning, I had days when I went without lunch or fancy furniture to invest my money in ways that could grow. But I wouldn't gamble with my child's school money. The way I work through anxiety is I don't allow anyone to intimidate me. I learned early on that there are people out there who will criticize you or take what you've earned if you let them. I don't give away my trust easily, and I don't pay attention to other people's shenanigans. I have strong boundaries. At the end of the day, I invest in self-care, so I never reach high levels of anxiety or panic when there are challenges.

I've had the same accountant since the inception of my business. Over time, I put her in charge of all the financial aspects of my businesses to the point where I stopped overseeing everything she does. I learned to trust her, and she has been my right hand since the beginning. We are very different, and I think that's why we are the perfect yin and yang. She's introverted and likes to work behind the scenes; whereas I am a connoisseur of everything beauty, she's into animals and her horses.

Being in Silicon Valley, I've always had to stay in touch with technology. Given the number of years I've been in business—over 40—I've had to refresh and renew many times. I'm never afraid to reinvent my business. I don't sacrifice my core, a hard work ethic and a can-do attitude. I shun negativity and always envision best-case scenarios. It doesn't matter if there is an earthquake or a pandemic, I know I can get back on my feet. One of my primary roles with my staff is motivation. They often need to be reminded of the end goals. I push my team to always envision a bright future. My family came out of the holocaust. I was raised with my grandmother telling me that the only thing that's a real problem is living through the holocaust. When I remember that, it puts all difficulties into perspective.

I am an avid consumer of books by strong women. I love stories about women from other cultures who succeed. I study their trajectories and learn how others achieve their dreams. I also believe that making time for fun helps you be more successful. Whether it's Netflix or YouTube, I always make space for me-time, watching my favorite shows. I rely on my techies to tell me when there are new developments, at which point I consciously incorporate them, whether it's updated online booking or check-out systems; if something makes sense, I learn and adapt.

People are the most important resource to growing your business and reaching financial milestones. You can't do anything without a good network and strong relationships. No matter what the technology, ultimately the beauty and wellness business is first and foremost about people helping people. You have to be reliable and consistent. So, I would say the most important resource is having integrity in how you deal with people so that you are dependable.

A woman should strive for her independence, no matter what. Even if she doesn't need money, abundance comes from her knowing how to take care of herself and having her own world to be content in. Especially now with this pandemic, we are all reminded how important it is to be able to entertain and keep yourself happy so outside forces don't bring you down. Wealth and abundance are relative to a person's individual needs. Be honest with yourself and unapologetic about what you need to be happy, then believe you have the power to give it to yourself. No one is going to do it for you.

• • •

Looking back, I spent my working life being a perfectionist. I always drove myself hard and demanded the utmost excellence from my team. At times, I took the harder road. The five things I wish someone had told me are:

1. Take it easy on yourself. If you don't, you'll burn out. Success needs to be a sustainable endeavor, otherwise it's fleeting and won't last. In the beginning, I would never take real vacations, only working vacations. I micromanaged from afar. Constantly calling, having employees check in with me about every decision. It took me ten years to realize that I can trust my employees to run the business on their own. I realized that, even if they make different decisions than I would, they'll learn in the process. Nothing is irreparable.

2. Ask employees to do things or to change with kindness. Be soft on your circle of devoted employees. They're doing their best, and change isn't easy for anyone. If you are too hard on people, it's demotivating and creates an environment of constant fear. When I was too tough on my team, they wouldn't tell me the truth in difficult situations, and then we couldn't grow or improve. In that kind of ambiance, people crack, pick up and leave. When you accept that no one is perfect and that, at their core, everyone, other than a few outliers, wants to do a good job, it's much easier to react gently to situations.

3. Don't build loyalty through fear but through respect. It's one thing to scare people and something else to inspire them. People want to work for you when they're inspired by your role modeling. The loyalty I developed from my team was from those who wanted to work hard. People who respect hard work stayed with me because they saw that I work hard. I don't ask them for anything I'm not willing to do myself. Otherwise, you spend your time policing instead of growing

your employees' strengths. When they feel safe, they take on more responsibility.

4. Passion is the key to success. Money will come afterward. In order to succeed, you have to be willing to work hard and enjoy it. You can only enjoy working hard on something that interests you. Remember, your job is where you spend most of your time physically and emotionally. Even your friendships are often built through your work. So, wouldn't you rather spend time with people you have commonality with? This is the heart of success. Be true to who you really are. Then working hard comes naturally and is full of pleasure. If I had taken my economics degree and worked in banking, for instance, I wouldn't be happy, and I would have failed. That's not me. I love beauty, fashion, women, and fun. It's easy for me to work consistently through goals even when there are struggles because it's the core of my essence.

5. A politician once used a famous Russian proverb, "*Doveryai, no proveryai,*" which means "trust but verify." Give people the benefit of the doubt. Start on the right foot and be pleasant with everyone. However, trust your gut and double-check before making decisions. No one will ever be able to tell you what the best decision is. You are your own best judge. This is true even of professionals. I have trusted contractors, scientists, managers, doctors, and lawyers. They are all a part of my success and have qualifications and talents that I don't have. But, no matter what another person's title is, I listen to my gut because I know my goals best. I apply this to every aspect of my business and life. If I consult an architect and they tell me I can't have the fountain that I want at the entry to my spa, I won't take no for an answer. I have no problem saying, "Are you sure? Try a little harder. I think there's a way to make it work."

I am in a place now where all I do is make choices that I enjoy. Money is no longer my motivation because I've achieved all that I wanted financially. Now, I focus more on how I invest my money, the future of my brand, and the happiness of my loyal employees. Once you've reached the top, it's important to use your success wisely. I have a trusted team of financial investors that helps me invest in stocks, funds, and real estate locally and internationally. I'm expanding certain aspects of my business. I'm adding a new hair salon to my existing Town & Country spa and remodeling it. I focus on doing what I love most in terms of hours I work and which parts of the spa I put my energy into. This is a stretch for me because I used to value my life in terms of how productive I was instead of in terms of how fulfilled I was.

I am also thinking about future generations now and making sure my family is well provided for. It's important for me to continue to work so I can be a role model for my daughter and grandson. I don't believe one should ever stop creating as long as they are here on earth. I continue to create new products, refresh my spas, revamp my services, and create new treatment protocols. For the first time, I'm starting to think about my exit. I aim to include more travel and enjoying more glasses of Chianti with a view of Capri to my schedule. My goal is definitely more *Dolce Vita*!

To follow my work, visit the press section of both my websites: LaBelle-DaySpas.com and BellaSchneiderBeauty.com.

• • •

Bella Schneider is the innovative beauty guru, clinical esthetician, and cosmetic formulator behind Silicon Valley's premiere LaBelle Day Spas & Salons and international wholesale and retail cosmetic company, Bella Schneider Beauty. Her multimillion-dollar business spans forty years, dozens of awards, hundreds of employees, and world recognition in the skincare field. She trains and supplies professional cosmetics to hundreds of salons around the world and is the recognized esthetician of famous Silicon Valley personalities in the political, educational, technology, and show biz spheres. She is a laureate of the esteemed LNE lifetime achievement Crystal Award for her contributions to beauty science.

How I Started with Nothing and Created
a Million-Dollar Agency

I grew up in Lake Tapps, Washington, where my parents both worked at Boeing. Despite raising us on lakefront property, they were always very frugal. The only country we ever visited outside of the US was Canada (a short drive), but we traveled often domestically. I played a lot of sports, primarily volleyball, where I learned a lot about teamwork and leadership. Through sports and school, I encountered many different personalities and learned how to work those personalities. I went to the University of Washington, graduated from the business school, and experimented with a multitude of professions before I landed in digital marketing.

Being frugal was a generational practice in my upbringing. My dad is an engineer, and his father came to the US from Hungary during the Holocaust. My grandma was always very frugal. One time when I was visiting her in New York, she took me to see *Rent* (with tickets she got on the cheap at TKTS day-of). She wore a sweatshirt to the theater. Their kitchen was filled with canned food, and her favorite place to eat was McDonald's.

I discovered digital marketing after I worked at a hotel doing sales. After teaching it to myself, I successfully convinced the VP of Marketing at Blue Nile that I was the right pick to run their affiliate program because I had essentially done the same thing at the hotel by creating partnerships with local theaters and airlines. Once I landed at Blue Nile running the affiliate program, I never changed careers again. I ran the affiliate program, then oversaw international marketing. After that I oversaw the affiliate program at Expedia. I hired an agency for support when at Expedia, and after I decided not to stay in the corporate world, I was recruited to join that small startup agency. I worked closely with the leadership team to grow their business, and after three years I knew I was capable of doing it on my own. I started LT Partners in September of 2018 and haven't looked back since.

Because of the perspective I've had working on the brand side, as well as at another agency, I saw an opportunity to create something unique and more consultative, starting in the affiliate industry. By taking a customized, strategic approach to our work, we think of ourselves more as part of our clients' teams than as a vendor. The key to my success has been bringing the right people onto our team to share in that success and help create more of it. We strive to create innovation and use technology in the most strategic ways possible. We focus on data and make recommendations for our clients in their best interest, regardless of whether it's in our best interest today, tomorrow, or next week. I know from working in this industry for more than 12 years, doing the right things for people will always work out in the long term. Many people with whom my team and I have worked in past roles have reached out to us because they trust us to manage their business in their best interest. It's not just about doing the right things; it's about having the right character, the right ethics, and the right moral compass.

I've always felt as though I wanted to start my own business or be an owner of a business in some way. I thought the company I was at before I started mine was a way to do that. After about three years there, it became apparent that was not going to happen. I have two daughters, and I decided that I needed to pursue my goals on my own terms to show my girls that women can achieve their dreams, even in an industry that many refer to as a "good ol' boys club." I was very fortunate in my roles at Blue Nile and Expedia to have incredible mentors and leaders. I learned so much from them that I retain today. I also saw many things through my experiences as an employee that I want to refrain from doing at my company. We operate with transparency, and I am an open book. I have regular check-ins with everyone on the team. I'm excited to have promoted some incredible people and provide a financial opportunity to many that outweighed their previous expectations. I don't believe the people at the top need to make all the money while those below struggle along. The work we do for our clients is the obvious priority here, but I truly don't believe an agency can do exemplary work in an old-school environment where the team is not valued and not kept in the loop with authenticity.

·   ·   ·

Honestly, gathering interesting stories that have happened to me since I began leading my company is so common, I pinch myself. The fact that I'm answering these questions is pretty interesting to me. I suppose the story I think is the most interesting is sort of a David and Goliath tale. A large retailer was introduced to me and, when I spoke with them, they shared that they had already spoken with 11 other agencies and no one would do what they were requesting. Being consultative in nature, we will always create solutions that are outside of the box. We found a way to support them, designed an economic model that worked for everyone, and went to work. We both operate with respectable transparency, so whenever we've had challenges, we discuss it and find a way to overcome them. Although we've grown quickly since working together, we've continued to exceed expectations and have been working together now for over two years.

I seldom think of mistakes as funny because a funny mistake might be not catching something in my teeth in a video call, but I don't really think of things like that as mistakes. Real mistakes are usually not funny and have serious consequences. In the beginning I had Statements of Work (SOWs) that were pretty generic, and we didn't use Master Service Agreements (MSAs). I worked with a couple of companies that decided to let us do a lot of work and then not pay us for it. Trusting all people to that degree in business is a mistake, but it's not funny. We quickly remedied that mistake and don't work with companies that don't honor their agreements.

My first client was a husband/wife team. The woman worked in public relations at Coca-Cola for 14 years. On one of our first calls together, she told me about a woman in leadership course she took when she was at Coca-Cola. One of the things they taught her was that women inherently believe they need to have 100 percent confidence before starting a company, whereas men do not. I think that is primarily the mindset obstacle any woman, including me, has to overcome to continue to thrive and grow. We must understand that we don't have to know everything, that we can take chances without being completely confident. As with any mental mindset, being conscious of the obstacle is the first step and doing the work to make sure you don't let it get in your way is second. I've spent time working with a coach who was fantastic at helping me remove those barriers and take the chances I've needed to take. I think that, by seeing the results, the mentality is further reinforced.

March 30, 2020, was our general manager, Steve Tazic's, first day. COVID had caused the country to go into lockdown, no one was traveling, and there was a lot of speculation about how this was going to affect everything. We had to make choices on a daily basis based on the information and facts we had without knowing what the future held. It was scary, but we came together as a team to focus on doing the best we could under the circumstances. A couple of our clients were hit hard, but, for the most part, online businesses did not suffer like many other industries. Several of our clients said, guiltily, that COVID was good for their business, and the partnerships channel in particular thrived. We still don't know what lies ahead with the pandemic and the economy, but I have confidence that our team will navigate any challenges as wisely as possible.

One of my favorite quotes that I carry with me every day is from *The Hard Thing About Hard Things: Building a Business When There are No Easy Answers* by Ben Horowitz:

> Whenever I meet a successful CEO, I ask them how they did it. Mediocre CEOs point to their brilliant strategic moves or their intuitive business sense or a variety of other self-congratulatory explanations. The great CEOs tend to be markedly consistent in their answers. They all say, 'I didn't quit.'

Quitting is not an option when you run a company. You must remove that word from your vocabulary. Every day you have a choice to show up and be happy to make difficult decisions and either embrace the journey or hang your head. What's ultimately best for every person and every company is the former.

Every single person in my life and at my company plays a crucial role in shaping what our company becomes. There is no one particular person because it truly does take a village. I've thought about drawing out a web of all the people who have helped build this business into what it is today. Obviously, my parents had a big part in shaping who I am, and my husband and family support me on this adventure, which is no small feat.

There are several former managers, colleagues, or people I've met through work who have spent extra time mentoring and guiding me on my journey, including Joanne Lai, Lisa Riolo, Vijay Talwar, and Doug Siegel. My first employee, Molly, took a huge risk after having worked at eBay. She believed in me and my vision and is now our Head of Operations. Julia Stanley worked at Footlocker for 23 years, 16 of which were in affiliate marketing. Going from a huge corporate environment to a relative startup is a big change. It wasn't an easy change, but she has navigated the shift masterfully. Rachel Jones was at Saks, Lord & Taylor prior to joining us as employee number six. Ashlee Smith came from Hotels.com and Expedia to become our Head of Client Services. I could go on and on. Every person on the team contributes to our success, and after hearing about and seeing many business partnerships fail—sometimes in a vile way—I could not be more grateful to have Steve Tazic by my side. Our brains are wired the same way, and the world needs more men like Steve.

My first clients were referrals from a former manager of mine, along with the agency I was at prior to starting this company. Every single one of our current clients came from a referral of some sort and many have referred other companies to work with us, which is a huge component of our success. Several of the partners we work with have either referred clients to us or team members, and there are some like Elizabeth Shipley, Jacqueline Wlaydis, Mark Lipson, and Melissa Corliss who paid attention to us when we had just started, even though they didn't have to.

• • •

At the end of the day, the core values I grew up with—especially those I learned playing sports—have been the most important resources I've used to build my business to where it is today. When I binge-watched Ted Lasso, I was reminded of those mindset strategies. Because I've spent my whole life practicing them, it isn't necessarily a conscious, daily effort anymore. It just comes naturally. I do spend a lot of time reading quotes and talking to the people on our team about those values. We're an organization founded on transparency. We must have the hard conversations in a constructive way if we're going to be the strongest team. No team can simply go through the motions and win. We need to always be learning, improving, and helping each other get better. Due to this mindset, we are constantly evaluating and testing tools to use as well as building our own. The constant reinvestment into resources for our team is what keeps us efficient and effective.

My favorite book is still *The Four Agreements: A Practical Guide to Personal Freedom* by Don Miguel Ruiz. It's not a business book, but I believe that, if you operate your business and your life under these four principles, you almost can't fail:

1. Be impeccable with your words.
2. Don't take anything personally.
3. Don't make assumptions.
4. Always do your best.

Out of all the things I just listed, if I only had one resource that would help me grow my business and reach my next financial milestone, it would definitely be my team. The team is all that matters at the end of the day.

•   •   •

I haven't done all the research, but I have done some, and based on that and what I've personally experienced, I have a hypothesis that companies owned by women and/or minorities are more likely to hire partner companies owned by women and/or minorities, and companies owned by white men are more likely to hire partner companies owned by white men. I suspect it's a company culture thing and not an intention, and I've certainly seen phenomenal anomalies. One of my favorite videos about feminism in the workplace is with Tim Armstrong about his conversation with Gloria Steinem. However, in general I would say it is a challenge for everyone in our society to remove their natural bias when making decisions in real life or work. Although I suspect this to be true, I also know that there are enough opportunities out there for us, and we must focus on the possibilities rather than the hurdles. I think in general the mentality of knowing there is abundance is the most important part of finding it.

There is so much business advice out there and I love to absorb all of it, but I think that the way companies do business right now is changing. Employees want to work at companies with values, clients want to hire partners they respect, and leadership is evolving from the archaic model of top-down management being highly overpaid.

The five things I wish someone had told me are more about the environment and culture of the company:

a. Gratitude goes a long way. When I first started the company, I'd send a bottle of wine or champagne to new clients when we kicked things off. It was a small gesture, but taking the time to place that order was a nice surprise and helped things get off on the right foot. We had just completed our first all-company offsite, and the impact it had on our team to have a wonderful experience together was priceless.

b. Never make fear-based decisions. A mentality and decision-making process based on fear will never result in abundance.

c. Difficult conversations are mandatory and need to be mature, respectful, and constructive. Maintaining open dialogue is the best way to ensure nothing is a surprise down the road. If we're not all constantly learning and evolving, we can't achieve success.

d. Even when you kill it, sometimes things don't go your way ... and that's okay. One of my favorite quotes from Ted Lasso is: "You know what the happiest animal on earth is? It's a goldfish. You know why? It's got a 10-second memory." We had a client who was extremely happy. When we found out they were moving to another agency, we were shocked. We got on a call and discussed it with him to get feedback. He told us we are amazing; he loved working with us, and he literally could not think of any negative feedback to provide or room for improvement. It was a situation where a new CMO came in who had a previous relationship with the other agency, and we never really had a chance. It doesn't happen often, but when things like that happen, dwelling doesn't do any good. Onward and upward!

e. Never underestimate the power of your network and the reputation you've built.

Our next short-term goal is channel expansion. There is so much that can be learned across all paid marketing channels, and having the right infrastructure and team in place to share those learnings, along with building tools that create efficiencies in doing so, is not a small undertaking. We hope to get it done this year. Additionally, we came up with a tangential Software as a Service (SaaS) business model that we'll be building and taking to market. It's something our industry has needed for a long time and will bring innovation and ease but will likely take investment.

You can follow us at https://lt.partners/ or https://www.linkedin.com/company/lacie-thompson-marketing/ for more info on what we're up to.

•   •   •

Lacie Thompson is the founder/CEO of LT Partners, a leading digital marketing consulting agency. Lacie has worked in the digital marketing space for over 12 years, with much of her career focused on performance marketing on the brand side. She founded LT Partners three and a half years ago and has quickly grown the company to a team of 32, running programs for 47 brands across a variety of verticals.

CHRISTINA
JANDALI

I grew up in a quiet little country town on the outskirts of Vancouver, Canada called Langley.

My mom's Polish grandmother would keep rolls of cash tucked in her purse, just in case. I can still hear her words ringing in my ears in her strong Polish accent, "You no work, you no eat." It was an expectation that we would earn our keep and work hard for our money. During the war, my grandfather gave my grandmother carrots instead of flowers, as there was not enough food to go around. My grandmother's eyes held a perpetual sense of lack, and she was always saving food and money for a rainy day.

My mom's father, a Dutch farmer, would use twine from a bale of hay to tie his pants and walk about in his big orange clogs to buy and sell animals to squeeze in profit. He'd go to swap meets, bartering for the best deals and wheeling and dealing his way to making a few bucks. Despite going through hard times while trying to feed 16 children, he had a major heart of generosity and would give the shirt off his back to help someone in need.

I remember visiting the farm and meeting new stray people and animals he had taken in since the last visit.

My mom started and failed at many businesses. She got suckered into many different get-rich-quick schemes along with several network marketing companies. I remember a diet cookie business she started. She filled the study with boxes piled high to the ceiling of these super dry, meal replacement cookies. My brother and I were forced to eat them right down to the last one, so we'd get our money's worth.

I was the kid who had just enough but went without all the niceties. At Christmas time, I would pretend I got presents so that I didn't feel left out when my friends bragged about their abundance of new toys. I remember wanting to buy a gift for my teacher, but my parents said no. So, I took one of my dad's pens, wrapped it up, and gave it to my teacher. I hoped she wouldn't notice the branded writing on the pen, giving away the fact it was not new.

One of my earliest memories of my grandfather on my dad's side in England was of him booby trapping alarms around the VHS player and near locations where he stashed cash in the walls. My grandparents didn't feel safe putting all their money in the bank, so they kept it hidden in the house. I remember setting off the alarm while playing darts with my brother. My grandfather jumped off the toilet, pulling up his pants as he ran down the stairs, whacking his elbow on the way and drawers dropping to the ground, only to find there was no burglar, only me and my brother's big guilty eyes looking straight at him. We were in major trouble!

My father always wanted to be a writer, but his parents told him there was no money in writing and to get a real job. So, he got a job as an insurance salesperson and later in pharmaceutical sales. He always regretted not following his true passion, especially after he got laid off and fell into depression. He realized he was living a life that he didn't want. Before he could do anything about it, he died in a sudden car crash at 50 years old, leaving this world with his dreams still inside him.

I busted my butt and worked my way from an administrative assistant to a financial planner investing wealthy people's money. After growing up very cash poor, my world opened up to wealth and prosperity. But even though I had all the boxes checked—husband, house, money in the bank, 6-figure income—something still felt missing. I knew I was meant for something bigger, but I didn't know what. I wanted to build my own dreams and not someone else's. But I was scared, and I didn't know how.

When my daughter was born, I cradled her in my arms in the hospital room, listening to the humming of the air conditioning and beeping of the machines. I looked into her large, innocent, sparkly grey eyes and felt a rush of love like no other flood through my veins. I wanted all the world of possibility for her. And that's when it hit me. Who was I to want that for her when I was playing small and not living that myself? So, I made a promise to her and to myself that I would pave the way of possibility for her. I would demonstrate to her what it was like for a woman, her mom, to unapologetically go after her dreams.

•   •   •

I'd love to say it all changed at that moment, but it took me a few years, until my son was born, before I actually started my business.

In the beginning, being the example for my daughter was enough to push me through the frustrations and failures to keep going, but I hit a point where I lost my motivation. I looked at what it would take for me to hit my next level income goals. The hiring, the training, the risk of investment into ads, the launches, the stress, and the time. I wasn't sure it was worth it. Do I need more? Nope. Will making more money change my life? Nope. Will I feel better? Nope. So why bother? What will it give me? Maybe this is good enough. It's comfortable here. I can stay here.

By then, I had already surpassed my corporate salary, so even though I knew I wanted a million-dollar business, it wasn't a strong enough pull to keep going.

That's when I finally understood my real mission. My true vision. I realized that what broke my heart was seeing so many entrepreneurs just getting by. Overspending. Hoarding their money. I saw what a privilege it was for me to have spent 15 years working in finance, surrounded by wealthy people. I began to think like them. I had made my first million in real estate in my mid-20s, lost it and then rebuilt it again.

But something about building my own business felt more personal. I came up against some major limiting beliefs: Can I really do this? What if I'm not enough? What if I fail? What if people don't like me? Who am I to be doing this?

It occurred to me that I could combine the old with the new. I wanted others to experience true wealth. Not just money in and money out, but a lifestyle of wealth. To be able to do what you want to do when you want to do it, how you want to do it, because you can. To have a network of millions, having your money work for you, versus you working for your money.

Alas, I am called to create millionaires, so why hadn't I built a million-dollar business yet? Well, I had a net worth of over a million dollars. I could help entrepreneurs create a net worth, and I would build a million-dollar business along the way and teach them how I did it.

•   •   •

At first, my vision of building 1,000 millionaires seemed terrifying. I remember my knees getting a little wobbly, words sputtering out of my mouth, but soon enough, it started to seem possible.

Could I really do this? Yes!

Just this year, not only did our business cross multi-7-figures only six years after getting started, but I was able to celebrate my first two clients becoming millionaires!

I started my business to demonstrate possibilities for my daughter but also to create freedom to have more time with my kids. Yet, I would teeter totter back from mom guilt for working when I should be with my kids to spending time with my family and experiencing the nagging feeling that I wasn't getting the things done that I needed to get done. I had to believe I could do it all—run a successful business, be a great mom, wife, friend, and daughter and that I wouldn't have to give up one for the other.

I also found that I censored my voice, trying to be polished and perfect rather than fully me. *I can't say that!* I thought I had to look like others, fit in, be likeable. Truth was, I had to like myself enough to not care what other people thought. I had to be the leader who prioritized my mission over being liked, a leader worthy of being followed because of my confidence in my own method of obtaining millions and carving out my own way. When I stopped caring about negative comments and pissing people off, my following turned from mediocre interest to raving fans.

In an airy-fairy world, we see building a business as a linear process, starting at the bottom and building, building until you arrive. But there is no

"I have arrived" nor a linear path. The journey is full of obstacles. I certainly have had my share.

•   •   •

The year I crossed a million dollars in my business started with January being my worst month in years. I made $16K in sales, and I felt like a failure. My husband had lost almost a million dollars in a stock investment that went sour, and we had a line of credit that was racked to the brim. We had two mortgages to pay, and I was in a major tailspin of fear and blame towards my husband for his failed investment. It was a moment of choice. I could choose to have my husband's back and be a team when he needed me or be right and wallow in my self-pity and continue to spiral into fear and blame. I chose to have my husband's back. I chose not to expect him to figure his way out on his own, that we would do it together. Just four months later, I had a $300k month! Later that year, I crossed a million dollars in sales. We paid off both mortgages, the lines of credit, and cleaned up the mess, together. This was a major turning point for me and for us as a couple. It's how you choose to act and treat yourself and others in those downward spiral pressure moments in your life that make or break your next level of success.

Every single year in business I have thought about giving up. Yes, you read that right. It's not all fluffy unicorns and roses. You're human and we are emotional creatures, am I right? I've found myself asking, *Is this really worth it?* And often having moments where I wanted to throw my computer out the window and say, "I'm done!"

•   •   •

A few months ago, I fired a salesperson. She was a beautiful human but wasn't committed to her role. I could see her heart was in building her own business, not supporting mine, so I encouraged her to go after her dreams. The next day, my lead salesperson gave me notice. *Shit, now what?!* Then, a few days later, my last salesperson also decided she was ready to go all in on building her own business.

I threw my hands up to the sky and cried. This was not the first time I'd brought people into my company, and, through the influence of my work, they built enough belief in themselves and their possibility to venture out as a business owner.

I, too, had that yearning when I was an employee, even though I made a damn good employee and busted my tail to do the best I could at everything I did. I thought building a business looked easy and that I could do it with no problem. When I got started, I was quickly humbled about what it really took to build a business and how little I actually knew about it until I got started.

Here I was, faced with my own team falling apart and thoughts rushing through my mind: Maybe I should scale back. Do I need to keep growing? Do I need to build a big team? Do I need this pressure?

As you can imagine, the sales team is the engine that fuels the income for the business, and there I was, feeling stranded on a desert island with nowhere to go. I questioned my leadership. I thought about taking sales all back onto my shoulders.

I stopped. Took a deep breath. Put a pause on the downwards spiral of my thoughts to center back on my vision. Those 1,000 millionaires. To my daughter and my son seeing me lead by example.

My thoughts changed to: I know this is my calling. I know this is God's mission for me, and I am not going to give up. I prayed for strength and clarity. I asked mentors for support. I reached out to colleagues to get advice. I put on my big girls pants and committed to keep going and stay in action.

I hired a company to help me engage and train my salespeople. I did countless interviews. This time, I trusted my gut. I quickly decided, no, no, not the right fit. Eventually I hired two new salespeople. I took the reins of leadership back with the new sales team. As a result, my lead salesperson chose to stay on, and business carried on as per usual. Well, for now anyway.

• • •

I've realized building a business is all about building you. Your leadership. Your belief. Your trust in yourself and your gut.

Nobody ever tells you the healing journey you will go on as you build millions.

After piling up a graveyard of half-completed courses, searching for the magic bullet answers yet still struggling to have my major breakthrough, I realized that I was the only common denominator. Me.

Ouch!

I used to think that when I hit my next goal, I would then have made it. I would be happy; I would feel successful. But every time I failed, I felt worse. Less than.

I wouldn't give it my all, because I thought if I did and failed, then it would mean there was something wrong with me. I was scared that I was not enough.

But it hit me. I had to experience the feelings, process the emotions and fears, and not believe I was wrong for having them. I had to feel through them to release them. The more I avoided them, the worse I felt, the more I struggled, and the more I pulled back.

•   •   •

Up until you are about seven or eight years old, any information you hear, see, or receive is accepted as truth. Then, around that time, it's as if a lid is put on your subconscious mind, and all information you hear, see, or receive is now filtered through the lens of your belief system that was shaped as a child.

So, let's say that, as a child, you had a moment where you felt excluded from a group, as though you didn't fit in. You were probably hurt, sad, disappointed, and just desired to be part of the group.

Now, whenever you try to be bold and do something new like go on a live video to train and share about your unique perspective to the world, it would feel like neon flashing signs went into action saying, *Warning, warning, distract her, tell her it's not safe, people might not like this, danger of being excluded, threat to operating system.*

And, without even realizing this, the desire to pull back goes into effect, the message gets buffered, and the result is a plain vanilla message that people tune out.

So, the path to clearing old wounds that are unknowingly blocking your success comes down to taking your power back. Uncovering what old decisions or core beliefs you made up as a child or that younger version of yourself that continue to influence you, to stand in your way.

You can ask yourself: What am I most afraid of? What is my biggest fear? What am I pretending not to know? What am I ignoring?

Then what ...

Then what ...

Then what … Until the end, when you come up with the core belief or fear beneath it all. That is when you stop avoiding it. Instead, you get "present" and ready to face what is coming up for you. As you know, what you resist persists.

Fear is just evidence of separation between God and yourself as the powerful creator you were born to be. These fears are reflected in thoughts such as: I'm not good enough. I can't have it all. I don't deserve this.

You are simply a thinker of your thoughts. You are not your thoughts. Your default thoughts were created based on your past experiences. Your old thinking will keep you safe and will re-create your results from yesterday. Remember, your thinking isn't truth. It's not fact. It's only a potential perspective. If you want a new result, you must choose thoughts aligned with where you want to go next, not from where you were before. First, you want to get brutally honest with what your default thoughts and beliefs are.

Here's an example that I go through with my clients in my program:

> *Fear or thought*: Nobody will buy my programs.
>
> *Underlying fear:* If I am successful in business, it will cost me my relationship.
>
> *Then* … my marriage would be over.
>
> *Then* … my kids would blame me and leave.
>
> *Then* … my business would crumble.
>
> *Then* … my family and friends would hate me.
>
> *Then* … I would be all alone and wouldn't have a reason to live.
>
> *Underlying belief:* I can't have it all

These negative thoughts and feelings lead to a constant state of uncertainty, self-doubt, avoidance, inaction, undesired actions, or ticking things off the list but never believing or expecting them to work.

In order to shift into a new result, you need to ask: If I were the person who already hit my goals, what did I need to believe in order for my current reality to be what it is? How did I create this?

Then, you go to work to think, behave, and act like the person who already has the result. You make decisions from that place. You lead from that place.

The truth is that successful people have a different set of thoughts, beliefs, and ways of being than those who struggle.

A phrase I always tell myself is that I am only a thought away from my biggest breakthrough, so what is my new thought I will choose in this moment?

I spend time visualizing my future where I have all that I want to create. It's already done. And I practice thinking, behaving, feeling, and taking action as that person today.

It really is that simple, but that doesn't mean it's easy!

If I only had one resource to help me grow my business, it would be the commitment to keep going no matter what. It's one of our company's core values: Whatever it takes.

•   •   •

Everything epic that I have created in my life has come from never taking no for an answer and knowing there is always a way. And being resourceful enough to figure it out and do whatever it takes to make it happen.

It's never about your resources. It's about your resourcefulness. I remember watching a TEDx Talk where Tony Robbins asked, "Who in the room has failed?"

It was silent; nobody wanted to admit defeat in this high-power room.

After some coaxing, he asked again and added, "Why did you fail?"

People blurted out that they didn't have enough money, time, the right people, and then, at the back of the room, Vice President Al Gore said he failed and lost the presidential election because he didn't have enough Supreme Court justices.

In that election, Al Gore tied with George Bush Jr., and it landed on the Supreme Court to decide the fate of the president-to-be.

Tony Robbins looked at him and said, "That's not a very accurate answer."

He went on to explain that everything they had told him in that room, that they didn't have the right contacts, technology, people, time, money … those are resources.

He said that they were telling him they had failed because they didn't have the resources, but the truth is, a lack of resources is never the problem; the problem is a lack of resourcefulness.

The ultimate human resources are emotional states—creativity, decisiveness, passion, honesty, sincerity, and love. When you engage these resources, you can get any other resource on the planet.

Resourcefulness is the ultimate resource.

And, if you don't have what you want, stop telling yourself the story that it's because you don't have the money or the time. That is BS. It's because you haven't committed yourself, and you haven't burned your boats and eliminated any other back-up, fallback plan.

•   •   •

Consider this for a moment. Can you think of a person you follow online? A mentor or someone whose emails you read, or you watch their videos or listen to their podcast?

Ok, great. Now, why do you follow them? What is it about them that has you coming back for more?

When I ask this question, I normally hear things like, they're bold, authentic, tell it like it is, confident, real, generous, etc.

Notice that I didn't say that they have the best how-to tutorial on the planet or the best steps to get a result. No.

What keeps you following them are their resources—what I refer to as leadership qualities—and you have those already. They are innate in you. Those qualities you admire in others are already within you. Perhaps you've tucked them away, forgotten about them, or have masked them over the years, but they are there. Peeling back the layers of the onion, the years of adapting to meet other people's expectations to gain love, attention, acceptance, have molded you into someone that isn't fully you. No wonder things feel a little off.

Your job is to peel back those layers and authentically reconnect with all of you. When you do that, not only do you find true freedom by no longer pretending to be someone you're not, but you find true joy and happiness by simply being you. Remember, you don't look good wearing someone else.

When you carve out those resources, those leadership qualities, you are enough to create that big magic dream you have. You are enough exactly as you already are.

I highly recommend the following resources, which have helped me tremendously, for anyone who wants to build:

- *Big Magic* by Elizabeth Gilbert. A terrific reframe on fear and taking your idea and running with it before it expires;

- *The Big Leap* by Gay Hendricks. Understanding how we limit the level of success we believe we can have or deserve in our life;

- *Tapping Into Wealth* by Margaret Lynch. The best money book on busting through old money conditions and stories and resetting yourself with a new concept around money creation and your ability to hang onto it;

- *The Power of Your Subconscious Mind* by Dr. Joseph Murphy. A great scientific perspective on how the mind works for you or against you;

- *Can't Hurt Me* by David Goggins. I had no idea what commitment was until I read this book. Just, wow!

- *Go Giver* by Bob Burg. The principles whereby I approach life and business through generosity in a super fun, easy way to grasp tangible concepts;

- *You are a Badass* by Jen Sincero. If you're ready to own your worth, this is a must read!

And if you're already in business, check out some of these resources that have helped me tremendously with automating my systems: www.deliveryourgenius.com/resources.

A rock-solid step-by-step strategy, combined with coaching from a mentor who has created the result you want, is the fastest way to uplevel to the result you want while giving you the resources to help you quickly work through any blocks standing in the way of your success. You don't know what you didn't know when you are building a business. You'll get there much faster if you have a step-by-step process to guide you from idea to getting started and moving forward in the right order to grow and scale.

•   •   •

It took me years to figure out that most perceived solutions are missing at least one of these three things:

1. Results Based System: A step-by-step system to follow with simple tools to execute. In business, this might be swipe files to fill in the blank so you're not starting from scratch and you'll actually implement. This needs to be combined with skill development. For example, we teach skills to sell on camera, program design, how to write compelling copy, to name a few. When you look at the person who has achieved the result you want, they have already developed and mastered certain skills. Most programs say, do this. But the question becomes, how? That is where tools and skill building come into play. Without it, only a very small group will get results.

2. Coaching: This is where you get support to work through the thoughts, emotional triggers, resistance and limiting beliefs that don't serve you, so you can quickly shed them and create fresh clarity and a new empowering rock-solid belief in yourself.

3. Accountability and Accessibility: This is like your insurance policy to stay the course. To show integrity with your word, to do what you say you're going to do and have someone hold you to what you want, your big dream, that vision, no matter what. It's easy to falter and talk yourself out of your own greatest possibility when you are lone wolfing it. When you have someone who believes in you, sometimes more than you believe in yourself, you rise to the occasion.

A long-term program with all three of these ingredients is what I call a Results Based Transformational Offer or RBTO. It's the secret ingredient to fast results. I found myself investing a lot into coaching, programs, and courses, yet I was still missing at least one of these ingredients in each investment I made. Therefore, I was kinda piecemealing it all together.

I realized the best solution you can offer your market is the solution you wished you'd had on your journey. That's what I did. I chose to fill the gap, work with fewer clients on a deeper level, and focus on a client-for-life model. If you're missing one of these three ingredients, you're not equipping yourself with the best recipe to produce the quickest results, and you'll go looking to fill those gaps. Then confusion sets in. There are too many voices in your head and you can't see the "best" path forward. Same goes for your market—fill the gap and create a dream-come-true offer that is the one-stop solution they crave, and you'll create clients for life.

The biggest challenge for women with regards to creating wealth and abundance is feeling deserving of having it all. This leads to overthinking, overworking, overcommitting, undercharging, working for free, and feeling majorly overwhelmed. If you're falling into any of these traps now, stop. Pause and remember this quote from Marianne Williamson:

> *Our deepest fear is not that we are inadequate.*
>
> *Our deepest fear is that we are powerful beyond measure.*

Find a mentor and get into an RBTO program that supports you with a step-by-step strategy, coaching support to get you through mental games, and accountability to your big vision, so you can uplevel your belief that you *can* have it all.

You need to make four key decisions:

Number One: Just start. Done is better than perfect. Don't compare your beginning with someone else's end.

Number Two: Make it about them, not you. If you're thinking about getting it right, trying to control outcomes, then you are not present to the human on the other side of your interaction. Get present and make it about them.

Number Three: Be the scientist and get obsessed with landing your messaging, communication, value, and offer. It all starts with your very first following.

Number Four: Selling is serving. Selling is simply a tool. As an excavator can be used to demolish forests, it can also be used to dig a hole for the foundation of your dream home. The fact that you worry about being pushy or slimy already tells me that you will use selling as a tool for good. You have the key to change others' lives. Own that. Be unapologetic about selling your product or service, as if you had the cure to cancer.

You will create what you expect, so set your expectations wisely.

•   •   •

When I started my business, I told myself that the first year I would make $60,000, since it was a partial year, then my first full year $100k, in the third year $300k, and in the fifth year $1M. That's exactly what I did. I met my expectations. And I know now that I could have built faster if I'd expected myself to. Raise your standards, and you'll raise your results.

The big vision for my business is to create 1,000 millionaires. On my path to discovering how to create that result, I birthed the idea of my own RBTO program. It's a 12-month program called the VIP Cashflow Accelerator, and it serves as a 6-figure incubator. A stepping-stone. It's year one of a four-year millionaire-maker curriculum. I look at this program as building a large pool of 6-figure earners to pull from and elevate into millionaires. It's so clear to me now exactly what it will take to create those 1,000 millionaires.

As a stepping-stone for that, my company has a financial goal of hitting $10M in annual sales in the next three years. That volume of revenue means lives changed, 6-figure earners created, and millionaires popping!

●　　●　　●

Christina is a confidence-boosting, cash-creating Business Growth Strategist who helps coaches and course creators start, grow, and scale their digital business online. After becoming a millionaire in her mid-20s (and losing it and building it again) and working in finance where she invested wealthy people's money in the stock market, Christina realized she was done with the shackles of corporate. She was ready to break free to build her own dream business, not someone else's.

In just six years, Christina built a company from ground zero on maternity leave to multi-7 figures, selling thousands of digital products and programs in more than 68 countries across the globe and helping new, aspiring, and seasoned business owners create more freedom, impact, and income in their lives.

You can follow Christina at:

Facebook Biz Page: https://facebook.com/deliveryourgenius
Instagram: https://instagram.com/christina.jandali
LinkedIn: https://www.linkedin.com/in/christinajandali/
Discover 17 Ways to Monetize Your Knowledge: https://deliveryourgenius.com/womenandwealth

MANEET CHAUHAN

I grew up in a middle-class family in India, where the value of money was taught to us very early on. My dad kept a diary in which everything that was spent in the day was written down. The one thing my parents told us was that they weren't going to leave behind money for us. What they wanted us to learn from them was the value of money and the value of good education, because that would be our foundation for success.

In terms of money consciousness, mine came from a combination of my family and the culture/society in which I lived. We grew up in a community where the people were, you know, working people. They were engineers. There was no great economic disparity between families—everyone was pretty much the same. When we went to school, we encountered people from a different economic stratum, of course, but that never played into things because it was a convent school and we all had to wear uniforms. Everything was very standardized and equalized.

There were a couple of thought processes behind the vision for my multi-million-dollar business. Recently, I was having a conversation with one of my fellow chefs, and she said, "I want to open a business."

I'm like, "Why?"

She replied, "It's my passion in life."

"Why?"

"Because I love doing it."

"Why?" I repeated.

She asked me, "What answer do you want?"

I said, "The answer is to make money."

If you want to go ahead and indulge your passion, then go ahead. You can start charity work, right? But if you are thinking of your business, I need you to start thinking along the lines that you're getting into business to make money. And that is the success of business, right? It is not. That's how you *measure* your success. So, I think that, when we started it, there were a couple of reasons, a couple of thought processes behind it. One was definitely that you make exponentially more money on your own than when you are working for someone else. The second is that it's something you own. The third is you have the freedom to make the decisions and to steward the rudder of your business. Ship the way you want. Also, when you love what you are doing, then you're going to put more passion and more effort into it. And it was also very important to have that passion behind the business.

• • •

I think one of the biggest mindset obstacles I had to overcome in order to reach the place of consistently earning a million dollars a year or more is growing up in a household that depended on the check coming regularly. There was that constant that only grew by a very miniscule value over the years. Suddenly there was a big check and then there was nothing. Then there was a big check until this next date. Those kinds of things. You had to make the adjustment for it in your lifestyle and budget. My husband and I are business partners, and he is definitely the one who is bolder in the financial moves he makes; I have to kind of balance him like a yin and yang equation, which I think is very important. You need somebody who will be constantly pushing you and then pulling you, and we do that with each other.

I think one of the biggest external obstacles I had to overcome in reaching business milestones was the fact that we had come here as immigrants. Becoming an American citizen is a long and expensive process, but being a citizen is the foundation for getting more in terms of facilities and resources. That was one of the biggest obstacles, and it elongated the time before we could start making money. I think we started off at minus 10, not even at zero! For us to get from minus 10 to zero took a lot of time and expense. It was a much more emotional journey than the one from zero to where we are right now. And there were other external obstacles such as diversity ... being a woman in an industry where you didn't see many women or someone with my ethnic background. But to me, I think the biggest obstacle was the fact that we were immigrants.

• • •

Everybody has that low point where they think about quitting, but I don't believe I ever reached the stage where I thought, *Oh, my God, this is it. I just want to take a job.* I don't think that's ever happened, only because that's my personality. I get up and I'm like, *Yes.* What do we have to do to come together today? That is what keeps me going. Of course, there are moments of disillusionment. For example, COVID-19 in 2020? The fact that we had to lay off 250 people really scarred us. It really, really, really affected us. It made us wonder what direction we were going in, but it didn't stop us. It only inspired us to pivot. I think that is the key. To be a businessperson, you have to be constantly ready to pivot because you never know what you'll need to adapt to. One day we had bad thunderstorms and our entire restaurant got flooded. We had to shut down for a week. Another time a snowstorm shut us down. The idea is to always be on your toes and ready to pivot. That is crucial.

I believe the underlying mindset integral to success is to never get comfortable, no matter what. You think you've reached a place where you're comfortable, but no, don't get comfortable because you have to keep on pushing yourself. The only person who is going to push you to the next level is you. Right? To me, one of my biggest fears is stagnation. By the time you start to stagnate, you're not stagnating. You're regressing. You're going back, right? So, the only way to move is forward. And that is what you must do. In terms of a mantra, mine is so close to me that it was my first email signature—*Nothing ventured, nothing gained.* I don't know why I wrote that. I had just come from India to do my undergrad. I didn't know anybody in the university I was attending, and I was the only Indian on campus the majority of the time I was there. So there was that feeling of being the only person—of being lonely. But to this day I have that phrase on my Hotmail. That's the one thing I refuse to change. And I've given a couple of TEDx talks about it where the lesson is "Jump in the deep end and your survival instinct will kick in; you will learn how to swim!" If you don't have that—if you don't have the will to survive—then you will sink, and that's what it's all about.

If I only had one resource that would help me grow my business and reach my next financial milestone, it would be tough to choose. I think one of the biggest things is really good investors who are not afraid and who see the vision and also the hard work.

I am the kind of person who will read everything. I think a wise person is a person who will find inspiration anywhere—through Instagram, reading *Forbes* or *The Wall Street Journal*, watching television. If you are the kind of person who is inspired, you will find inspiration everywhere. I find a lot of inspiration talking to people. Because I travel so much, I get to meet a lot of people. I get the most from talking to my dishwashers or people who are hosting large events at the restaurant. I will get inspiration from each and every person. I want to be that sponge who is absorbing all the information and the education which is freely available in the world. If I spend one day without learning something, then it's a waste.

One of the biggest things I tell everybody is that we as women always pause, likely because of the way we've been conditioned for generations and generations. If a challenge presents itself, the first thing we think of is in the form of a question. *Can I do this?* An opportunity is put in front of you. It could be a big business deal, and you're like, *Can I do it? Can we do it?* I tell everybody to switch those two words around to *I can do it. We can do it.* Right? That's what I have seen, especially with men. Even if they think they can, deep down they believe they can do 0.05 percent of it. The truth is that of course we can do it! Right? A woman will 99 percent believe she can do it, but she thinks the 1 percent is going to weigh heavy. I believe that needs to change. Of course, we can do it. There are no questions about that. A second challenge for women is that they think family is something that puts a pause or a full stop to who they are or what they can do because they aren't sure they can multitask.

Come on.

We, as moms, are the world's biggest, most amazing multitaskers! You can do so much. Taking that ability and applying it to your business is incredible. I started my business when my daughter was born, and, to me, it wasn't a comma. It wasn't a full stop. It was fast forward. And you know it's worth it. The trick is to give 100 percent of yourself to the moment you are in. Don't get distracted thinking, *Oh, this is what I didn't do yesterday* or *this is what I have to do tomorrow. Right now, I'm having a conversation with you. This is getting 100 percent of me. Okay, once I'm done with the conversation, we're done. Over. My next event is in 30 minutes. This is what I need to do now.* That's how you've got to operate.

•   •   •

What I would tell my younger self is to not get so easily frustrated when things are not going my way. I think that's one of the biggest things when you're young and things are not going your way. You get really, really frustrated and that frustration seeps into your productivity. In hindsight, each and every thing that didn't work out my way … actually did. But I would have been a lot more effective and productive if I hadn't been as frustrated when things didn't go the way I perceived that they should have gone.

Five years ago, I wish I had known COVID was coming. I would have gone ahead and restructured the entire business accordingly.

My next big goal is to learn from how things have been the last two years with COVID. My immediate goal is to make sure that the businesses we have are very strong and very stable. When we opened back up during the pandemic, we literally started from ground zero, not on everything we had built so far. So, the immediate goal is to make sure that the businesses are thriving and the foundation is strong because the foundation is what we are going to build on. There are a lot of other projects on the horizon that we are working on, including expansion. And we're also working on diversification. It's not about all the eggs in the same basket. That is definitely not the way to go, and that was how we started off. There is a beer aspect, a restaurant aspect, and the TV aspect, and we may look into retail, etc. as well. All of those possibilities are on the table. There are so many rods in the fire; we just have to figure out which is the one we are headed towards first. We know that if this one business is successful, then the next thing will be successful, and we keep building on a strong foundation for our business.

Do I feel like our next big goal is a stretch? Absolutely. No questions about that. If I am comfortable doing something, that means I'm doing something wrong. There has to be that little twinge of *oh my God* because, when you operate outside of your comfort zone, you are more alert. And that's what it's all about. It is a fact. Think of the girl who grew up in this small community in India. At that time, it was a stretch of my imagination to even think of coming to America. And then, when I was in school in America, it was a stretch to think about getting a job and then to open a restaurant and then to open not one but four as well as a brewery on 83 acres of land. You must stretch your imagination to think about what is attainable and then work your frickin' backside off to go ahead and achieve it. That's what it's all about.

What will achieving the unattainable represent for me and others? To me, it would be more of a personal achievement … *Yes, I did it!* But for others, what has been very incredible recently, has been, especially due to COVID—the number of people who've reached out to me, especially young women, who want to start a business of their own. The ambition has to be there, but you must make an educated leap. You cannot get up in the morning and think, *I want to start a business and then do it.* First, make a business plan. A plan is very important because it gives you the roadmap to follow, and that is what is important. When women reach out and say, "We want to do this," I respond with, "You absolutely can and you absolutely must. But do your homework." That is very important if you want to succeed. And, if you do, other people can see and figure out that you can follow your dreams, even if you don't fit the mold of what people think of as a successful business person. You don't have to fit a mold to succeed!

•   •   •

One of the biggest things I'd like to leave you with is that everybody has their own journey—and you've got to embrace that journey. You can learn from other people's journeys, but one of the biggest things you'll learn from is your mistakes, so embrace them. Don't be hard on yourself for your mistakes. Learn from them. My biggest learning tools have been my failures as opposed to my successes because I know exactly what not to do next time. Embrace that.

My early experiences with money were ones of contrast—extreme wealth alongside poverty consciousness. White WASPs had the money, resources, and power. I needed to be like them in order to achieve the same. Shopping at Kmart and TJ Maxx while living one mile away from the Henry Ford mansion was our life.

I learned that, to make money and to succeed, I needed to push down my feelings and be like the successful white people, even if it didn't feel quite right. My feelings didn't matter. And, really, I didn't matter. What mattered was knowing what role to play and playing it correctly.

I am part of the Indian Diaspora. My family left India during the late 1930s because the violence in Punjab, the state in India we originate from, had been exacerbated by British colonization. My family left most everything they had behind. My parents were raised in East Africa, where they attended medical school.

Soon after marriage, they fled East Africa for England due to violence incited by Idi Amin Dada, losing everything they had once again. My brother and I were born during the few years my parents spent in England. Discrimination against Indians was intense, so we left everything behind yet again and came to America with a few hundred dollars.

As part of the so-called "model minority," my parents worked super hard and by 1976 had purchased a brand-new, custom-built home in Grosse Pointe Shores, Michigan. They went from abject poverty in India and Africa to the top 1 percent in the world in just one generation.

What this meant was, our money consciousness didn't match how much money we had. This theme continued into my marriage. We both had intense intergenerational ancestral trauma in our systems after hundreds of years of poverty and the recent huge trauma of partition.

Essentially, we had achieved financial freedom before we began to finally register that we had enough money, that we were and are safe.

My dad is a very unusual Indian doctor. He prioritized family and had dinner with us every night. In contrast, my friends rarely saw theirs. His main objective was patient care and *not* making as much money as possible. And he was always experimenting with personal growth, motivation, and investing on the side. There was always some plan or another going on.

So, when it came to creating a vision for my epic life, infinite possibilities were open to me, at least intellectually, and only on the side (meaning, it's okay to pursue your passion, but only in the margins). I did my life this way for a long time and felt as though I was dying inside. I filled the void by binging on food and wine. My life looked great on the outside and felt like a prison to me. I was desperate to find another path.

When I was little and we would sit down to pray at family Havan, my dad would ask us what the four aims of life are. I would excitedly yell them out. Dharma, Artha, Kama, and Moksha. Little did I know that these precious moments would turn into my lighthouse as I was navigating hurricane-level storms in my inner and outer world.

•   •   •

4 Pillars of Prosperity: When Divine Desire (Kama) Intersects With Divine Design (Dharma) That Is Where You Create True Wealth (Artha); And big bonus ... it's also the path towards spiritual liberation (Moksha) and elevating this reality.

- Dharma – Purpose, your calling, the reason you were born and the meaning of your life.

- Artha – Prosperity and wealth derived through following your soul's calling, the means to fulfill your purpose and your desires.

- Kama – Pleasure, play, delight, desire, and sensual gratification.

- Moksha – Paradise, peace that comes from spiritual liberation, and freedom from pain and personal reincarnation.

In the past, money, business, spirituality, and sexuality were all split and compartmentalized, but now they *must* come back together for true success.

What I've realized on my own journey is that, if you go after only wealth (Artha), you can end up feeling empty. I was a multi-millionaire in my late 30s who felt deeply unhappy and unfulfilled.

It was only when I started to activate my life with pleasure and purpose that the money came to life for me. I wish to share this wisdom with others.

Here are six actions you can take to activate your life:

1. Assess where you are right now with these 4 Pillars of Prosperity.

2. Tune into where you desire to be.

3. Be honest with yourself about the gap.

4. Journal about what you discovered.

5. Set targets based on what you discovered.

6. Do this planning ritual on every Solstice and Equinox!

Oddly enough, I had to realize that I actually had enough money before I could start to relax into finding more pleasure and purpose. Truly, what I discovered is that, if you begin with pleasure and purpose, it activates the path to true prosperity and freedom.

The hardest part has been overcoming the part of my programming that says I'm only meant to follow my passion on the side. True abundance for me is permitting myself to rest in the financial security we have built as I allow myself to go to graduate school in feminist studies, something that has no practical purpose in immigrant thinking.

I also know that pursuit of my passions will create even greater abundance than we enjoy already.

I used to think that the main obstacles to me following my dreams were my husband and my conditioning. What I realized is that the greatest issue was within me, in struggling to allow myself to go for my actual desires, and not just my programming.

Still, I have experienced significant family resistance to my choices. Being an Indian feminist is never an easy path! Being an outspoken woman is never an easy path, either.

•   •   •

There was a point in the journey where it was clear that I was going to remain in deep physical and emotional pain unless I took the risk of having some very difficult communications with family and friends. I'd been avoiding these shadowy corners in the relationships; however, it had become too costly to continue doing so.

As women, we are conditioned to hold our truth inside in order to keep the peace. I've never been good at that to begin with. Finally, I realized that the only way I was going to have any inner peace was to speak my truth. Unmuzzling myself and liberating my voice has opened up more flow of money, pleasure, and purpose than I ever could have imagined.

I overcame this obstacle by valuing myself enough to choose my well-being and happiness first, to finally do what the men in my life had been doing all along.

I've wanted to give up so many times because it's been really tough to even figure out what my true desires are. I can think I have a desire that's mine, I can begin to act on it, and then I realize it's not really what I want; it's what I'm supposed to want. I've gotten much better at this part, with practice.

There was a point on the journey when I was frustrated because I had so much of what I was supposed to want—financial freedom, family, career, nice home—but I still felt deeply unfulfilled.

I wondered if perhaps it would be best to just forget about going for my dreams because deep happiness and fulfillment weren't possible.

Then I realized I had fallen into the pattern of undervaluing myself again. I kept putting off what I most wanted, and I always had reasons to do that, to put me last. Now my child is off to college, and I finally am putting myself first. This shift makes all the difference in how I feel about my life. It went from black and white to technicolor HD with surround sound. And I didn't change anything, except the filter.

I used to gaslight myself, to hide parts of me in family situations because I didn't feel they would be acceptable. I don't do this self-harming behavior any longer. This shift allows me to bring more of my heart and soul wisdom to every interaction.

The most important shift I made was to realize that I had desires that were trustworthy. When I found my authentic desire and created my life from there, a true and consistent flow of love, money, and freedom ensued.

Make it a practice to connect daily with your desire. Find ways to fulfill your own desires—not just big ones, but small ones—every day.

•   •   •

If I only had one resource that would help me grow my business and reach my next financial milestone, it would be deeper and deeper embodiment. The more I become embodied as a soul, as a multidimensional being living in the third dimension, the more all that I desire, including my business, grows in flow.

I like listening to Elizabeth Peru's The Tip-Off Global Energy Forecast. It's the most useful, accessible, time-friendly energy and planetary shifts tool. It's very high-level and high-vibe and brings great insights to my day.

I love using the Shiv Yog app for spiritual practice.

Women have trouble believing they are worthy of having what they desire, which includes being wealthy. Our identity as women doesn't include all that many examples of super-successful, wealthy women.

Watch your inner dialogue carefully. How often do you devalue yourself? Discount yourself? Tell yourself you can't have something that you desire, even though other people are pursuing that perfectly reasonable desire?

In the noticing, I hope some shifts occur, that you begin to value yourself more. It's a subtle and long process. I still notice new ways daily that I can improve my self-regard.

When you are making a decision, ask yourself what you'd advise a loved one or a child to do. Women often value other people more than themselves, so this offers a good lens to zone in on your self-devaluation.

If I could coach my younger self just setting out with a dream and an idea, I would tell her *don't wait, go for it*. Don't sell out on your true desire as you follow that dream. Stay consistent and true to your heart and soul. Heart and soul always cut through the noise.

•   •   •

Five years ago, I wish I'd allowed myself to go in the new direction I deeply desired. I continued to lead with business coaching, when what I really wanted was to be a spiritual guide and unconventional leadership strategist. I was afraid to go all in and stayed on the fence for too long.

If there's something you know you want, go for it sooner rather than later. Don't stay in the in-between like I did.

Own your desire. Own it deeply. And go for it!

When I was 20 years old and doing my undergraduate degree at the Wharton School of Business, all I wanted to do was take psychology and South Asian studies. Instead, I chose the practical path and squelched my dreams.

I'm applying to graduate school in 2023 in the field of study of my choice! It's a huge stretch for me to give my mind this gift of following my heart and soul's desires, but it will support me in my goal of spreading Indian feminism, of liberating so many Indian women from the intense oppression of Indian patriarchy.

I'm also writing several of my own books. I'm soooooo excited! That's a stretch because I've never written an entire book on my own. It's something I've always wanted to do, though, and I am overflowing with ideas, so I can't keep it to just one project at a time. I finally feel my wisdom and voice is mature enough to share with others in a meaningful, impactful way.

•   •   •

Kavita Rani Arora, Esq. is an Indian Feminist living in the United States, a best-selling author and the founder of Epic Dream Academy. She supports high achievers to drain the emotional swamp within and transcend upper limits towards epic emotional intimacy, sharp self-actualization, and financial freedom.

As an Unconventional Business Strategist and Spiritual Catalyst, Kavita has developed a proven energy-based process, the Epic Dream Method, for creating vibrant health, wealth, and soul-driven success derived from ancient Vedic wisdom, neuroscience, the Quantum Field, and the Divine Feminine.

Kavita gave up her career as a lawyer and Fortune 500 director in favor of listening to her soul's true calling. For more than a decade, she's worked with thousands of people, including visionary entrepreneurs and high-powered leaders from UBS, Morgan Stanley, and Wells Fargo through her transformational programs, workshops, and retreats.

Kavita earned her bachelor's degree from the Wharton School of Business and her J.D. from Santa Clara University. She's a perpetual student, with at least 15 different coaching and leadership certifications (and counting). Prior to starting her own business, she spent 15 years negotiating contracts worth hundreds of millions of dollars for Fortune 500 companies like Avaya, AT&T, HP, and Sprint.

Kavita has spoken alongside such luminaries as Dr. Christiane Northrup, Marianne Williamson, Lynne Twist, and Gabrielle Bernstein. She is currently living her dream in her resort-like home in Southern California with her husband, Moneesh, and their black lab, Leo. Her son, Vijay, studies at Berkeley and introduces her to new feminist books.

You can follow along with Kavita at:

Web Site: https://www.epicdreamacademy.com/
FB Personal page: https://www.facebook.com/KavitaRaniSoodArora
LinkedIn: https://www.linkedin.com/in/kavitaaroraca/
Instagram: https://www.instagram.com/kavita_rani_arora/
https://www.instagram.com/the_quantumqueen/
FB Fan page: https://www.facebook.com/epicdreamacademy/

HAYLEY
HOBSON

Jersey girl here! Oh yeah. Big Bruce Springsteen fan. I grew up in Cherry Hill, an affluent suburb of Philadelphia. My dad was a doctor and I thought my family lived pretty comfortably. We had a nice home. My parents drove nice cars. We went out to eat.

But it's funny because I only remember the positive memories. My parents now tell me they were scratching nickels together in their early years. But by the time I remember, they were driving BMWs and my mom was wearing designer clothes and carrying Louis Vuitton bags.

They may have been trying to figure out how to pay their bills, but that's not what I remember. I never felt like I had to worry about anything. In fact, they paid for our private college tuition. And then, even graduate degrees.

Money just wasn't something I ever grew up questioning or wondering about. I knew I was taken care of, and I believed my family was secure. I think I used this to my advantage by promising myself to create the same kind of abundance for myself and my own family.

The vision I had for myself when I started my own business was to create more freedom and flexibility. I wanted to be my own boss. Play my own game. My dream was to create a life (and calendar) that worked for *me*.

In the beginning, I did get the J.O.B. I think it's what many of us are programmed to do. But, only a few years in, I ended up leaving this "secure," full-time job (as a corporate bankruptcy attorney) to follow my heart.

And yeah, I know … I'd spent a lot of time (and money) to become an attorney. But that career wasn't really my vibe. It didn't really suit my personality. In fact, it ended up actually wearing me down … both physically and mentally.

I literally reached a breaking point and knew if I didn't walk away and prioritize my own health, I'd be wrecked to the core. So I traded the courtroom for a health and wellness center. And the story keeps going.

While working on my own digestive issues and stress-related problems, I became obsessed with holistic wellness. And, I swear, I accidentally built a million-dollar business. OK, not a total accident. I worked my tail off. But the business model fell into my lap by accident. A friend shared essential oils with me and I was hooked.

I had never heard of "network marketing." But I knew I loved the product. And bonus, the oils actually worked. I started sleeping through the night. My moods shifted—I woke up happy! The distress in my gut went away. My immune system got stronger. And they gave me the strength to get off all my meds.

So off I went. To build my first million-dollar biz. And create the freedom I was craving in my professional life. For the first time ever, I saw the potential for an uncapped income. But listen … earning money is the easy part. I'll say that over and over again. It's your mindset that will hold you back from your earning potential.

I liked to hustle. I believed that if I wasn't working, I wasn't worthy, I had to overcome an ingrained belief that if I wasn't hustling and constantly creating … I wasn't producing. Or being effective.

Once I realized my success was not directly tied to my output, things began to shift. I was able to let go of unrealistic expectations in my life, protect my mental health, and actually work *less*. But produce *more*.

The result? The freedom I had been craving. Peace of mind. This enabled me to be creative about how to grow my business. And all of the relationships in my life.

And that creativity allowed me to overcome, before probably most, the belief that my success was related to the *physical* location of my work.

I knew I could reach so many more people. And share my message.

I was open to the idea of "going online" before what we now refer to as digital marketing existed. I started creating my identity in the online space. That's what we now refer to as a personal brand. And then optimizing social media to build my digital database. Or what we now refer to as an "email list." I learned that if you have a vision, and you lead with intention, 100 percent is possible. 100 percent of the time.

Yes. Of course, I've had a handful of moments where I felt like giving up.

In fact, most recently, my social media accounts on Facebook and Instagram were hacked and disabled. The accounts I'd spent a decade building and using strategically to build my business.

Gone.

The heart and soul of my revenue model.

To have them wiped out overnight, through a situation completely out of my control, was devastating. But I had a choice …

… Have a pity party for myself and then get over it. Or quit.

I chose the pity party. For a few days. So yeah, I went through the grieving process … and then I picked myself back up.

What pulled me through when I felt like giving up was leadership. And a flexible mindset. I realized that what I'd built was through the systems and frameworks I teach my own students … so I could build it again. And I did. And it was at that moment that all my accounts came back.

It's all about being resourceful. That's what I have learned from my own mentors. And I have always been a *huge* fan of *learning from other people* … and growing my network of friends and mentors.

•   •   •

I've never been afraid to learn. Or ask for help. Or collaborate with someone who's a few steps ahead of me. In fact, I would probably call myself an education or personal development junkie.

One of my biggest assets is my ability to see where I need more education, better leadership, or where I have the opportunity to hire someone to fill a gap. That's what's helped me continuously grow and scale over the years. In fact, if I only had one resource to rely on as a growth tool in my business, it would be my network.

Relationships are everything.

Being in a relationship is what I consider true wealth.

Whether these relationships are between your friends, your family, your partner, your spouse, a circle of like-minded people in a mastermind … having connections to people on the same path, (or even a little ahead of you), is so important.

I was always a huge fan of listening to podcasts, staying in tune with leaders in my own industry, and taking online courses in an area I wanted to grow. These resources gave me the foundational tools and knowledge I needed to structure my own online business in a profitable way.

I hope you're not looking at me and saying "she just got lucky." Because that's not the truth.

The story is: I created the time. And I made my dreams a priority.

•   •   •

I find the greatest challenge for women in creating wealth and abundance is the belief that they don't have time … because of their family, their work, etc. It's this belief that keeps them trapped in a cycle of burnout (and often caretaker) where they take on too much. Or, they don't take on enough. If you can flip the script on that mindset and realize you can *create* time by asking for help … outsourcing … automating … delegating … everything will shift.

So I am where I am now. And there are things I regret. Mistakes I made. A few choices that still haunt me. If that weren't the case, I wouldn't be human.

But I don't look back. I won't punish myself for making choices.

However, if I was coaching my younger self, I'd say, "Hayley, spend less time focusing on things you can't control. Instead, continue to just make a decision. And if you don't like the way it feels, change it later."

Just choose.

And remember, although things may feel out of your control, it's okay. What's in your control is how you show up. What's in your control is how you choose to respond. When you make choices that align with your core beliefs and intuition, you'll continue to walk along your own success path.

There are a lot of things I wish I'd known earlier. For instance, I wish I'd known how to launch a membership five years ago. I would have gotten in on the ground floor of that concept. When you can be an early adopter of something that shakes the industry like that (or TikTok, lol), it's a total game-changer for your business.

But why focus on the past? Or even the future. When you focus on the present, you are living. And that's when you get to create magic.

•   •   •

What's next for Hayley? Welllllllll, I'm glad you asked.

My next big goal is to expand into the next rank in my dōTERRA essential oils business while simultaneously growing my online educational programs.

My online programs and membership support entrepreneurs, coaches, and creative professionals who want to eat smarter, proactively rest more, and be way more productive in less time. Building healthier habits that stick, so they, too, can take their own biz online and thrive.

I know I have a big message to share. And thousands of people to still reach with my message. But I also know the world needs me.

And while that feels like a stretch to continue to bring my vision to life, I also know, once I achieve it, so many women will be served. And they, too, will be able to adopt that same belief, that with the right support and education, anything is possible.

•   •   •

You can follow Hayley Hobson on her social media sites:

www.hayleyhobson.com
IG: @hayleyhobson
FB: @hayleyhobsonwholeyou
TikTok: @iamhayleyhobson

AMY YAMADA

I was born and raised on a U.S. Naval Base in Yokohama, Japan, from the late 70s until the mid-90s when I moved to Seattle, Washington. My father was full Japanese, and my mother was an American elementary school teacher on the base. My earliest experiences with money were influenced primarily by my father. He had grown up as a post-World War II refugee who went from being extremely poor and homeless to creating success as a business owner and electrical engineer. When it came to money, he would say things like, "I don't need fancy things. Experiences are worth more. Seeing is believing." My parents were big on traveling (which I am truly grateful for!) but not buying things that were beyond what was considered practical. When I look back now, my thoughts around money were that I needed to work hard to earn my own and that life is more about experiences than material things. And, if I wanted to buy something, I would value it more if I earned the money to pay for it myself.

I remember at one point seeing a pink camera in a store display, and I wanted it so badly! I said to my father, "Papa, I really, really want that pink camera. Can I pleeeeeeease have it?" He replied with a smile, "I could easily buy it for you, but then you wouldn't *feel* the value of it. If you dropped it and broke it, it wouldn't be a big deal. But if you worked many hours to earn and save money for it, and then you purchased it, every time you used it, you would know the value of it."

I appreciated this lesson from a young age and started working when I was 12 years old so I would always have cash and be able to purchase what I wanted—including my pink camera!

In my family, culture, and society, my understanding was that men were the financial decision makers and breadwinners in the household. But, deep down inside, I knew I wanted to be my own financial decision maker and generate just as much income (if not more!) than what men generate. I didn't think it was fair for men to earn more than women. So, I decided from a young age that I would never let "being a girl" hold me back from anything I wanted in my life. I would see it as a strength and tap into my own unique gifts to create my best life. Of course, I fought many limiting beliefs along the way and still do ... but now those limiting beliefs come from within versus external circumstances or societal pressures. And with that, I have the power to shift!

I remember hearing the quote similar to: The problem is not the problem. The problem is the way I *think* about the problem. It's so true. We will all have obstacles throughout life. But what if every obstacle is a growth opportunity? What if the challenge exists to expand our possibilities? I love challenging my mind this way.

I was inspired to launch my business after going through my biggest life-awakening experience, which was losing my wonderful mother in 2010. I remember thinking, *We are really not here, in this life, forever. If there are things I want to do in my life, I'm going to do them, and I'm going to do them* now!

I had been working in the corporate world for about 15 years, and I knew I was meant for more. Initially, launching my business was about creating freedom. I wanted to become my own boss, create my own schedule, travel and work from anywhere. This evolved to creating transformational experiences, giving back to the world, and building my dream life!

I remember the year I decided to go "all in" on breaking through to 7 figures. My mentor said, "It's not about the million dollars. It's about *who you are becoming* as you break through the limiting beliefs along the way." That got me so fired up to just *do it*!

Instead of taking logical steps of scaling what I had already built, I shut down the group coaching program I had run for several years (a program that had been the bread and butter of my business; I just knew in my heart I wanted to build something bigger and better). That year, 2018, I launched three new offers: my high-end Powerhouse Retreats, Powerhouse Mastermind (my signature, ongoing group coaching program and community), and my "Dream Big" 3-day conference.

On the last day of Dream Big in October, 2018, I stood in a circle with my team, family, and some of my closest friends, as my event producer shared how many new clients had just enrolled in Powerhouse Mastermind. With tears in my eyes, I said to everyone, "We did it!! We crossed a million dollars!" My team and I had worked so hard on hosting our retreats and events that year, and it was such a magical moment for all of us. Not only had we just crossed 7 figures, but we also helped raise over $80,000 for "Josie's Well" (my stepdaughter's charity project) to build over ten wells in Ghana.

Now, my *why* is that I am super passionate about making a difference for the difference-makers—coaches, mentors, guides, healers. If I can empower them, I feel as though I am making a ripple effect in the world. And, on a personal note, I am passionate about supporting my family and building an extraordinary life together.

•　　•　　•

Ah, yes … the mindset obstacles. I've had so many limiting beliefs run through my head over the years, and they tend to circle back around every time I stretch myself to a whole new level. These inner gremlins sound like this:

What if it doesn't work?
What if I run out of money?
What if I can't do it again?
See? That launch was a total flop. I shouldn't employ that strategy ever again.

On a deeper level, my limiting beliefs come from an old story of not valuing myself, thinking I could never do enough, feeling "not enough." As a young girl, I created a belief within myself that, in order to be loved and accepted, I needed to be "perfect." A perfect student, a perfect daughter, a perfect friend. I thought I needed to show up the way others expected me to show up instead of being my authentic self. I carried this belief for decades until I decided that the most important thing was for me to be me.

The external obstacles I had to overcome were also many. In the spring of 2019, I tried a new strategy where I ran Facebook ads to "cold traffic" (people who do not know me or follow me) promoting a free, 2-day event in La Jolla, California. I invested tens of thousands of dollars on this event and campaign, with the goal (and plan! It *had* to work!) of enrolling a group of new clients into my mastermind.

At the event, there were about 35 attendees (which I was okay, but not thrilled, with). I only enrolled two new clients, and, within a week or so, both of them canceled! Soon after, I enrolled a short-term private coaching client (and even offered a discount) whom I had met at that event, so I generated a few thousand dollars. Still, I lost so much more and felt like a total failure.

Several months later, I was having a conversation with my love, Ken, when I brought up that particular event, since it was still living in my head like a dark cloud. I was having a multi-month pity party about it. With a surprised look on his face, he said to me, "You thought you *failed*?"

I nodded, thinking, *Obviously.*

He said, "I've seen you speak on a lot of stages. And I've *never* seen you as powerful as you were at that event, on that stage." I looked at him with, I'm sure, a totally confused look on my face. He continued, "At the beginning of that event, you had a room full of complete strangers. Skeptics even. By the end of Day 1, everyone was having Happy Hour and dinner with you at the hotel restaurant as if you were old friends. By the end of Day 2, you had a standing ovation, and everyone was in tears."

His words gave me a whole new perspective on that event. I realized that I had *only* based my success on sales and hadn't looked at it from the lens of the impact I had made, the lessons I learned, the growth I experienced. It was a game-changer.

On the financial side of things, I had a few uncomfortable months after that event, but I was able to get back up on my feet through setting a powerful intention for my next big event, which was my 2nd Annual Dream Big. I came up with a revenue-generating plan to create and sell sponsorships, event tickets, and VIP Days to cover the hard costs. I have learned that anytime I want to create anything, it's about starting with a clear and committed vision, deepening my trust within myself, and knowing that, no matter what happens, I will figure things out!

•   •   •

I never experienced a point of wanting to give up on my multimillionaire dreams. I've had moments where I've been afraid of losing everything, but, even then, the one thing I remind myself of is this: Nothing can ever take my dreams away from me. And no one can take *me* away from me. I will commit and recommit to my dreams, however long it takes. It's a much more exciting way to live!

What has helped me build my business to where it is today the *most* is what I call "Deep Connection" (which is at the heart of what I teach, as well as how I live my life). Deeply connecting with my authentic voice; deeply connecting with my vision and big dreams; and deeply connecting with others. I connect with my authentic voice and vision through journaling and creating quiet space for myself. I connect deeply with others through having thoughtful and meaningful conversations with them. I love breaking down barriers and seeing if people I meet throughout my life will let me see who they *really* are, and continuing to peel back my own layers, vulnerably, to let people see me, too. Anytime I've had the courage to go a little deeper, I've seen the greatest gifts and beautiful imperfections within others—and they've been able to see mine, as well.

The most important investment I have made has been investing in my own mentors and masterminds. Finding a coach I resonate with and surrounding myself with other, like-minded, badass entrepreneurs have been the best investments I've made. And I don't only mean financially but investing time, money, energy, love, contribution … all of it. I don't believe we are meant to do life or business alone. I believe we're meant to rise together!

•   •   •

If I only had one resource that would help me grow my business and reach my next big financial milestone, it would be to have full-time sales team members. As I write this, I currently have an awesome director of sales and two talented, seasoned, part-time salespeople. But sales and enrolling new clients are all about connection and consistency. They require having time every single day (at least Monday-Friday) dedicated to connecting with people and following up in a timely manner. I'm excited about implementing that this year so we can serve more people, make a bigger impact, and take my company to a whole new level!

I'm currently reading Jen Sincero's *You Are a Badass at Making Money*, and I'm loving it! My other all-time favorites are *Living With a Seal* by Jesse Itzler and *Choose Yourself* by James Altucher. My favorite apps are: Slack for team communication instead of email; Voxer for voice and text coaching my top-tier clients; Google docs for sharing/reviewing/editing copy; Kajabi for hosting my mastermind portal and online training programs; PipeDrive for sales tracking and communication; Infusionsoft/Keap for email marketing and payment processing through WePay (through Infusionsoft/ Keap); WordPress for my website and some of my landing pages; and ClickFunnels for other landing pages, sales web pages, order forms. My team uses Asana for project management and Airtable for tracking our clients and planning themed content. The list goes on and on, but the above are the best!

•   •   •

In my opinion, the greatest challenge for women and creating wealth/ abundance is the infamous "imposter syndrome." Within the first few years of coaching entrepreneurs, I realized something. Nearly every person (including myself!) that I'd had the honor of coaching said to me at some point, "Who am *I* to think I can do this?" Clearly, we all have this limiting belief within. It's fascinating when I think about it.

If I could give advice to anyone who is feeling blocked by this obstacle, here it is: Know that you are not alone. Of course, you feel this way because it's very likely that the thing you are about to do is something you've never done before. The secret, though, whenever this inner gremlin comes up and says, *"Who am I to think I can do this? What if I can't do it?"* is to remember that this is only your inner voice trying to keep you safe. Still, in doing so, it keeps you small. Something that has really helped me shift my thoughts in those moments has been to remind myself that I can either spend precious energy on my limiting beliefs, or I can focus on making a difference.

Regarding your bigger dreams and goals, I recently heard the incredible speaker Rex Crain say, "Decide that it *will* happen. And then write down three reasons it *will* happen!" I love that. I used it this past month, and my four-week goal happened within one week. It's amazing what happens when we are open to the possibility of it!

If I were to coach my younger self, I'd say, "Trust yourself. Trust your soul's journey. Don't overthink things too much. It won't all unfold the way you think it will, but it will ultimately be better than you ever imagined! You will create your most extraordinary life, with people you love, and adventures that will provide you with the best memories. When you have moments of self-doubt, reach out to those who believe in you and ask for support. Get coached and be coachable. Be committed but unattached. Be kind to yourself. Go above and beyond for others. And, by all means, have fun along the way. You've got this!"

If there was something I wish I'd known five years ago that would have accelerated my growth, it would have been to hire a project manager. Before I had a project manager on my team, I hired contractors to take on specific roles like executive assistant, web and graphic designer, copywriter. I gave myself the job of project manager and my team members asked me questions and needed my attention to manage the projects *and* manage them. Hiring a talented project manager was a game changer. She took so much off my plate so I could focus on the vision of my business versus getting into the weeds of every project and being there to answer questions and hold people accountable to deadlines.

For example, over the past year, I hosted twenty live virtual events, and this was on top of all our group coaching calls and workshops. I was never overwhelmed by this quantity of events because I didn't have to concern myself with all the nitty gritty details of each funnel, promotion, graphic design element, link, or piece of copy. Having a project manager to lead projects, test funnels, and create systems (as well as other team members creating systems and processes) allowed me to focus on creating content and experiences for each virtual event.

When I thought about my next big goal for my business, I thought I *should* write about my big, stretchy, multiple-seven-figure financial goals or talk about how many lives I want to impact. And while I do have these as a consistent, growing vision, I'm going to share my vulnerable, personal goals, which are to focus on health and fitness and spending more quality time with my family.

I fully trust I will expand my business, serve more beautiful souls, and continue to give back, because it is my passion! What I get to work on is developing consistent, healthy habits and creating the best memories with my three precious loves.

The plan I've put in place to achieve these two focuses are: working out with my awesome personal trainer three times a week and swimming laps at the pool with my stepdaughter once or twice per week. (She's inspired me to become a stronger swimmer, as she's on her high school's swim team and continues to stretch herself, too!) And when the kids come home from school each day, I am committed to spending our evenings together, hearing about their day, and doing fun family activities together like game nights, movie nights, or going out to dinner and chatting away. We love spending time together, and quality time with the people we love is life's most precious gift!

This is a stretch for me because I can easily slip back into "workaholic mode," but, at the end of the day, I didn't become an entrepreneur to be tied to my laptop or phone 24/7. I did it to make a bigger impact and to be able to create life on my own terms.

These two focuses are important to me now because I don't want another year to go by that I haven't been consistent with healthy habits. And I want to create more wonderful memories with my family. Life is so precious, and time with our kids is so fleeting! Achieving these important goals will represent self-respect and appreciation for my family members who have brought so much love and joy into my life.

• • •

Amy Yamada trains coaches and service-based entrepreneurs to master the power of deep connection through their words and messaging, high ticket packages, and sales conversations, so they can create the impact and income they've always desired.

With over twenty years of experience in marketing, sales, promotions, and broadcast media, Amy has created her own, signature "Create, Connect, Offer" system that empowers entrepreneurs to break through all the marketing noise, deeply understand and connect with their audiences, and make a massive difference for their clients. As a result, Amy's clients, colleagues, and entrepreneurial friends have gained clarity in their message, confidence in how they communicate, and increased cash flow in their businesses. Beyond business, they have created a deeper connection with themselves, their big dreams, and who they get to show up as to bring their dreams to life!

JULIE
THURGOOD-
BURNETT

*W*ho would have thought that the city girl, who has three main loves, family, cars, and shoes, (in that order) would own a lavender farm and a
*full line of skincare products that soon followed? Julie Thurgood-Burnett knew
that she wanted to make her brand special and different, and she has achieved
that with Hereward Farms. With a background of over 25 years in marketing,
cosmetics, and retail, Julie built this brand with the notion of "farm to skin".
Going back to nature and creating these spa-quality products that are researched,
created, developed, and marketed by her.*

• • •

I grew up in a small town with an older brother and two amazing parents. We were a middle-class family; my dad was a teacher and my mother
was a legal secretary. My love of cars came from my dad :). I watched my
parents, who both grew up with very little and had very little family support,
make a life for themselves and their kids. We didn't have a lot, but we surely
did not go without.

Life was pretty amazing, and then life kinda went on another path for me, and maybe that is why I am where I am today because, well, it didn't define who I am but it sure did carve out who I was. I don't really talk about these things because, like I said, it didn't define me, but it sure did change how I viewed the world and how I was going to navigate it.

I had three defining moments in my life that definitely have put me where I am today. When I was nine, I was attacked by a dog and ended up having 72 stitches in my face and two plastic surgeries. My parents were incredibly supportive, and that really did get me through this stage in my life. However, the kids I went to school with weren't so kind, and I never quite understood why people could be so mean. Then, when I was 14, my father died in a tragic accident, and that definitely was the day I changed. Four years later, my mother became ill and lived in the hospital till I was 30, then she passed away. From there, my brother and I were on our own with little to no family support or guidance.

This is not about feeling sorry for myself, but it made me realize that I was solely responsible for my success, career, and life. I could have made a decision to feel sorry for myself and take a completely different direction, but that is not how I am built. I have fought long and hard for where I am today. If a job didn't fit or if I lost a job, it was up to me to fix my life and make it right. And here I am!

•   •   •

We were taught that you didn't have to spend money to be happy, and that you should only spend what you have. I grew up in a home that had one car and camping was our vacation until we got older—but we were happy, and money wasn't the center of our lives.

My first real investment was possible because of the insurance money I got from the dog attack. My mom gave me some and told me she was hanging onto the rest so that I could invest it down the road. I am glad she did. I bought my first home at 24, and have invested my money ever since. It hasn't always been easy, but it sure did ensure that I had the fundamentals financially to look after me and my family.

Well, this Hereward Farms really did start out on a whim. You see, I co-owned a marketing agency called Green Monkey Creative with an amazing business partner. In 2015, I was not happy at my current agency and knew

I had to get out. I was about to resign on Monday and they let me go the Wednesday before. I took my severance, learned to be careful what I thought out to the universe, and started up an agency by myself. In 2017, I launched Green Monkey Creative.

Hereward Farms was something I never really thought it would be. The agency was going so well, but a thought occurred to me during the lockdown in Ontario in 2020: *I wonder if we can grow lavender on our 150 acres.* So I bought 40 plants and tried my hand at farming. Then I researched and went back to school and really was winging it all the way through. When I wondered what I was going to do with all this lavender, we came up with a skincare line. We sold out immediately and started to plan how to expand. Today we have over 4,000 plants with another 2,000 coming on just over two acres of land, and we offer over ten products. I am still in shock at how quickly we have grown and taken off so much. I have now sold my half of the agency and am now running Hereward Farms full time with my family and staff.

I just knew that I had to keep listening to my heart and my values. Remember, this started as a whim, and I just went with the journey of where this was taking me. I wanted an all-natural skincare brand that was high-end and didn't look like a typical "Mom" brand. The "Why" is because it opened up a passion in me that I can't even describe and that wasn't present in other positions that I have carried or other companies I have owned.

I did know I wanted to honor the land we live on, as my husband's ancestors settled here during the Potato Famine in Ireland. The Hamlet of Hereward was a small little stop that had a hotel and post office that my husband's great-great-great-grandfather started with his brother.

I married the two thoughts: the heritage and the branding and products. I source out every ingredient and every recipe to make our products. For the products we do not make, I wanted to partner with other women-led Canadian businesses. I do not want my business to be about competition. I want the business to be about us walking the same path holding hands and gaining success together.

I also didn't think we would have a store. We were doing well online, but when a local magazine did a feature on our farm, people started showing up the day it hit their mailboxes. We now have a Lavender Lounge + Boutique that we run as a family as well.

•   •   •

I think the most interesting story I have had along this journey was when the tables shifted. When I was quietly launching this business, I wanted it to be abouts its brand and not about me or my name. When it finally came out, I was at a dinner party when someone said, "Did you hear about that new lavender farm and skincare company called Hereward Farms?"

I answered, "Yes, that is my baby."

The cat was out of the bag, and we haven't looked back.

When we did our first big harvest in 2021, I really underestimated how much lavender we would have. We harvest by hand (in 2022 we will harvest both by hand and machine) and after I was done cutting all the lavender, I didn't quite realize how much we had until I went to lay it all out. Let's just say my husband came home from work and the whole floor of his area of the barn—approximately 1000 square feet—was covered in lavender. He couldn't access his tools without tip-toeing around all the flowers for four weeks. Now we know, and I have tons of drying racks now—ha-ha!

•   •   •

I own a couple of companies that contribute to this success, and they are such a variety that I love it. I think mostly just the sheer fact that I can do it. Nothing is stopping me from achieving success. I remember that, on LinkedIn, a career coach (or whatever he was, cause he "wasn't worth remembering") sent me a private message and said, "Wow, you sure do have your hands in a lot of things. Hopefully, you don't neglect Green Monkey Creative and stay focused."

My response is probably not suitable for this story, but I wondered, if I were a man, would his response have been the same? Many people are partners in several businesses, so why is it different for me?

Time and balancing everything were probably the biggest mindset challenges. I have to say I was pretty exhausted last year, working extremely long days running two main businesses in and out. I felt like two different people at times, but my family pulled together and helped out.

•   •   •

I have always invested in my own companies. I have not borrowed a single penny to be where I am today. I am always conscious of what is going in and what is going out. For the first year, everything I made went back into my company so that I ended the year even. This year will see us doubling or even tripling that.

Being in the position I'm, with great success, I've had to deal with that nasty imposter syndrome that we obtain from the sudden shift in success. We all deal with it: Are people going to see right through me and know I am a fraud? But I am not! I knew what I wanted to do. I knew in my heart that passion and hard work would pay off. That doesn't mean I was not afraid; fear was allowed to come along for the ride, but she was not allowed to change the channel on the radio or tell me where to go.

• • •

Starting a new brand is tough enough, but a beauty brand is even harder. There are a thousand new products launching every day and so much noise to cut through. My marketing expertise has had to be invested in me this time to prove that I knew what I was doing all those years. E-commerce was a completely different beast to me. Not only was I trying to grow this business and its amazing brand, it was how to tell the story and make sure that I was getting that across. We have a backstory to why we are doing what we are doing. I also have taken so many courses on the things that I need to sharpen with regards to e-commerce, so it has been a learning experience every step of the way. My brain hurts some days.

It was never about money; it was about communicating and making sure that I was navigating through the digital space effectively so that I knew I was spending my time and money appropriately. When I took one course, the teacher reviewed my website and digital marketing and he asked me why I was even there because I was well on my way. I knew then I was in the right place and doing all right and could start to believe in myself.

Was there ever a point where I wanted to give up on my journey to becoming a multimillionaire? Oh god. Yes. You have to make many sacrifices to fight to the top. My social life sucks, and I am pretty sure my family life suffers at times.

When I broke down in tears while running both companies, I knew I couldn't do it anymore. Something had to give. Did I take the easy road and close up Hereward Farms because I wasn't expecting this success so soon (I was thinking I still had another year) and go back to just owning a marketing agency? That would be easier, right? It was successful, we were growing, and it was a half-a-million-dollar company.

But I knew I didn't want to own Green Monkey Creative anymore. I knew in my heart that Hereward Farms was where I needed to be. On that day, my mind was made up—to the horror of my husband, who wondered how I could give up my secure agency—and I was throwing my hat in the ring.

I have been scared. I have been doubtful about this. But on December 31, 2021, when I "retired" (I like using that word) at 48 from the agency, I knew I was doing the right thing.

•   •   •

I was wondering where I could put some accolades in here about the person who I'm grateful towards who helped get me to where I am today. Honestly, it was my husband. He has supported all my dreams and ideas and grown with me. He is the person who is silently watching me from the side, as I shine and he does a lot of the hard work. He is the man who oversees all the operational things, and I am the one who runs the marketing, design, products, photography, and PR—and we work like a well-oiled machine.

But I do owe a big part of this to him. He could have told me my idea sucked, and maybe we wouldn't be here right now. It was his insane idea to go from 40 plants to over 4,000, so you can blame him for that.

I also want to say, my kids! They have been there whether we need to make 500 lip balms for an order, open the Lounge for guests, deliver orders, or help plant or prepare the plants for winter. I keep telling them that this will someday be theirs, so they need to know how it all works. I am very proud that my family is behind me, supports me, and helps me out when they can.

I plan for everything. Everything is thought out, resourced, and planned. That doesn't mean that I don't rush into things and make things happen, but I certainly don't sit back and just wonder. I never invest in anything that I can't get back, and I definitely don't spend the money with no results. You have to learn to pivot (gosh, I am starting to hate that word) when you need to. If something isn't working out, you need to be able to adapt.

For example, when the first batch of infused oil was done, people would ask me why it didn't smell like lavender. Well, it isn't supposed to be all smelly and grandma-like, but I was always having to explain the difference between the lavender varieties and why it wasn't a strong scent. I remember sitting on the stairs, perplexed about a client who had complained about it. And my husband said, "Will it really hurt you to add a little bit of lavender essential oil to the product if that is what people want?"

I struggled with that because I knew what I wanted this product to be. But it wouldn't be successful if I was trying to convince people what they wanted wasn't what I was going to give them. So, I made changes to the product. I changed the branding a bit and the ingredients, and I am glad I didn't just stick my heels in the ground. Customer feedback is key, and if we don't listen then we aren't winning.

I am learning all the time. There are a few podcasts, books, and other learning resources that stand out to me the most. Clikk newsletter always sends out tips and tricks and trends to help you stay on top of things. I also thoroughly enjoyed Zack from Smart Founder with his website and marketing tips for e-commerce brands. I have also recently started the Jilly Academy and am looking forward to learning more about stuff I may not know. Never, ever stop learning.

I also think that looking at what you do and ensuring you are looking at your financials, what products are working, what needs to change, and adapting to that are the keys to our success. You need to examine your social media stats, your audience. You have to see what is working. I listen to my customers—whether they are happy or have suggestions for new products—and I tuck that away. I don't have a vision board; I just have tons of post-it notes and scribbles in my books that I will revisit almost daily.

•   •   •

Out of all the things I just listed, if I had one resource that would help me grow my business and reach my next financial milestone, it would have to be branding and marketing. That alone is what probably led to the success of Hereward Farms. When I was taking a course on lavender farming from the University of Michigan, the one thing that they said was, "The downfall of lavender farmers is they don't know how to market." I started to research other lavender farms and what they did. I then took what they didn't do and did it. I knew I wanted this brand to stand alone; it wasn't about the farm, although the farm is part of it.

I wanted a brand that I would buy. I love every single thing about this product and what it stands for. And communicating that love story, the brand, and the way I market it is key to our success and will help us reach our next financial milestone.

•   •   •

I think the greatest challenge for women and creating wealth and abundance is Imposter Syndrome! When women tell me I am an inspiration to them for having the gall to do this, I am taken aback because I just did it. It hasn't been easy and I knew it wouldn't be. But the road less traveled is successful if you believe in yourself and what you can do.

I knew I didn't want to be known as a "mom" brand. I knew that I was more than just a woman creating a product.

I have also surrounded myself with some pretty amazing people, and I have made many sacrifices personally and professionally to be where I am today. I wasn't doing this to put another notch in my belt, and I wasn't going to fake it till I made it. I gave myself no choice but to make it. There was no option other than success. I knew when I worked for someone else doing the 9 to 5 grind that it was not for me. But I didn't believe in myself nor did I have that purpose.

Then it changed.

The only regret is that I didn't do this ten years ago, but you learn from your mistakes. If you don't, then you keep making the same ones. This isn't easy and it will sometimes keep you up at night with ideas and problems.

I have to hold myself accountable for all that I do ... successes and failures.

•   •   •

5 Things I Wish Someone Told Me Before I Started:

1. *Take time for yourself.* I very rarely take downtime, and when I do I feel guilty. There is always something to do, but if I don't take the time to recharge my batteries doing something other than work, then I would be pretty empty and wouldn't have much to give others or my business. It is okay to sit still and do nothing.

2. *Let Fear Come Along.* It is okay to be fearful about things. I think it makes you feel more grounded and aware that you can make mistakes

and you may not know everything. Fear is just not allowed to make decisions or make you change your path.

3. *Don't Dig Your Heels In.* Adapt. Adapt, Adapt. For the last two years, if you didn't adapt to the changing world, you were going to be left behind. You have to evolve and be ready to change. For instance, when supplies were being impacted, I could have easily gone to plastic bottles, but I knew that we needed to continue to be eco-friendly and felt quite strongly I wasn't moving from glass. I spent hours sourcing Canadian products and finally found them and discovered a new, amazing supplier.

4. *It's Okay to Make Mistakes.* But only if you learn from them. For example, when we first launched, we had four varieties of lavender-driven products. I had to explain each time what the difference was, and then it dawned on me that what is important to me is not important to the consumer, and I was confusing them. I simplified my line and now people get what we are selling.

5. *You Don't Have to Compete.* Sure, I am competing with thousands of other brands, but we are unique and we stay in our lane. I may be influenced by others, but each product is our own. Partnering with others so that they can be successful instead of us taking business away from them is key. Let's go on this journey together.

Now that my focus is 100 percent on Hereward Farms, I have lots on my list to achieve this year. Our next big goal is to register as a natural health product so we can talk about more of our health claims and work on our wholesale business that has been neglected this past year. We have been growing our retail and online presence, which didn't leave much time to focus on this side of the business accurately.

The plan is to map out what markets we want to be in, and we don't want to be everywhere. We still want to remain unique and a luxurious product. This will definitely give us much more brand exposure and reach more people.

•   •   •

You can find us through our website at herewardfarm.com or on Instagram https://www.instagram.com/herewardfarms/ and Facebook https://www.facebook.com/herewardfarms.

Personally, you can find me on LinkedIn https://www.linkedin.com/in/juliethurgood/

I was raised in Washington, DC at the height of the crack/cocaine epidemic. My parents did everything they could to keep me away from all that, even though we didn't have much money. Although my parents worked hard and often had two or three jobs at a time, we never had much. I always wore hand-me-down clothes, and I was often teased because I didn't sport designer clothes at school. I remember early on that I started selling things like bracelets and candy just to make some extra money. As a child, I remember wanting to be a bus driver because all I knew was that the bus driver collected all this money in his token box, and I knew we needed money. Conversations about the fact that "money doesn't grow on trees," that it was hard to make and even harder to keep, were a big part of the consciousness that I grew up with. There was never enough money and there was frustration around it being scarce and hard to come by. Not getting locked up or selling drugs but going to college and getting a good government job and working at that job for 20, 30, 40 years was a success where I came from.

Because of the neighborhood I grew up in, I didn't know anyone who was a millionaire, nor did I ever consider that it was possible for me. I remember my high school sweetheart (now my husband) was the first person I met who wanted to be a millionaire. He talked about it and it inspired me to start to dream bigger. It wasn't until many years later, after landing my dream job as a TV reporter and becoming disillusioned with the "good government job," that I started to aspire to be an entrepreneur again. The big inspiration for me wasn't to make millions ... it was to have more flexibility to be with my newborn. At the time, I thought if I could just match my salary, then I would be good. As time went on and my business grew, I learned different strategies and got clear on what my contribution was to the world. That's when things really picked up. Interestingly enough, I never thought that my 7-figure business would come in the way it has. It turned out being that my work was deeply rooted in a childhood tragedy that I experienced, and the lessons I learned from that became my movement and work in the world.

At the age of six, I lost my younger sister in a fire. We were both staying at my grandparents' home for the weekend and a fire broke out. The firefighters rescued me but did not find her in time and she died. For years I battled with survivor's guilt, and it wasn't until I was doing work on the trauma that I realized my sister gave me a beautiful gift. She died hiding under the bed, and I felt that her message to me and the work I had been doing to help people get featured and step into the spotlight was to ensure that others don't die hiding. They don't need to live a life where their gifts and expertise are hidden and they aren't making the impact they want. When I finally healed from the trauma of losing her and stepped fully into the purpose I was put here to advocate for, I opened up to making millions.

· · ·

One of the biggest mindset obstacles that I had to overcome in order to reach the place of consistently earning a million dollars a year and more is that it was not only possible but that it was possible *for me*. Those are two different things, and therein lies my mindset shift. I am smart enough, and I don't have to wait until I feel ready enough or good enough or smart enough to charge what I am worth and richly receive all that God has in store for me. You know, my grandfather was the only entrepreneur I knew growing up.

He was a mechanic and a cab driver, so I always joked that he knew how to fix things and get you where you needed to go. However, he died penniless and worked himself into the ground. I had to let go of the idea that I have to work myself into the ground or that only by working hard can I make great money. Don't get me wrong, I do believe there is a level of hustle, grit, and resourcefulness that you need as an entrepreneur, but I believe that God establishes the work of our hands and wealth is available to you as your birthright.

For women who are raising families, I think it's especially important to factor in their spouse and children. They have been the main reasons why I've wanted to reach certain milestones but also the biggest impediment at times. I still remember the first time I told my husband that I wanted to hire a coach and that the investment would be the size of a luxury car payment. He was not in agreement, and I remember feeling so strongly that I had to do it that I moved forward even though he wasn't on board. He was livid and would only "let" me if I didn't take any money from the household budget. I still remember feeling powerless, even though my job was the main contributor to the household budget. It took me deferring my student loan payments and borrowing money from someone else during those first few months in the coaching program. Despite my husband being really upset for days, I knew it was the right decision, and it wasn't until months later that he saw that it was too.

I often think about that moment because it would have been easy for me to be the "good wife" and not have moved forward, but there is no way we would have ever built the empire we have today without that coach. I always tell women that you've got to go with what's in your gut and what your vision is, then ask yourself, *Is this decision in alignment with my vision?* Meaning, will it get you closer to your vision or take you further away? If the answer is that it is in alignment with your vision, then it's up to you to problem solve the money and investment piece.

•   •   •

I remember when I first left my government job when my second child was born and we had to go on food stamps just to make ends meet. I felt so ashamed because I had spent so much time talking about how awesome it was to be an entrepreneur and we couldn't even figure out the finances of running and growing a business. I had to learn how to manage cash flow, how to factor in the finances of a business, and ultimately started following a method that taught me to put profits first. That completely changed things for me, and because I was able to save and properly allocate the money that was coming in, it allowed me to show up more powerfully in service to our clients and honor my commitments to my loved ones.

There are so many tools that have helped me over the years, but if I had to boil it down to two, I would say first re-committing to my faith in God and taking time daily to pray and read my Bible. In so many moments, having that Scripture planted in my heart and mind has supported me and affirmed many of the decisions that were happening in my business. The power of prayer has been another, and the book *The Circle Maker* by Mark Batterson and the devotional guide gave me an entirely new outlook on what was possible for my business and my life. That book is centered around the power of a single prayer, and it encourages you to be praying around your biggest dreams and greatest fears.

•   •   •

If I only had one resource that would help me grow my business and reach my next financial milestone, it would be how to build an audience of some type and then understand how to influence that audience to say yes to what it is that you are offering. Often people think that it is enough to have a large social media following, but unless you know how to inspire that audience to take action around your offers, it's pointless. My favorite way to grow my audience is doing media interviews and creating an email list because, at the end of the day, any social media platform can shut down, and unless you have a way to contact those people outside of that social media platform, you are jeopardizing your business's success.

Books I keep on my desk and read often:

- *The Law of Divine Compensation* by Marianne Williamson
- *Be Obsessed or Be Average* by Grant Cardone
- *I Declare: 31 Promises to Speak Over Your Life* by Joel Osteen
- *The Circle Maker* & *Draw the Circle* by Mark Batterson
- *You Can Heal Your Life* by Louise Hay
- *Profit First* by Mike Michalowicz

I've got a whole list of apps and tech that I recommend and use regularly: Voxer, Asana, Infusionsoft, Calendar booking systems, electronic signing systems, etc.

* * *

It takes a certain level of audacity and determination to create wealth and abundance. Decide today that you don't need anyone's permission to do so. One of my favorite quotes is from Eleanor Roosevelt: "Well-behaved women never made history." I believe that for more women to push past the blocks, we've got to be willing to jump out of the plane and build our parachutes on the way down.

Go for progress over perfection and visualize yourself at the top. Know that we are built for this and can and are victorious. I used to feel some kind of way when people would call me bougie or say I had high standards, and now I own it. I like to have the best, and it's taken me working on my money mindset, activating my wealth consciousness, and deciding that I get to be a successful, wealthy woman who deserves to have everything she's worked for and more.

* * *

If I could, I would tell my younger self to build residual income. This is the one type of income that not many know about or even factor into their wealth-building journey. Residual income means that you do something once and you are paid for it for years to come. Artists know about this because of the royalties that they are paid from their albums. However, most people don't know that there are opportunities out there to build this type of income, especially if you are partnered as an affiliate for the right services or products. Even as a coach, I have to go out there and enroll clients in another program or do a big launch, and most clients stay for two to three years. With residual income, you often have to take a good three years or more to build it, but once it is built it can cash flow any project that you need funding for.

Ten years ago, I used to think that if I only worked hard and was the smartest, I would be successful ... but success is about so much more. It's about building great connections, being and not just doing, visualizing, and affirming what you want to create. The other thing I know now that I wish I would have known sooner is that sometimes God answers your prayers in ways you don't expect, so you've got to be willing to follow the breadcrumbs even when others might look at you like you're crazy. That happened to me a few years ago in 2019.

Six months before the pandemic, my husband signed us up for a network marketing company. At the time I rolled my eyes! I was a multiple six-figure award-winning coach, and I honestly had so many crazy experiences in the past with the MLM industry that I didn't want any part of it. But God knew. He knew that a pandemic would happen, and I now believe he sent us back into that industry—after I had sworn in my 20s that I'd never work that model again—so that we would be there to help other coaches and influencers create another stream of revenue that would help them, especially when masterminds and speaking engagements were being canceled left and right. What's more, God allowed us to make multiple 6 figures in the MLM industry—in record speed; it took 12 months to be exact—earning a rank that only 20 others held, helping 70+ people hit the executive level, and becoming a household name in our company … all during a pandemic. If I had known how powerful a network is and put myself in places where there are large networks, I would have probably been at multiple 7 figures by now.

My next goal is to build generational wealth so that we forever change the legacy in my family tree. This is important to me because I feel like I owe it to our ancestors for all the struggle they went through. I also want my children to thrive, and I believe money gives you choices, which ultimately leads to freedom.

JEANA
GOOSMAN

Family has always played an important role in my life. I grew up a farmer's daughter where my parents taught me the value of hard work and dedication at a young age. I grew up on a farm in Northwest Iowa as the 5th kid in a family with entrepreneurship ingrained in our DNA. My father, Frank Seitzinger, was an entrepreneur and farmer in northwest Iowa. He was resilient and never too concerned with the meaning of "normal." This drove him to be one of the first in Iowa to take on "no-till" farming, earning him a reputation for innovation. He didn't wait for anyone else to take the lead; he would always dare to be the first. He grew his business into a farming operation that included a grain warehouse bigger than the local mall.

My mother, with her entrepreneurial spirit, was Queen of the Daughters of the Nile, a women's organization that raised money for the Shriners children's hospital burn unit. Having toured the burn unit, my mom had a strong drive to raise the money to help these kids that had suffered so much. These ladies made and sold 800 boxes of peanut brittle. I still remember the year when the humidity caused the peanut brittle to get sticky. The ladies moved the 800 boxes of brittle to our basement to keep it from sticking all together. It was the same year the price of ingredients soared, and my mom worked with the owner of the ice cream manufacturing plant, Wells Dairy, to buy ingredients in bulk through them. The hustle was to help the children. To *give*. Your ability to help others because of your business success is part of what makes it *worth it.*

My childhood and education were all about getting me ready, a foundation for being equipped to do what I've done.

My vision was and still is to ultimately feed America through Agricultural and Estate Tax Legislation. My experience as a lawyer taught me how to be proactive, and that in return helped to guide me when I started my own firm. I had previous experience as a law firm partner, so I had seen the hard work required to keep a successful firm running. I had great mentors who encouraged and guided me along the way, and this allowed me to envision myself starting my own firm. I began thinking, *I can lead the firm,* and the more I believed in myself, the easier it was to go out and start a firm of my own.

• • •

I started the firm in 2009 with a vision to provide strategic legal advice with big-city style and small-town service. I defied the risks of starting my own firm, and in 2013 I launched "Trust Law Counsel" to give clients a full-service experience to ensure they receive the most personalized estate plan that helps preserve their wealth and legacy. I wanted to create a boutique estate planning department that was unique, with fixed fees, collaborative team approach, and business mindset. As an approachable firm, with the understanding of family and all of life's events, I strive to provide exceptional service to clients in life's most sensitive moments. I sold the vision I had to my team early on, and they see the passion we have for what we do every day. I not only care about our clients, but I care about what they care about. I get to know them as people and find out what matters to them.

One of the most important mindset strategies is to foster a "giving culture" within your business. Hire a team of givers, not takers, and treat them well. This impacts your culture and client experience. A strong team is more productive as a whole than having that one superstar. Working on a great team makes everything easier, more satisfying, and more productive. When you give to others, the universe sends it back to you in some other way. Executing with a giving mindset helps you win in life.

I had to overcome the additional hurdle of commanding the respect of others as a young female professional in the first year of my business. As any young professional knows, people may see you differently than a professional with 20-plus years of experience. Learning to be confident in myself, even when others doubted me, helped me to earn the respect of others. Respect is something that is not always given freely.

•   •   •

Giving up was never an option for me. As a leader, you will have difficulties, and how you respond to those is key. When you respond to failure with compassion it gives your team room to grow and develops a culture of trust rather than fear. With a team of high achievers, they are way harder on themselves than you could ever be.

Once, when I was a new lawyer, I did a presentation project for a partner, and when the partner returned to the office after having stumbled on an audience question, she ripped me apart for not having prepared her enough. It made me feel small, hurt, embarrassed, and ashamed. I try to remember this moment often. While we are human and not perfect, take a deep breath and work to be emotionally patient. As a leader, look at what you celebrate. These are opportunities to set up culture building moments. Your job as a business leader is to see to it that your team is successful, that they have what they need to win. Because when your team wins, so does your business.

I found that asking questions of the right people and strategically thinking through decisions helped me to become the business owner I am today. Seeking advice from a credible professional, one who can also serve as a mentor, will be one of the best decisions you make for your business.

Have great ideas, persevere, and work hard and you will eventually reap the rewards. After all the risks, challenges, and trial and error, I am now at a team of 65 and growing! I have not been afraid of letting go or embracing change, and I know that the decisions I have made have led me to where the Goosmann Law Firm is today. I have gained the respect of my community, led my team to think big, and I have never steered away from my vision. I was recently told by someone that I am a business owner who just so happens to be in the legal industry. I found that comment extremely rewarding.

With a business mindset, hiring and promoting the right people, developing a strong professional culture, and capturing hot markets, I have been able to beat the odds, defy the risks, and watch my firm grow.

My education and dedication to continuous learning is the foundation on which everything else is built. Without it, I wouldn't be where I am today. You can learn from others' experiences and make them your own. Learning, being innovative, pulling from your education and being teachable are all part of being ready for what comes next and willing to put that plan into action.

•   •   •

There are many tools that have helped build and boost the success of my business. One is the Clifton Strengths by Gallup. As a strengths-based firm, we're able to identify and utilize our own strengths and the strengths of others to collaborate, innovate, work together as a team, and win as a team. Another helpful guide in navigating common but all-consuming business problems is a book called *Traction* by Gino Wickman. It outlines practical methods for achieving the business success you've always envisioned with more focus, growth, and enjoyment.

One of the biggest challenges for women is that we want to do it all—run a business, volunteer, be a good friend, raise a family, support your spouse—and do it all really well. It's not just about work-life balance, which is why I use a strategy called MashUp. It's been a guiding principle in my life and has allowed my entrepreneurial spirit to thrive, but not at the expense of the rest of my life. The MashUp strategy is born through the acknowledgment and acceptance that life is not static; it's not simply a screenshot in time. You don't ever stop being you. I'm still a lawyer when I'm at my kid's soccer game. I also need to figure out how to eat well when I'm traveling for work. Life is a dynamic reality, with seasons that come and go, constantly shifting. Once you embrace your own unique rhythm and cadence, you'll find all the elements of your life coming together and you flow from one area to another with ease.

•   •   •

If I could coach my younger self, I would tell her to be bold and stand confidently in your decisions. As a business leader you must be willing to take those risks that others are not willing to take. While others may question what they are doing, if you are bold and confident you will already be busy actively making moves. Persist in your dreams and constantly overcome the obstacles.

When we invest ourselves in something that isn't worth it, we fail, because eventually we realize that it isn't worth our time, our personal sacrifice, our investment of our resources. Several years ago, we opened an office in Fargo, ND. I did not go all in. I hired one associate and rented space in the Regus center. We made a minimum investment financially and with our time. There were opportunity and client needs in ND. Yet, I was not fully invested personally, and I did not commit the firm to its fullest potential. The office closed nine months later ... in December, just before its break-even point. The minor attempt at a satellite office failed. The opportunity compared with the opportunity cost wasn't worth it with the five hours of travel through tunnels of snow and closed interstates and being stranded in the dead of winter. The firm had better opportunities that were worth it. We learned. The Fargo office was part of getting ready for what was to come.

Now in our 13th year, I still see the big picture of where the firm might be in the future. Our goal is to grow ten times in ten years; we will not get there remaining stagnant, or with those who do not see my vision. Over the years, I have seen business owners get complacent. Suddenly, their business stops experiencing growth, and they and their staff are no longer motivated. To overcome the risks of stagnation, a business owner must set the tone for her team to see growth. Involving my team in a pep rally where I hand out praise or surprising them with a new quarterly bonus plan can spark their motivation. Do not let yourself or your team fizzle out. Keep growing and continue working toward the "bigger and better."

MICHELLE
TASCOE

Growing up, we didn't have very much money. In fact, my parents came from the Philippines dreaming of green pastures and Elvis and the land of opportunity. I know these three specifically because my 5th grade report was on my dad and his experience coming to America. My parents were hard workers. As one of seven children in both families, they experienced a hard life where there wasn't enough to go around at times until my grandparents' entrepreneurial ventures of a rice mill, apartments, and a farm panned out well. When I look back, I remember bags of hand-me-down clothes as my new wardrobe for back to school. I remember my parents sharing one car and my mom working graveyard while my dad worked a day shift so that there was always a parent home with us three girls. To work in this country, my mom, with her Bachelor of Science, took a housekeeping position, and my dad did maintenance at the same hotel. He was actually qualified to be an engineer through his college education in the Philippines but humbly took this job to provide. This is how I grew up.

We lived in a little two-bedroom apartment of a four-plex in a cul-de-sac in Anaheim, which is known as the happiest place on earth because it is where Disneyland is located. We didn't have money for new clothes but we were happy, and my parents did the best they could with what they had access to. My fondest memory was waking up to so many balloons in my room. Apparently, there was a big party at the hotel and my dad gathered all the balloons after the party to surprise me when I woke up on my birthday. This taught me that, although we didn't have much, we had each other, and my parents were always finding ways to celebrate the present. This was their gift to me to that day.

I didn't know it was possible to make $1 million on my own. It seemed like that was something that only happens in the movies to the pretty blonde girl who was dressed up like she walked out of a magazine. In my heart, I really wanted to be happy, and when I think about it, I can still feel that deep, deep down inside there was something more that I wanted out of life. Secretly, I felt like I was meant for more, but I didn't know what that more looked like. I just knew that I felt something inside that was big and I couldn't describe it.

At the time I had four credit cards in collections and a car repossessed through a series of wrong decisions. I had just gotten married that year, and my husband, Jeribai, and I had our first son, Angelo. I knew that I wanted to contribute to the household, and after trying and failing at network marketing and doing okay at direct sales, I read this book, *Leadership Coaching: The Disciplines, Skills and Heart of a Christian Coach*. It was one of those moments that seems really cliché, but after I read that book, something inside me woke up and I believed that I had found what I was meant to do: be a life coach.

My goal really was to see how I could bring in an extra $2000 a month to help out with bills and to take a family vacation that year. Little did I know that I would have $2000 afternoons in coaching a decade later. And that's how it started. I coached five people for free, just pouring into them, and one of the five told me that I was helping her so much through our coaching that she had to pay me something. She asked if $25 a session would be okay. That $25 meant more to me than the $50,000 that I'd earned in corporate America the prior year because I created it out of the air with just myself. As I kept showing up to coach, some clients referred new clients to me. And with each person that I coached I was also coaching myself and getting my own life completely on track.

My big "why" behind my coaching is that coaching saved my life! I had a colorful past—my 20s were full of parties and "finding myself" in Los Angeles, escaping using alcohol, people, and TV to do so. When I dove into personal development, I started unpacking the mess and found my message of creating true success from the inside out.

I tell my life coaching clients all the time that if you don't have a plan for yourself someone else will have a plan for you. And for my financial coaching clients, if you don't have a plan for your money someone else will have a plan for your money for you. Coaching helped me create the plan for my life and discover that there was a life that I was meant to be living and that I could reach for it. Even though I had a colorful past, I learned through coaching that my past doesn't equal my future and that each day is a brand-new day. Because my life is now completely transformed by coaching, my big gift is to lay my life down each day working with clients so that they can find theirs. I am fulfilled every day seeing my clients transform before my eyes, as coaching had done the same for me years ago.

• • •

Your inner game will make you or break you. There were three specific ways of thinking that molded my mindset to one of a millionaire. I giggle as I remember events where we would say affirmations over and over like a broken record: "I have a millionaire mind." Saying the right things is not the same as thinking the right things. The first obstacle in my mind I had to overcome is the mindset of faking it 'til you make it. You see, when you fake-it 'til you make it, you're always operating from a place of inauthenticity and it never feels aligned, real, or true. Instead, I learned to fail forward, and that it was OK to fail because I learned how not to do something. With that new approach, it wasn't enough to know the right thing to do. As the saying goes, knowledge is power, but I recognized that it isn't knowledge that's power. It's *applied* knowledge that's power, because if you just know a lot, you are a walking encyclopedia; when you apply the knowledge that you know, you become a risk taker, a history maker, and a world changer.

Once I learned to be authentic, I tackled the mindset of comparison. In Los Angeles and other metropolitan areas, there's always going to be someone who has a nicer car than you, better clothes than you, a fancier purse or watch, and more letters at the end of their name if they had access to a college education. The mindset of comparison leaves you always comparing and emphasizes where you're not good enough. It leaves you wishing and whining and operating from a place of reaction, trying to keep up with an unspoken self-imposed competition with everyone else.

The mindset of comparison is so tiring. It never goes to sleep, and when you're always comparing, you never feel rested because what you're doing is never enough. When I realized this, I realized that everything that I was focusing on with comparison was festering, instead of me focusing on taking action and having a vision of what I could manifest. When I stopped focusing on what festered and started focusing on what I could manifest, the comparison shifted to celebrating everyone around me who was winning. As I celebrated everyone around me who was winning, some of it rubbed off on me and I began to win. I stopped wishing and I started working. I stopped being reactive and I started being proactive. That made all the difference!

Finally, I stared the mindset of "I don't matter" right in the face. This was a mindset belief that had haunted me ever since junior high. At that time, I had a group of girlfriends, and we were a clique. Our group had the funny one and the pretty one and the sarcastic one, and I was the quiet, studious one. I'll never forget when everything changed. On one ordinary day in my eighth-grade year, my so-called girlfriends thought it would be funny to pretend that I was invisible.

Let me paint you a picture.

I would walk up to them and say, "Hi" and the sarcastic one would say, "Did you hear something? Oh, it must've been the wind," and they would walk away.

This transpired for two weeks. I was devastated because it confirmed the deep down fear I had that I didn't matter.

Fast forward to today, and it was such a gift! Yes, honestly! It was truly the best gift in the world because it taught me that people want to feel special and important and that they matter. It seared inside of me that listening and acknowledging people is the biggest way to love and honor them and to create trust. I now know that the greatest currency in the world isn't actually money, it's relationships. You build relationships by being a giver.

Giving your time and giving your attention matters most to the people around you that you know and want to get to know. It makes sense to me now why people would say it's not what you know but who you know that will help you to be successful in life. So much of my success came from clients introducing me to their friends whom they believed I could help. Success comes from knowing you matter and treating people around you like they matter so much. I couldn't agree more!

•   •   •

When you're making your first million, it feels like an uphill battle in the beginning, and it seems as if the building phase lasts a long time. As my four-year-old, Leilani, would say, "Mom, this is taking *for-ever*, like a million years!"

As mentioned, I started off with four credit cards in collections and a car repossessed. What a way to build my résumé of qualifications to be a financial life coach, right? But that's where I started, and it is what shaped me into the coach that I am today. As I learned how to address those cards in collections, learned how to create a budget, demystified my credit score, and navigated my husband and I buying our first home despite my tarnished credit, it gave me hope that, if I can do it, I can show others how to do it too. And that's how it started. Just one foot in front of the other, taking one step at a time, realizing that when I was at the top of one step I was at the bottom of the next one.

In the last 12 years, we have purchased seven houses. Some were bank owned, one was from an auction, another was with an investor, and the last two were cash purchases. Here's the biggest lesson I learned with overcoming the ruined financial state that I was in at the start: As long as I was breathing, I could be resourceful. I could learn what I never learned around the dinner table about money and wasn't taught in the classroom with my private school college education.

Money is a tool with which you can leverage and negotiate. I negotiated my $64,000 in credit card debt down to a payoff of $24,000. That brought it down to paying only 37.5 cents on the dollar. The first house that we bought, I crunched the numbers and realized that if my husband sold his BMW, that car payment and our current rent would be equal to a mortgage payment. That's how we got into our first home in 2008, when the market was so high.

Since we bought a bank-owned home, we were able to buy at below market value, and with a little sweat equity, some paint, some handyman skills, renovation realities, and a whole lot of vision, we fixed up that house and in three years sold it, pocketing $74,000 … and I bought my husband a BMW X5 with cash. Real estate investment meets with reward. I recently read a book by Marie Forleo titled *Everything is Figureoutable*. It's so true! Life is one big test that is figureoutable! You just need to take the time to be resourceful and diligent and consistent and disciplined to figure it out.

•   •   •

I wanted to give up so many times when I was getting close to the finish line. In the beginning, I had a hunger and desire that seemed to refuel me every day, but the longer that I worked my business, the longer the finish line to $1 million seemed to be. It's almost like you're pushing a boulder up a hill and all you can do is stare at your feet, taking one step at a time in front of you. You're making some kind of progress but not knowing if you're really getting anywhere.

One day, I was working with my coach, Will, who was from Minnesota. I was frustrated because life felt like whack-a-mole. As soon as I navigated how to enroll a client, I had to navigate who was making dinner tonight, and then I had to figure out how that laundry was going to get done. Then, around the corner, what was waiting for me was how to figure out that formula on the spreadsheet for a client to get a grasp on the profitability of her company this month.

I told Will that there was only one of me, and how would I ever make it to $1 million?

Will has this funny way of saying something that you know is true, but because he says it sarcastically, it anchors you in the truth that is deep inside of you. "Well, Michelle, it's not like you're going to impact people one million at a time!" But that was it!

When he said that, something woke up inside of me like a sleeping giant. That sleeping giant is like that scene in the movie where you can't tell how big this giant is, and you're zoomed in on the screen as a camera is getting closer to its eyes resting through the night. But a squeak is heard and the sleeping giant's eye opens up like it's wide awake and scanning the room for the source of that sound. That is how I felt. I was awake and I knew it through and through—I wanted to impact people one million at a time! That was a vision. In fact, in that moment it wasn't that I had the vision—the vision had me.

Since then, every time something gets hard, every time something is thrown off, every time it doesn't seem like something is going to work, I think about the vibration inside of me that resonated in my soul to impact people one million at a time. It is that very thing that keeps me going to find the answer on the other side and continue the journey onward and upward to reaching the millionaire destination that I knew was possible.

•   •   •

Growing up, I loved the TV show *MacGyver* because MacGyver would be stuck in an abandoned barn in the middle of nowhere, and, as long as he had some duct tape, a paper clip, and a piece of foil, he could find a way to free himself. In building my business to $1 million, I had my own version of MacGyver's tools. Although mine didn't fit in my back pocket and were not part of a Swiss Army knife, they were so handy that I teach my clients these tools every single day to help them reach the same level of success and beyond.

The first tool is *knowing your numbers*. You see, the numbers don't lie. They're neutral, they're realistic, and they will tell you exactly where you're at financially and what's not working and why. When you get competent with your numbers, you will become confident with your finances! Knowing your numbers looks like creating a budget to tell your money where you want it to go. It looks like understanding your conversions in your business so you can project your revenue of how much your business can generate. It also looks like understanding how much income you're bringing in on paper and how much debt you have against it so you can strategize how to buy a home and stop throwing money down a hole with renting.

One year, I helped 12 clients buy their first home. Most of them didn't know they could even afford to buy a home because they didn't know their numbers well enough. After coaching them, many of them bought houses within the next 90 days because they were armed with the competence and confidence of what was possible for them financially. Making decisions with your money is best when you have full certainty around your finances.

My other MacGyver tool is a *goal-setting strategy*. When I goal set with clients, we design the 2.0 version of their life. But what I have discovered is that, in order to reach the 2.0 version of their life, they also have to get clear with who the 2.0 version is that they will need to be to achieve the 2.0 life.

You see, your 1.0 version, who you are today, won't be able to achieve the 2.0 life because they don't have the mindset, capacity, habits, action-taking ability, and thinking to get there. I love the quote by Jim Rohn: "Don't make it a goal to make $1 million because of the money but because of who you'll become on the way to reaching that goal." What's funny is that he never said to earn $1 million, he just said to make the goal $1 million. This is an important distinction; it is that very shift in mindset for the goal to be $1 million that compels someone to be the person that can achieve making the million. It's the same as asking the question, "What would a 7-figure me do?" If you ask yourself what your 7-figure self would do every day, chances are you will come up with new actions, thinking, and ways of being that will enable you to operate as the 7-figure you; hence, you actually manifest the 7 figures. This is such a huge gold nugget if you are getting this!

The last MacGyver tool I have is more of a mindset universal truth: *If it's meant to be, it's up to me!* I would lean on this whenever there was something that I didn't want to do but had to do because no one else could do it but me. "If it's meant to be, it's up to me" was such a saying of accountability to myself that it helped me to develop my own integrity. That is crucial because if you're not following through on your word to yourself, on the thing that you say you're going to do for yourself, then you're not in a position of self-trust or self-leadership. I learned that I had to trust myself to follow through in order to lead myself to making the million.

I see life in pictures, stories, and experiences, and when I think about growing my business and what it's taken me to get to where I'm at today, there is one resource that made all the difference. I believe that when we reduce things down and reduce them even more and more and more, success for each person comes down to one thing. For me, the answer is faith.

Faith is often described as something to hope for even though it's unseen. Reaching for $1 million in revenue requires faith. I personally am a God-girl. For those of you who know the same God that I know, I am one of those girls who is Spirit-led and Word-fed.

I remember moments in my business when my focus was purely coaching. Because I built my business around birthing and raising my three kids, all I honestly had the bandwidth for was to coach my clients. I told God, "If you can put a line of people in front of me who need help with their finances and life, I will do my best to coach them with all my heart to success." He answered just that, because when you Google "financial coaching Los Angeles" I come up four times on the first page. Therefore, my one resource that I relied on the most was my faith in God. He was my marketing plan; He was my operations manager; He helped me with sales; and He helped me with all the aspects of my business that I didn't know how to do. I was able to show up in the one area that I was talented in: coaching my clients to succeed wildly with their finances.

There is a scripture that I lean on that actually was spoken over my husband and I on our wedding day. Proverbs 10:22 (ESV) says, "The blessing of the Lord makes rich, and he adds no sorrow with it." As I leaned on my faith for over a decade, being diligent and consistent and, more importantly, faithful to grow my business each year, I consistently reached a new financial milestone well beyond the year before.

• • •

Every successful person has their Inspector Gadget tech and tools that have helped them reach the top of the mountain. I don't think anyone has reached success without some kind of help from someone else's zone of genius. For me, I love me Google Sheets. Seriously! I have learned over the last decade to be a spreadsheet ninja as I navigate all of my clients' numbers and transactions and goals.

In my other back pocket, I love using my daily planner by Tools4Wisdom. It's funny because I know myself; I am a piece of paper and pen kind of girl. My husband, on the other hand, is more of a Photoshop and Illustrator kind of guy. For me, if it's out of sight it's out of mind, and I don't remember it. But when I write something down in my calendar and I put pen to paper, something happens that's cathartic—I'm connected with my time and how I'm using it. It is the way that I have been the most productive; just like how I have a plan for every penny with a budget, I have a plan for every minute with my planner. It's my playbook for my day, and every day I run the plays from my playbook all the way to reaching the goals I committed to achieve. I know now the truth of what I heard for the first time many years ago: failing to plan is planning to fail.

And don't forget my journals! All 36 of them since 2005!

I once heard that documentation beats conversation. People talk and talk and talk and talk, but they don't write it down to take action on it. I love to say to my clients when we're goal-setting, "if it's not written, it's not real." That is truer than true! When you think about it, what transaction occurs out there that you don't sign on the dotted line for, whether you buy a house, a car, get married, or sign a birth certificate for your firstborn child? If it's not written, it's not real, and if you're not writing down everything and anything that is important to you, then there's no guarantee that you will follow through on it.

Writing in my journal since 2005 has transformed the way that I think, expanded what I know, and inspired what I believe. If the question you are asking is, How can an empty book give me the path to my success? The answer is, the path to your success will come from what you fill the book with.

Even as you're reading this, I hope you're taking notes to fill your own journal, because, as Tony Robbins says, "Success leaves clues." It's like this amazing game of following the breadcrumbs. In other words, if you're putting enough popcorn kernels in the popper, at some point a kernel will pop and then another one and then another one and then another one, and then all of them are popping! It is working! All the things that you are writing down and following through on are reaping results. At that point, you know that you are on the path to success because you took the time to write out the goals, the strategy, and the action steps to get there.

As a Christian woman who is doing well financially, over the years I really struggled with hiding my success and playing small. There's something about feeling ashamed of making a lot of money. It's almost like wanting to make a lot of money as you serve God is wrong, selfish, and self-seeking.

Recently, I was coached by a Christian woman, Shanda Sumpter, who is a business coach running an 8-figure business. On our coaching call, she said some things that caused me to stop hiding and share the shame I was feeling about wanting to succeed wildly financially. It was such a freeing conversation because she unapologetically showed me by example how to own my success, own my faith, and own my destiny. I thought, *If she can do it, I can do it.* And if I can do it, you can do it. If you've ever felt shame around making a lot of money and you're hiding your gift, I am talking to you from deep in my spirit!

You get to choose to sit on the bench or get up, get going, get to work, and be "up to something" that is bigger than you that only God could be calling you to. Be the unstoppable, faith-filled business woman that you are. You are able! Discover and use your God-given voice to change the world. Be aligned with who God called you to be. Rise up and keep rising—in your finances, in your faith, in your family, for your future, and for your freedom. It has been time to do so for a while and you are called. Now go and do!

• • •

I've envisioned a handful of times talking to my younger self who is full of dreams and goals and wanting to be anything and everything she imagined. Oftentimes, when I coach clients who remind me of my younger self, I shift into big sister mode and tell them, "I'm gonna say something to you as a big sister" and give them advice as if I was giving my younger self the same advice. Sometimes advice is actually passed down traditionally from one generation to another. I still have my red journal where Dani Johnson, a multi-millionaire woman of faith who taught in the marketplace, wrote "never ever give up!" That would be the first thing that I would say to my younger self: "Michelle, never ever give up!"

Over the years, as I've grown wiser and stronger and clearer, I would now say this: Gain clarity in these three areas as fast as you can.

1. Get super clear with who you are because that is your identity by design.
2. Get crystal clear with what you want because that is your destination by destiny.
3. Exercise discernment daily because life is full of decision making. This is your decision-making ability by discernment.

When you know who you are, when you know what you want, and when you have a strong ability to make decisions on how to get there, nothing can stop you from accessing and becoming all that you're called to be. I will always be cheering you on in the background, so you're never alone, never not thought of, and never not seen. I love you and I am proud of you!

• • •

Recently, I was getting a download as I was writing in my journal number 35. I really think that this download came from heaven above because so many things connected for me in ways that I never saw the dots connecting before. If I had known this sooner, it would have cut ten years off my learning curve in building the business that I have today and becoming the person that I am today. This was the download:

- Self-Trust
- Self-Integrity
- Self-Leadership
- Self-Care
- Self-Worth
- Self-Confidence
- Self-Joy
- Self-Accomplishment
- Self-Fulfillment

When you have a low level of self-trust, you typically have a low level of self-integrity; you're not trusting yourself to follow through on the things that you say you're going to do for yourself. It isn't that you have no integrity, it's just that you don't have the level of self-integrity to keep your word to yourself. This leads to a low level of self-leadership because you are not following through on the things that you say you're going to do.

When you are not in charge and you are not leading your life, then you most likely have a low level of self-care because, if you're not keeping your word to yourself, you're also most likely not taking care of yourself. A low level of self-trust, self-integrity, self-leadership, and self-care most likely results in you having a low level of self-worth because not following through for yourself is not valuing yourself. And if you're not valuing yourself and you don't feel good enough, then you likely have a low level of self-confidence.

If you have a low level of self-confidence, you're not feeling so great about yourself, therefore, you have a low level of self-joy; the joy within is gone, and you may feel unhappy or even depressed. If you're not happy and you're depressed and not following through for yourself, you probably have a low level of self-accomplishment because you're not leading and guiding yourself to get things done; therefore, you're not accomplishing what you set out to do, which leads to a low level of self-fulfillment. You're not satisfied with who you are and what you're up to and how you're showing up.

Now here's the gold in the download I got:

When you start trusting yourself, you'll start following through for yourself because you're trusting yourself to follow through on the things that you say you're going to do, which increases self-trust and your self-integrity. As you're keeping your word to yourself, you are now showing up as the leader of your life that you're meant to be. And as you lead your life in a direction toward success, you'll be taking care of yourself along the way, being good to yourself, being kind to yourself, and, of course, loving yourself.

If you trust yourself and you keep your word to yourself, leading yourself and taking care of yourself, then you are telling yourself that you are worthy. Your self-worth then goes up, and if your self-worth goes up, your self-confidence goes up because you see yourself and you're hearing yourself so you are secure in yourself. When you have self-worth and self-confidence, then you'll have self-joy! You are now happy, but this happiness comes from the inside because that's how joy works.

Joy starts within.

This leads to self-accomplishment because if you're clear with your worth, clear with your confidence, and clear with your joy, then you're taking action and getting things done. You're up to something, and you're accomplishing what you set out to do. All of this allows you to also grow in self-fulfillment. There is a self-satisfaction that you now can taste and experience as much as you so desire.

This has everything to do with accelerating progress and building a business faster. How? Truth be told, I used to be one of those people who didn't trust my decision making, and I would go to ten different people to get confirmation, advice, and input on decisions. I came to find out that everyone has an opinion. It took me a while to realize that, if I buy someone's opinion, then I also buy their lifestyle. Why? Because the opinion that they're giving me is a combination of every decision they made to reach the life that they have today. If I don't like the way they're living, then I don't want to buy their opinion, as it will, in some way, shape, or form, lead me to the same destination.

Looking back, I could have saved myself so many years of taking advice from people instead of trusting myself at a level 10 and following through on the things that I knew to do to succeed faster and higher. Deep down I knew it was possible, but I lacked trust in myself.

My recommendation to you is learn how to trust yourself at a level 10 as fast as you can. Here's a picture for you: Do you want to walk for 40 years, or do you want to run for four? It will take as long as it takes because you are the one who sets the pace. Trust yourself!

•   •   •

My vision is to lead an army of faith-filled, heart-centered financial coaches around the country to create a movement of helping families across the US with establishing the financial structure to support their goals to live a life of financial freedom. Together, we will link arms to equip our clients to learn how to create a budget that works, learn how to pay off their debt quickly and efficiently, and strategize how to buy their first home. We will shift economies in each household, so their money will no longer cost them money from credit card debt with high interest rates and finance charges, but they will learn how to have their money make them money to secure their financial future and build wealth and a legacy for generations within their family.

To accomplish this, I am creating the infrastructure and the team to be able to offer moneyschool.com, an online education platform to learn about money. Through this hub, clients all over the country will learn about their money personality type, so they know what their spending tendencies are with how they handle money. Clients will learn how to conquer their credit score so it's not a mystery but a vehicle to give them access to leveraging other people's money. They'll also learn my better budget blueprint, which helps clients create a budget that actually works. Finally, there is training on real estate because real estate has made the most millionaires in all of history. Each person will be educated on how to buy their first house, their first investment property, and how to leverage other people in real estate so you can profit from their effort.

Quite honestly, this is a stretch for me because the original goal for coaching never went beyond my reach of coaching clients one on one. But when the vision had me with impacting one million at a time, I realized that this is bigger than me and that it will take a team to be able to reach and impact more households for good. In the 2.0 version of this vision, I can see having my own franchise in every community around the country. These Tascoe

Financial Freedom locations could help transform households within each community. People will be able to learn the lessons about money that, unfortunately, are often not taught around the dinner table or in the classroom. They can learn how to create a budget for their growing family, learn how to get out of debt, and then learn how to position themselves strategically to buy a house.

In addition, business owners can learn how to grow their business to be more profitable and have the ability to use our bookkeeping services and accountants to file their taxes and learn how to legitimately mitigate their tax liability. And for those who have an entrepreneurial spirit, and have an idea for a business, they can get help to determine if their business idea is viable and profitable. Achieving this would represent a world in which there are no excuses for any household to not be financially secure.

I was taught that excuses are well-planned lies. Instead of planning excuses, we can plan their family's financial future. My hope is to live my life pursuing my calling, and, in doing so, I hope to inspire every girl to know that her voice can change the world.

JONI
ROGERS-
KANTE

Growing up, my early experiences and perspectives about money weren't necessarily around consciousness but having a solid work ethic. We knew if we wanted something we needed to work for it. My siblings and I took a great amount of personal pride in earning the things we wanted. It gave us a tremendous sense of empowerment and self-worth. I started working for my father at Sav-On drugs when I was 15 and have been working ever since.

I have owned and operated SeneGence®, a global direct selling cosmetic brand, for the last 23 years. Our flagship product, LipSense®, was the first long-lasting lip color ever to hit the market. Right now, we have a massive global expansion plan to bring SeneGence® products and the business opportunity to more countries. In addition, we are looking for new and exciting product categories to launch in 2022 and beyond. Innovation and expansion are at the core of our growth strategy, and we are excited to see what the future holds.

When I wrote the SeneGence® business plan, I was a newly single mother who had taken nothing from the marriage but full custody of my son. I knew I had to provide for him, not only emotionally but financially. However, I wanted to be present and a part of his life. So, I knew I had to find a way to work from home, have scheduling flexibility, and create income. Direct sales was the perfect fit, but I couldn't find a product line I was proud to represent. I wanted to know the products I was sharing really worked. That is when I wrote the SeneGence® business plan and started looking for products that "really worked' and delivered on their promises. When I met the product formulator of LipSense®, I knew we were destined for greatness and success.

I've gathered so many interesting stories on this journey that I can't list them all, but the thing that stands out to me most is how many lives SeneGence® has transformed. With our line of Long-Lasting Color Cosmetics and Anti-Aging Skincare and other personal use products, we have created an opportunity for women to be in business for themselves, but not by themselves. They receive support, training, encouragement, and recognition from our SeneGence® community on an ongoing basis. The story is about lives we have changed and been positively impacted over the last 23 years.

As far as mistakes go … you only want me to share one!? I think the funniest mistake I made turned out to be the most positive thing that could have happened in the company.

After I wrote the business plan and founded the flagship product, LipSense®, I thought I needed investors. No one was interested in investing money in a single mom selling lip color. Go figure! In order to launch this company, I had to take the products on consignment, go to trade shows and home demos, sell the products, pay back the formulator, and re-invest the profits to get more products to sell. While I thought I needed investors, I really didn't. I have never taken on debt and have fully self-funded SeneGence®.

People say I am the most boring person in the entire world, as I do the same things every day. However, this gives consistency, predictability, and security to the company and to our independent distributors. The obstacle I had to overcome was that this trait didn't make me boring—it made me successful. I lived up to all my commitments and created a structure our independent distributors and corporate employees could depend on.

•   •   •

Direct Selling / Multi-Level Marketing tends to have a stigma to it. People often think this industry is a get-rich-quick scheme. By taking the time to educate our distributors and customers, being an active member of the Direct Selling Association, and always basing our business practices in absolute truth, we have overcome the perceptions of an industry that has been around for over 150 years.

Giving up is not in my nature. There were often many people telling me to give up, pack it in, go live a much simpler life. However, when you are as committed as I am to helping women find the freedom and flexibility they need to have the life they want, you don't just walk away. At one point, we had lost our country manager in Australia. The easy thing would have been to shut down the operation. However, by partnering with our independent distributors, we found creative solutions to keep our operations going and are still in that market today!

• • •

My father gave me an incredible work ethic and taught me how to create a business. My good friend, Carmen Holladay, helped care for my young son in the years I was traveling to earn the funds we needed to start SeneGence® and my husband, Ben Kante, was one of our first employees who set up our computer platforms, accounting programs, and our marketing department. Without him, there would be no SeneGence®.

Acknowledgements

Huge and terrific thanks to everyone that made this book possible.

To Joe Vitale: I haven't met you (yet!). However, your work showed me that a book can provide a transformative energy even more powerful than the words it contains and inspired me to write this book.

To the wonderful team at Muse Literary: Jeremy Brown, Mike Owens and Alle Byeseda.

Thanks to our amazing team at Thought Leader Academy: Dominique Swanquist, Alexis Reyes, Alex Kusis, Laura Granato and Kavita Arora and all our Thought Leader Academy clients.

Enormous gratitude to my mentors Fabienne Frederickson and Shanda Sumpter.

A great thanks to our incredible contributors: bad asses all. To the metaphysical and neuroscience teachers who paved the way for the process and strategies in this book, I thank you deeply.

Endnotes

1. "60+ Stats About Women and Money," *Ellevest,* June 26, 2020, https://www.ellevest.com/magazine/disrupt-money/stats-about-women-money.

2. Tucker, Jasmine, "Equal Pay for Native Women," *National Women's Law Center,* September 2019, https://nwlc.org/wp-content/uploads/2018/11/Native-Women-Equal-Pay-2019.pdf.

3. Kay, Katty and Claire Shipman, "The Confidence Gap," *The Atlantic,* May 2014, https://www.theatlantic.com/magazine/archive/2014/05/the-confidence-gap/359815/.

4. "2022 State of the Gender Pay Gap Report," *payscale,* 2022, https://www.payscale.com/research-and-insights/gender-pay-gap/.

5. "New Research from FreshBooks Discovers a 28% Wage Gap Among Self-Employed Women and Men," *FreshBooks,* https://www.freshbooks.com/press/data-research/women-in-the-workforce-2018.

6. "COVID-19 Cost Women Globally Over $800 Billion in Lost Income in One Year," *Oxfam,* April 29, 2021, https://www.oxfamamerica.org/press/covid-19-cost-women-globally-over-800-billion-in-lost-income-in-one-year/.

7. Delamater, Eleanor and Gretchen Livingston, "More Than Statistics: How COVID-19 is Impacting Working Women," *U.S. Department of Labor Blog,* July 21, 2021, https://blog.dol.gov/2021/07/21/more-than-statistics-how-covid-19-is-impacting-working-women.

8. Rothwell, Jonathan and Lydia Saad, "How Have U.S. Working Women Fared During the Pandemic?" *Gallup,* March 8, 2021, https://news.gallup.com/poll/330533/working-women-fared-during-pandemic.aspx.

9. Alon, Titan, Matthia Doepke, Jane Olmstead-Rumsey, and Michèle Tertilt, "The Impact of COVID-19 on Gender Equality," *National Bureau of Economic Research,* April 2020, https://www.nber.org/papers/w26947.

10. Karageorge, Eleni, "COVID-19 recession is tougher on women," *U.S. Bureau of Labor Statistics,* September 2020, https://www.bls.gov/opub/mlr/2020/beyond-bls/covid-19-recession-is-tougher-on-women.htm.

CPSIA information can be obtained
at www.ICGtesting.com
Printed in the USA
BVHW031616220622
640289BV00025B/1626